PENGUIN CANADA

POWER

Born in Prince Rupert and raised in Calgary, Gordon Laird has written for *Saturday Night, Canadian Geographic,* the *Far Eastern Economic Review, This Magazine, Outside* and *Mother Jones,* and has won two gold medals from Canada's National Magazine Awards. His previous book was the critically acclaimed *Slumming It at the Rodeo: The Cultural Roots of Canada's Right Wing Revolution.* He lives in Toronto with his wife and son.

# POWER

*Journeys Across an Energy Nation*

# GORDON LAIRD

PENGUIN
CANADA

PENGUIN CANADA

Published by the Penguin Group

Penguin Books, a division of Pearson Canada, 10 Alcorn Avenue, Toronto, Ontario,
    Canada M4V 3B2
Penguin Books Ltd, 80 Strand, London WC2R 0RL, England
Penguin Putnam Inc., 375 Hudson Street, New York, New York 10014, U.S.A.
Penguin Books Australia Ltd, 250 Camberwell Road, Camberwell, Victoria 3124, Australia
Penguin Books India (P) Ltd, 11, Community Centre, Panchsheel Park, New Delhi – 110 017, India
Penguin Books (NZ) Ltd, cnr Rosedale and Airborne Roads, Albany, Auckland 1310, New Zealand
Penguin Books (South Africa) (Pty) Ltd, 24 Sturdee Avenue, Rosebank 2196, South Africa

Penguin Books Ltd, Registered Offices: 80 Strand, London WC2R 0RL, England

First published in Viking by Penguin Books Canada Limited, 2002
Published in Penguin Canada by Penguin Books, a division of Pearson Canada, 2003

10 9 8 7 6 5 4 3 2 1

NATIONAL LIBRARY OF CANADA CATALOGUING IN PUBLICATION DATA

Laird, Gordon, 1967–
    Power : journeys across an energy nation / Gordon Laird.

Includes bibliographical references.
ISBN 0-14-029003-6

1. Power resources—Canada. 2. Energy policy—Canada. 3. Environmental degradation—Canada.
4. Laird, Gordon, 1967– —Journeys—Canada. I. Title.

TJ163.25.C3L34    2003    333.79'0971    C2002-904651-3

Early versions of "One Last Boom" and "Closing Kemano" were originally published in *Canadian Geographic* magazine. Parts of "The Oil Patch War" were first printed by *The Globe and Mail*, as well as Toronto's *NOW*. Sections of "New Storms" and "The Arctic Vortex" were first commissioned by *Outside* and *Mother Jones*. "Another Nation" was first published in part by *This* magazine.

Visit Penguin Books' website at **www.penguin.ca** and Gordon Laird's website at
**www.gordonlaird.com**

# CONTENTS

# PHOTOGRAPHS

# ACKNOWLEDGEMENTS

AT SOME LEVEL, EVERY BOOK is a collective effort and this one is no different. I would not have travelled a kilometre were it not for the following people.

Thanks go to Cynthia Good and my former editor Jackie Kaiser at Penguin Books Canada, whose idea for *Power* launched me on my energy odyssey. Diane Turbide shepherded the project through its early stages and helped with the first draft. Cheryl Cohen completed the edits and skillfully wrangled a sprawling manuscript into its current form. I am one lucky writer. Martin Gould and Sandra Tooze also provided much-appreciated production assistance for the book's photographs.

Westwood Creative Agents—first Jennifer Barclay, then Hilary Stanley and Bruce Westwood—ably managed the project and continue to keep me in the writing business.

Hong Kong photographer Justin Guariglia travelled with me during the first two chapters, an excellent adventurer inland and offshore. Andrew Murray, a skilled and patient cartographer, drew my map. My scientific readers, Drs. Robert Caton and Norman Rubin, helped parse the subtleties of atmospheric chemistry, climate change and radioactive waste.

Across Canada, people generously aided with my research and travel. Jacklyn MacDonald and Alan Boras at PanCanadian Petroleum guided my passage to the *Rowan Gorilla III*; Survival

Systems Limited made sure I got there knowing how to escape a submerged helicopter.

Joan Waldron at Sable Island Trust provided valuable information on the island's many mysteries. David Waugh, Meteorological Service of Canada, assisted with offshore environmental data. And Mike Mcphee introduced me to Cape Breton. As I followed the coal trail west, the staff at the Frank Slide Interpretive Centre in Alberta were exceptionally helpful, as were the Coleman Museum and the Fernie District Historical Society.

Hans Fast at Environment Canada generously opened up a bunk at Eureka's Astrolab, where part of the fourth chapter, "The Arctic Vortex," was written. Other Arctic angels include First Air; Zipporah Kalluk; Al Gaudet and Vivek Voora of Environment Canada; Bea Alt; Wayne Pollard; Terry Fenge of the Inuit Circumpolar Conference; and Claude Dicaire of the Canadian Ice Service.

In Quebec, Marc Thibodeau of *La Presse* gave sound advice on hydro politics and Marni Thompson hosted me in Val Saint-François. In Toronto, friends Wayne Roberts, Paul Webster, Andrew Johnson, Loic Jounot, Olivia Chow, Sue Zielinski and Shannon Thompson all provided valuable feedback.

Up in Uranium City, Denise Bougie and Bill Holland of Holland's Motel and U-Drive helped me make the most of a too-short stay, as did an anonymous government official who provided useful information beforehand.

In probing the unwritten parts of Alberta, the following people were invaluable: Andrew Nikiforuk, Tom Marr-Laing, Gail MacCrimmon, Scott Thompson, Gillian Steward, Kevin Taft, David Finch, Tony Hall, Martha Kostuch, as well as the folks at the Parkland Institute and the Pembina Institute. Tina Fox and Aaron Young brought me inside the world of Stoney Nakoda; Terry Munroe introduced me to Victor Buffalo. Brenda Erskine and Harold Roth at Suncor were gracious hosts in Fort McMurray, despite everything else; Tony Punko, Bertha Ganter and Ken Shipley were all generous with their time. Paul Tough encouraged me to dig better and further.

Out on the West Coast, Liz Hardy and Don Timlich at Alcan opened up Kemano to its last journalist. Photographer Peter Bennett was an excellent collaborator and Kitimat elder Tom Robinson was patient with a clumsy line of questioning.

I'd like to thank everyone else who helped me rediscover Canada, particularly those forthright people who braved possible repercussions and spoke honestly.

Finally, a number of my favourite editors supported my work along the way: Rick Boychuk and Eric Harris at *Canadian Geographic*; Patrick Martin and Val Ross at *The Globe and Mail*; Jay Stowe at *Outside*; Monika Bauerlein at *Mother Jones*; Ellie Kirzner and Glenn Wheeler at *Now*; Dianna Symonds and Sarmishta Subramanian at *Saturday Night*; Julie Crysler and Judith Parker at *This Magazine*. Thanks to all.

And there would be no book if not for Lisa and Addison, who continue to make my life whole.

Fernie, British Columbia
August 2, 2001

# PREFACE

ENERGY IS ONE OF THOSE THINGS that both vexes and sustains us. After travelling 75,000 kilometres across Canada to research this book—and a year after its initial publication—I am left with some nagging questions. *What have we lost in the wake of our material gains? What is the real cost of progress?*

Energy, economic growth and unsustainable practices are deeply intertwined in Canada. The epic battle over the ratification of the Kyoto accord simply underlines this troubling fact. During the first half of the twentieth century, Canadians revelled in the advent of mass electrical networks, cheap power and affordable automobiles. But by the 1960s, energy had faded from our collective consciousness, surfacing briefly during the oil shortages of the late-1970s.

What was lost—now so clearly evident—was the capacity to apply common sense to the forces that shape our material world. During the twentieth century, Canadians became passengers in the nation-building process, unquestioning consumers of power. Our at-home power sources leaned heavily on non-renewable power and expensive megaprojects, even as pollution and waste became a public health liability. Our homes and our cars grew larger, as did our per capita share of consumption and emissions, despite technological advances in energy efficiency.

Simply put, many Canadians were simply unable or unwilling to address the trouble that brewed behind decades of generous nuclear subsidies, continued dependence on coal power, failure to manage growing energy demand, and the advent of regional power monopolies from Cape Breton to Alberta. When it came to energy, governments did not govern as much as expedite an incomplete vision of progress. Consequently, today's status quo demonstrates little in the way of coherence, resulting in a mess of vested interest and uneven growth that has flourished in the absence of close scrutiny.

Now that Canada has begun to address climate change, among a plethora of other issues, it has found itself short of convenient alternatives. Transportation, housing and industrial practices common to many European countries, for example, are still quite foreign to a nation that actively subsidized urban sprawl and protected its environment with a patchwork of inconsistent and sometimes invisible regulations. Conversely, the mass lobby against Canada's ratification of the Kyoto protocol—arguably the largest mobilization of business interests since the free trade wars of the 1980s—has its roots in a deep nostalgia for the twentieth century, back when pollution and inefficiency were considered tolerable by-products of economic progress. The truth is that Canada is so unaccustomed to mediating its growth impulses, deeply ingrained from its colonial days, that the mere suggestion of national emissions standards, smaller cars and an economic price for pollution have inspired predictions of apocalypse unseen in generations.

Luckily, the end is not so near. While any regime of energy efficiency and reduced emissions will inevitably have an impact on economic growth, the long-term benefit of moderating our energy footprint will, under most scenarios, furnish future generations with a fighting chance for health and environmental security. When global oil giant BP announced a windfall of twenty per cent greenhouse gas reductions in 2002—with triple returns on cost savings expected in future years—it showed that many of Canada's business leaders have much to learn about the opportunities of the twenty-first century. Sir John Browne, BP's CEO, even predicted that half of the world's total energy demand will be met by renewable power—solar, wind, hydro—by 2050. It also showed that BP, with its ongoing plans to produce more oil than ever before, has a really smart public relations department.

In the wake of the Kyoto protocol and growing public awareness, we live in a time of escalating environmental gestures. Take, for example, the giant wind turbine plunked down next to Ontario's leakiest nuclear reactor at Pickering. Each year, there are showy demonstration projects like that one, but some of our most effective solutions remain profoundly under-utilized: national incentives for energy efficiency upgrades, stable support for public transportation and policy reform that recognizes the full cost of fossil power.

Real progress is being achieved across Canada, often without fanfare or glossy ads. Car-sharing cooperatives, green power plans at public utilities, as well as victories against lax regulators and chronic polluters are all tipping the balance forward. Many options exist locally and municipally, along with a rich literature on energy alternatives that has been building since the 1970s.

Perhaps the most underestimated challenge of a post-Kyoto world will be the ever-seductive draw of tomorrow's technology—impractical applications that herald tremendous promise. Hydrogen fuel cells, for example, will likely not offer significant advantages over other technologies for several decades. The problem lies with the fuel: there is no alternative to mass hydrogen production outside of our existing power grid. This may explain why many American leaders have taken such a profound interest in fuel cell technology, while refusing to improve American fuel efficiency standards, a policy measure with the greatest potential to reduce pollution across North America. An estimated billion dollars has already been spent in the USA on federal auto efficiency and fuel cell research, yet real-time results show that overall rates of gas consumption haven't been worse since 1975.

With the exception of Canada's federal government, which hopes to enforce more rigorous auto efficiency standards in the face of stiff American opposition, jurisdictions with retrograde environmental policy have pointed to hydrogen power as a newfangled solution that could keep private sector companies awash in public funds. Hydrogen power has potential, but only if we address fundamental problems first. The fetish for unproven technological fixes helps to explain Alberta's "made-in-Canada" climate change plan: substantial public investment in technology without real pollution limits, graced by ever-expanding oil sands megaprojects across its most distant frontiers.

But here's the good news: in a world so accustomed to energy waste and needless consumption, rapid gains can often be achieved with a modest application of investment and hardware. Common sense has a way of prevailing when people consider their lives in the decades to come. On this count, Canada is rife with possibility.

Calgary, AB
October 2002

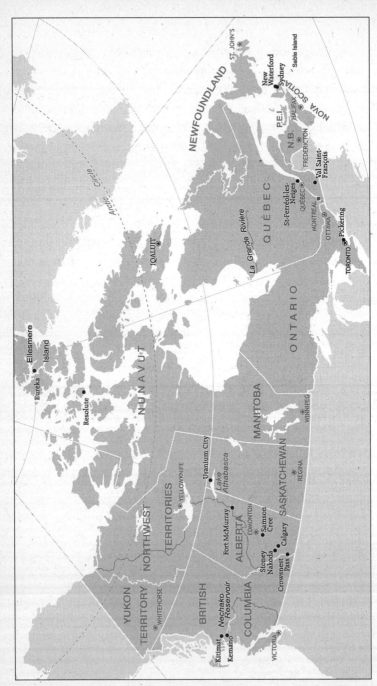

Across the Energy Nation: Selected Sites

# INTRODUCTION

Ellesmere Island

AFTER KICKING STEPS up the snowbound western edge of northerly Fosheim Peninsula, I pause on the crest of a ridge that rises six hundred metres from the pack ice of Eureka Sound. A few more steps up the slope and a view unfolds: to the north, the jagged black mountains of Ellesmere Island and the distant ice of Nansen Sound that feeds south into Eureka's narrow passage from the polar cap. Directly east is Axel Heiberg Island, an undulating and uninhabited span of ice and rock shaped by lava flows from another eon. Just beyond the horizon is the open ice of the North Pole.

This is the polar desert of Canada's eightieth northern parallel, an exotic collection of ice caps, massive permafrost and barren earth. It's nearly minus fifty Celsius as I gaze across the choppy first-year ice of Nansen and Eureka. After the worldwide heat records of 1998, polar ice floes flushed south through these channels along the edge of Ellesmere, clearing out twenty-year-old pack ice in a single season. Multi-year ice is usually about three metres thick—it does not move easily or quickly. Nevertheless, it was the biggest melt in the forty-five years that Canada has measured Arctic sea ice and it was brought about not only by several years of unusually warm temperatures but also by unusual atmospheric shifts.

Fourteen kilometres down the mountain at Environment Canada's Eureka weather station, readings from the 1950s onward chart steady increases in temperature, though it's not quite a heat wave: the average February temperature is still minus 41.4 degrees. But during summer months, station staff are warned about mudslides. Permafrost melts in the vicinity have seen ten-metre blocks of frozen earth liquefy over the course of several seasons.

I travelled to Ellesmere Island in the darkness of winter to explore what has become the most foreboding prediction of a generation: that humans are forcing unprecedented changes upon the planetary balance of oceans, land, ice and sky. It is just a few weeks since the Intergovernmental Panel on Climate Change released a comprehensive survey projecting "much more significant" climate change over the next century than anything seen in the past ten thousand years. Moreover, energy production and consumption is now understood to be the single leading source of carbon dioxide, accounting for two-thirds of the increase in all greenhouse gas emissions since 1980. And fuelled by traditional energy sources that continue to grow, Canada is expected to experience a temperature gain of as much as five degrees Celsius before 2100—twice that above the Arctic Circle.

I began my journey thousands of kilometres south, charting the legacy of Canada's first industrial century. From the offshore rigs east of Halifax to hydro projects hidden deep in the fjords of northern British Columbia, Canada is a country that has always been steeped in energy. From the beginning, turbines tapped the raw force of Canada's largest rivers; primitive oil wells drilled into surface seepages and turned the explosive hydrocarbons into rich fuel; wartime scientists pioneered today's CANDU reactor in the race to build the first nuclear bomb. By the 1950s, Canada was well on its way to becoming a major energy nation, launching successive megaprojects that created an immense network of dams, power plants, oil rigs, pipelines and high-voltage transmission lines.

The truly disquieting message from Canada's Arctic is that global warming appears to be accelerating. Based on energy demand and fossil fuel emissions, the earth's atmosphere is expected to see concentrations of carbon dioxide unequalled in

420,000 years. Dire scenarios have been projected: an increase in tropical disease, a decrease in arable farmland, water shortages, bouts of extreme weather. Not everyone agrees on what the future holds, but when old pack ice disappears from the glaciated reaches of Canada's High Arctic—one of the greatest collections of ice in the world—there's serious cause for concern.

Canada now finds itself at a crossroads. In 1995, we became the world's second-largest per capita producer of greenhouse gases—quadruple the world average—and the seventh largest in absolute greenhouse output. Though our world status has improved, emissions continue to grow, even after Canada's historic 2001 accession to the Kyoto climate protocol to limit greenhouse gases. The National Energy Board estimates that emissions could explode by 44 percent in the years 1997 through 2025.

The estimated cost of adapting to climate change ranges anywhere from $1.6 billion to $17 billion each year. It is Canada's biggest economic challenge since the Second World War, according to federal cabinet documents. And greenhouse gas emissions aren't our only concern: air pollution in Canada's major cities cause an estimated five thousand early deaths each year. Consumers pay an ever-increasing portion of their household income for heating, electricity and transportation. Debt carried by power utilities is at an all-time high.

Yet economic inertia behind conventional power remains strong. "We have energy to burn and we are willing to share," Alberta Premier Ralph Klein told American Vice-President Dick Cheney at a historic June 2001 White House meeting. As the number-one supplier of energy to the United States, Canada's future prosperity is increasingly defined by power exports: energy accounted for almost two-thirds of Canada's large trade surplus during 2000. Consequently, the incredible economic growth that quadrupled oil and gas profits between 1999 and

2001—reaching a record of $7 billion—has its roots in markets to the south.

This fact, say critics, is fundamental to explaining Canada's perpetual flip-flops on energy and environmental policy. Like water, energy is an increasingly valuable but problematic commodity. And Canada still controls some of the greatest untapped energy resources in the world, from the vast, frozen coalfields of Canada's High Arctic to the huge hydro potential of northern Quebec and Manitoba, as well as Alberta's oil sands, the largest hydrocarbon deposit on the planet.

The wealth of power means that we often fall prey to the perils of excess. Second only to the United States, Canada is now the most energy-intensive economy in the world. (And it's not just our cold winters: Denmark and Sweden use far less energy.) And with plentiful domestic sources of fossil fuels, it's possible that we'll push the environmental limits of our own economy—a critical carbon load that could precipitate costly climatic consequences—well before Canada actually runs out of oil and gas.

The solution is likely somewhere in the fundamentals: establishing a more efficient economy, effective environmental reforms and investing in more sustainable power sources. By some estimates, Canada already possesses the technology to cut its greenhouse gas emissions by half and significantly reduce air pollution: public transit, low-emission vehicles and a large-scale deployment of renewable power. The shift to a climate-friendly future could even prove profitable, as consumers and companies learn to live in a high-efficiency, low-cost world.

Back atop Ellesmere Island, a research outpost shrouded in blue twilight across the mountain collects a mass of data that is broadcast to scientists around the world. The island's erratic ice and melting permafrost, though distant, echo an emerging, troubled dynamic that connects just about every living thing on earth. In the deep cold above Eureka Sound, it's hard not to wonder if we've somehow lost control. What began as an improvement on nature—light, heat, power, speed—now presents itself as an intractable and essential series of challenges.

Behind Canada's energy riches and its deep dependence on fossil power stands a question: power built Canada's first century, but will it undo the next?

# OFFSHORE

# The North Atlantic

THE SUN SETS over the North Atlantic and another drill string is dragged from the ocean. They've been at it for twelve hours and they'll keep pulling pipe for eighteen more until they reach the end of the line: a shiny drill bit, a clenched steel fist with diamond teeth that's gone prematurely dull after a tough run of quartz. Mud sprays everywhere as three roughnecks grapple with huge hydraulic tongs that hold the top end of an emerging section, a twenty-five-metre pipe that forms a link in the kilometre-long drill string. It's still steaming from the heat of the earth's crust. They grab the pipe, anchor it securely, then steady another section that's been dangling just a few centimetres from their faces while swinging slowly in the glare of floodlights.

Twenty-seven metres above, the derrickman steadies the pipe and reads a signal from the floor. Standing on a small platform, he's almost invisible in the darkness and he leans out over the abyss as if he's ready to jump. He pulls the huge pipe sideways. It flies several metres over the deck and, guided by hand, gently sets down on a growing stack that leans against the inside of the derrick.

Tonight, the boys of the *Rowan Gorilla III* are tripping. By sometime tomorrow they'll have emptied the foot-wide portal in the ocean floor, replaced the bit and started back down again, ever hopeful that they'll hit a vast pay zone of porous rock that will feed natural gas to the hungry furnaces and electric turbines of Boston and New York. It's September 2000 and as North America faces the biggest natural gas crunch since the 1970s energy crisis—tripled and quadrupled prices in some markets—there's a race to tap the estimated 372 billion cubic metres of gas that lie beneath the Scotian continental shelf, some three hundred kilometres east of Halifax.

It is methodical, painstaking work. The roughnecks, the driller who runs controls in a nearby booth and the assistant driller who reads a bank of dials and printouts—all focus intently on the spinning rotary table, a metre-wide circular vise that screws and unscrews sections of pipe. One wrong move and the whole string—now nine hundred metres of steel—could fall back into the hole, more than a kilometre to the bottom, causing millions of dollars in damage. Worse, drillers continually reckon with the poison gas that bubbles beneath a protective layer of artificial drill mud at the bottom of the hole. A lost string could puncture the pressurized mud balloon, sending sour gas up the pipe and over the drill floor, poisoning the rig with sour gas, or hydrogen sulphide, a naturally occurring neurotoxin that kills instantly at several hundred parts per million. Everyone here knows that there is enough hydrogen sulphide in a small gas deposit to kill everyone on the rig several times over. No one lands on the *RG III* without vigorous survival training, partly because there's nowhere to run but the ocean.

From above, the *Rowan Gorilla III* looks like an industrial trailer park on stilts. But it's really a nautical fortress: two football fields wide and nineteen thousand tonnes, the rig was until recently the largest in the world—the largest, the *RG V,* now stands a few kilometres east, part of a twenty-rig fleet of Gorilla-class rigs that roams the globe in search of drill contracts.

Thirty metres below the drill floor, black waves wash against the three girdered legs of the rig that plunge ninety metres to the ocean floor. During the day, roughnecks can peek down the moonhole in the middle of the floor and see everything from pilot whales frolicking in the surf to great white sharks eviscerating seals. At least once every few years, a storm will roll through that slaps the bottom of the platform with spray from rolling whitecaps—a handy but unsettling way of charting the legendary thirty-metre waves of the North Atlantic.

We're perched on the edge of the continental shelf in about sixty metres of water. Due east is deep ocean. Thirty kilometres to the northeast lies Sable Island, a sandy mass that's surrounded by a huge collection of shipwrecks, some 350 vessels lost since 1583. This is one of the world's most forsaken parcels of sea: bordered by pack ice on one end and Florida on the other, the western edge of the North Atlantic is the stuff of legend. Especially the area that surrounds Sable Island on the Scotian Shelf, where tropical hurricanes run broadside into northern gales and anonymous winter storms fall out of nowhere, breaking boats, it would seem, out of sheer spite.

It's also one of the hottest energy spots on the continent, blessed with plentiful natural gas reserves and proximity to the world's largest markets. And besides petroleum companies that have paid upwards of $100 million on exploration rights alone out here, the arrival of this "Alberta-on-the-sea" has also attracted the interest of electricity generators in Nova Scotia, New Brunswick and New England that are planning to set up a fleet of gas-fired turbines to feed the crisis-ridden American electricity grid. Despite its remote location, the Scotian Shelf is a central node in a continental scramble for more energy, a boom fuelled by some of the highest and most unpredictable power prices in history.

I've journeyed out here during the middle of hurricane season to witness this convergence. Up close, it's an unusual neighbourhood: five heavy-duty drilling rigs circle an island populated mainly by wild horses. Here, stray icebergs and sharks mingle in the island's shallows. The offshore rig itself is a sulphuric geyser capped by a $900-million collection of girders, drill parts and bunk rooms.

I'd heard stories about the rigs. It used to be that platforms were the wild frontier of the industrial world: oil spills, gas blowouts, open liquor, gory accidents. They were lawless places, considered a hazard to anyone or anything in their general vicinity: during the 1970s and 1980s, roughnecks had some of the highest occupational mortality rates in the world. But strict corporate discipline and a raft of government regulations have forced the rigs of Atlantic Canada to become tightly run operations, with military-issue hardware and safety protocol. Aside from greenhouse gas emissions from dirty diesel generators and waste gas flares, their environmental impact is surprisingly subdued: spills are now relatively rare and drilling waste dumped into the ocean is considerably cleaner than in previous decades. Indeed, the worst pollution seems to come from the mainland: urban-industrial smog that blows over from the eastern seaboard and coats the island in acid fog, noxious ozone and assorted aerosols.

In a world marked by extreme weather, growing demand and short-term fuel shortages, today's offshore rig seems oddly well-adapted. Out here, everyone has a well-paying job and free cable TV, and no one goes hungry. If the ocean should rise suddenly as part of a cataclysmic shift in the earth's heat balance, as some climate scientists say is possible, it wouldn't slow drilling operations one bit. We could just jack up the legs of the rig another half metre and pretend nothing had happened.

Then it hits me: I'm not standing on an ocean-bound piece of steel—this rig is an evolution, an industrial oasis in a sea of change.

I ARRIVED EARLIER THAT DAY on a Sikorsky S-61, a large school bus of a helicopter favoured by offshore operations around the world. It sets down on the broad helideck of the *Rowan Gorilla III;* a cargo of other passengers and I amble out in our orange survival suits, gawky and huge like a pack of wayward Teletubbies. The daily helicopter flight delivers fresh crew, mail, machine parts and company missives from the mainland. More importantly, it offers the only quick ticket off the rig: beneath the helideck, poker-faced drillers and roughnecks are lined up, ready to jump on the waiting chopper after a punishing three-week shift. A sullen bunch, they seem halfway to shore already, inwardly contemplating the awkward first moments as returning fathers and husbands—or the first several hours of a raging tour through the strip clubs of downtown Halifax.

We pass the outgoing passengers, ditch our sweaty drysuits in an antechamber and don overalls, steel-toed boots and hard hats. The cold-water drysuits are mandatory for helicopter flights, as are a whole host of other precautions, thanks to a raft of offshore disasters during the 1980s that forced industry and government to address the many dangers of open-ocean drilling. The worst incident was the *Ocean Ranger,* a floating drill platform that capsized in 1982 during a fierce winter storm on the Grand Banks, 265 kilometres east of Newfoundland, killing all eighty-four aboard. It was the first disaster of its kind. Lucky for us, the *RG III* stands steady: its three retractable legs are firmly planted in the murk of Sable Island's outer banks, oblivious to the sway of the ocean. (Even without legs, our rig floats and can propel itself short distances in moderate ocean.) Nevertheless, the Scotian Shelf saw a number of serious blowouts and spills during the 1980s when rigs first arrived at Sable to drill for oil—including the world's most expensive blowout to date, a wild well that spewed hydrocarbons for almost eleven months in 1985.

Most of the natural gas is still underground, along with some 600 million barrels of undiscovered oil. With recent advances in geological mapping and directional drilling, there's plenty of opportunity for anyone who can afford $150,000 to $250,000 a day to rent a reinforced "super-class" rig like the *RG III.* PanCanadian—one of Canada's largest independent producers, with headquarters in Calgary—has launched a $1-billion exploration and production plan that, along with other companies like

Mobil and the nearby rigs of the Sable Offshore Energy consortium, may soon dot this lonely stretch of continental shelf with rigs, platforms and pipelines. The pull of southern markets is intense: following energy deregulation in 1985, Canadian gas exports to the United States quadrupled and now account for more than 15 percent of American consumption. Canada now exports more than half of all its gas production, worth more than $11 billion. Already, the Sable Offshore project moves fifteen million cubic metres of gas to the mainland by subsea pipeline, most of which is consumed in New England.

After negotiating a small maze of catwalks and open stairwells, I descend to the main deck where operations manager Paul Sykes stands amid a clutter of shipping containers, drill strings and dumpsters. It's his job to make sure that the *RG III* discovers as much gas as humanly possible. Twenty-five years ago, the Mississippi native took an offshore job in the Gulf of Mexico. "My first job was roughneckin' right on the floor—on my graduation night out of high school."

Sykes intended to be an accountant, but he stuck with rigs, gradually working his way to on-site honcho—a round-the-clock posting that involves hurricane watch, drill operations, marine logistics as well as ensuring the care and safety of a rotating crew of 180 men and women. It's a big responsibility—when things go wrong, they can *really* go wrong.

"When I first started out, safety was not the number-one concern," admits Sykes. This was back in the dark ages of offshore ops: open lifeboats, inadequate life preservers and minimal emergency training. Deemed unsinkable, the *Ocean Ranger* was outfitted with only four wooden lifeboats and no survival suits. Many, it was speculated, died jumping off the doomed rig into waters that sent them into immediate hypothermic shock. (One lifeboat, bearing eight men, did come within two metres of a rescue craft on the morning after the *Ranger* disappeared from radar, but 90-knot winds capsized the boat and the rig's last survivors were lost to the ocean.)

Now, all offshore visitors must undergo twelve hours of intensive survival training—including submersion helicopter escapes and poison-gas briefings from former British commandos, Canadian military rescue and other paramilitary operatives. I received my training the day before at Survival Systems, a private operation in Dartmouth: in a seminar including several engineers, technicians and roustabouts, we reviewed what happens when a helicopter goes down. It wasn't encouraging news. After a splashdown, top-heavy choppers like our Sikorsky will often roll upside down before quickly sinking, leaving crash survivors about five minutes to exit the flooded fuselage before it disappears.

Moreover, all passengers have to rescue themselves. Our trainers strapped us into a mock-up fuselage suspended over a deep indoor pool to see what would happen under simulated crash conditions. The drill goes like this: the mock chopper is dropped into the water and turns upside down quickly, just as in a real-life accident, leaving us locked upside down and underwater in our seats, hindered by bulky survival suits with nothing visible but bubbles and darkness. Following the instructions given in class, we wait for the compartment to fill with ocean water and pressurize. Then we unhook our flight belts and punch out the nearest window, trying not to lose orientation or breathe in too much water. Hanging upside down, with my nasal passages full, I knock out the window on my second try and swim to the surface. It's a little like drowning, except scuba divers and about twenty other people are watching.

This exercise must be repeated twice more before we're legally allowed to board an offshore rig in Nova Scotia. Full-time roughnecks must complete a week-long course that runs through several more catastrophic scenarios such as rig abandonment, sour gas explosions and open-water survival.

Crashes don't really bother Sykes: helicopter mishaps are still relatively uncommon. The thing he fears is geology. An ill-placed pocket of pressurized gas can blow the top off a rig's rotary table and, worse, potentially send the whole rig up in a fireball. It's happened before. "Been in blowouts in the Gulf two or three times," says Sykes. "We were lucky. Sand and rocks come out of the hole and cut through your lines. The gas can go anyplace."

On land, drillers would try to plug a wild hole with heavy drilling mud or a rapid cement injection. But offshore, a capped blowout can still escape through the silt of the ocean floor. "If you shut it in, the pressure is going to blow the gas out around the legs and your rig will fall in. Then it's all over." An offshore drill team has only minutes to decide whether to vent a blowout or try to wrangle it back down the hole. And you pray that nothing ignites or turns sour. "If it's a kick up the hole, it's now."

Despite all the hydrogen sulphide that lies beneath the *RG III,* the offshore manager would likely dry-vent the poison gas and put everyone in emergency oxygen masks—any attempt to burn the gas could incinerate the whole platform. The best outcome in this worst-case scenario is that the ensuing fireball would combust the noxious gases, but not so intensely as to melt the escape capsules that have dropped off the burning rig into the ocean.

On a clear day like today, the prospect of disaster seems distant. It's business as usual in the North Atlantic: a large crane pulls cargo off the deck of the *RG III*'s support ship, and the derrick booms and creaks above the roar of the rotary table.

"Here, you got to understand what's going on," drawls Sykes as containers plop down behind him. "The biggest danger is that you ain't got anywhere to go."

LOOKING OUT OVER THE DARK ocean from a catwalk near the drilling floor, I search for signs of Hurricane Gordon, a nasty bit of weather that's supposed to touch down in less than twenty-four hours. Yet there's nary a cloud in the sky. Weather is the source of constant fascination out here, not just because it is constantly changing—deep fog one hour, blazing sun the next—but mainly because an offshore rig is a sitting duck for whatever the ocean serves up.

With rogue waves, sandbars and winds that gust to 190 kilometres an hour, Sable still strikes fear and respect in the people who ply these waters year-round. It is a ground zero, of a sort, a meteorological explosion periodically broken by bouts of sunshine. No one is immune: vessels of all sizes have foundered, sunk or beached here, including the *Andrea Gail,* the doomed ship of Sebastian Junger's *The Perfect Storm,* which is thought to have disappeared in waters east of Sable in 1991.

"Under the scourge of the hurricane, for twenty, thirty, even fifty miles out from Sable Island, the Atlantic becomes a chaos of spouting maelstroms, with no rhythm to their range," wrote one shaken sailor in 1928. "As though it were some writhing dervish of sand, Sable shoots out sand bars like feeders and suckers, there one hour, gone ere the next tide. No man can chart these. They make the maddened ocean harder to stem than the Niagara whirlpool. There is no regularity in the violence of wind and wave then, nothing but violent uproar."

None of the fancy computers and expensive hardware aboard the *RG III* changes the fact that we're far out into the North Atlantic, way past quick rescue, out where the ocean usually has the last say. During a February storm several months earlier, the *RG III* was temporarily evacuated, the first time in recent memory; even during the "perfect storm" of 1991, the crew of the *RG III* stayed put. During the 2000 evacuation, the only ones who were left behind were the mariners who ran the support ship—they motored through monster seas as their empty rig swayed and groaned in the distance.

Down below, boat crewman Don Lutwick waits on the small deck of *RG III*'s quick-rescue craft, a small eight-person punt that's sealed and specially rigged to be virtually unsinkable. Soon, we're bobbing on the ocean near one of the rig's legs— waves have long ripped off ladders, external pipes and anything else that wasn't welded down with heavy steel. Above us looms a massive grey triangle that hovers over the waves at an unwavering altitude of thirty metres. This is the business end of the rig, the part that's built to fend off one-hundred-year storms.

Lutwick has worked the waters around Sable for most of his life, first as a fisherman and, lately, as a mate on offshore support ships. He has no regrets about leaving trawlers behind. While oil companies can usually write off exploration expenses, they can't afford to come back without a catch. "I've been fishing off and on for the last thirty-five years," he says. "When you're fishing independently, it's hard to go ashore no matter what the weather is doing if you figure you're going to get a load of fish, right?

"I've seen people picked off by seas," he says, shaking his head. "I was on one boat where the whole front of the hull and wheelhouse had been destroyed." After five days' battling Scotian Shelf storms, Lutwick's mangled boat pulled into Halifax. "We tied up at the dock and ran ashore. And she sank at the dock. I didn't go back on the water for a whole year after that."

Now he sticks with oil and gas—at least the companies have the money for proper flotation suits. We turn out from beneath the rig and speed towards a nearby production platform. We pull up alongside the steel tower of the rig on the Panuke field; it's an unmanned tangle of pipes and girders topped by a helipad that, until recently, sucked crude oil out of a subsea well.

Lutwick explains why Sable throws up such troublesome seas: first, there's the ambush factor. Winter storms and tropical hurricanes have plenty of open ocean to build up steam before slamming into Sable Island's weather station, which may well be the first reliable source of information on a storm—but by then, it's already blown over the island and whoever might be bobbing about nearby. As the only fixed points in an ever-changing oceanscape, the *RG III* and Sable Island frequently serve as guinea pigs in the ongoing effort to map the storms of the North Atlantic. The rig alone sees about five to twelve weather bombs every year.

We circle back towards the *RG III,* rolling up and down gentle swells that are the closest thing to perfect calm you'll see in these parts. But the peculiar marine topography of Sable ensures that big waves appear in the most benign conditions. As the only exposed portion of North America's outer continental shelf, Sable Island is an unconsolidated mass of sand that runs roughly two hundred metres deep and whose submerged sandbars are almost longer than the island itself. It is a plateau of shallow water at the edge of deep ocean, says Lutwick, "and if you have a big storm someplace else, the sea might carry the storm: you get a big mass of water that hits the shallows and moves up.

"Now the 'Perfect Storm,'" he says, in reference to the demise of the *Andrea Gail,* "that was just over the other side of Sable.

Whenever you get shallow water coming up to deep water and you got a big sea on, you're going to have shit happening. Then, if you get the tide coming one way and the wind blowing the opposite way, you don't need much wind at all to make it nasty."

Rolling over deep blue waves, we skirt back under the shadow of the rig. Overhead, one of the cranes lowers a basket towards the waiting supply ship, my ride off the water. Lutwick sends me off with a message. "This is life working a living on the ocean," he says. "The Perfect Storm can happen any time. Some guys live to tell about it and some guys don't. Those guys weren't so lucky."

Suddenly, he smiles. "Just don't let George Clooney drive."

THROUGH SOME MIRACLE of good planning, the *RG III* has never lost anyone to the sea. But it's taken a military-scale assault on the North Atlantic—fleets of helicopters, highly trained crew, strict discipline and one of the world's largest offshore rigs— just to punch a hole in the ocean floor with no surprises.

And despite all its home comforts—satellite television, a gym, recreation room—the main pursuits on the *RG III* are still working, eating and sleeping. Inside the four-storey weatherproof cocoon that serves as living quarters, mess hall and operations control, an endless cycle of twelve-hour shifts marks the passage of time: dinner is served several times every day, as is breakfast. This is a place where you can wake up at 2 A.M., trundle downstairs and find a herd of hungry roughnecks scarfing down prime rib in the cafeteria.

From the helideck that's cantilevered high over the back end of the platform, the *RG III*'s topside appears as a tightly organized maze of drill strings, containers and heavy equipment, all scattered between the living quarters on one end and an eight-storey derrick on the other. Everyone goes about his or her work, unfazed by the scream of the derrick and the rumble of diesel engines and the ever-present cranes that lift and move objects off the water and around the platform, as though a giant hand were constantly re-arranging a large steel puzzle.

But there is a system at work amid the chaos. As an engineer explained to me, the modern rig fixes the odds by employing every available technique to discover new hydrocarbons. In recent years, their success rate has been boosted by precision instruments that enable advanced directional drilling—where a drill team can literally weave horizontally and vertically through the earth, making Swiss cheese out of geologic pay zones. With advanced mapping technology, drillers and engineers can find and exploit deposits that would have been impossible ten years ago. Not only has this extended the life of known reservoirs across Canada—witness the record number of derricks in Canada's western oil patch in 2001—but it also greatly improves the chances of a major find out on inhospitable frontiers.

In the end, the operators at PanCanadian make an educated guess whenever they decide to drill another well in the ocean floor. But sure enough, headlines trumpet a major find several months later. Two wells tested on the *RG III,* drilled horizontally, plus two others nearby, burned more than 1.5 million cubic metres per day, including one that sent measurement equipment off the register. There was just too much gas.

Offshore drilling is more than just an expensive turkey hunt. Tended by a disciplined crew and fuelled by deep financial resources, the modern rig is the cathedral of the fossil age. This is where our industrial economy renews itself, pushing ahead into the future, ever hopeful of plentiful, long-lasting supplies of energy. Out here, faith is a precious commodity: not only do storms sway the rig, sometimes pushing it several metres sideways, but there is incredible pressure to find and secure paying subsea wells. Millions can be lost in a day's mistake and the prospect of a dead hole is always looming. People don't talk about failure out here; it's just too costly and potentially career-destroying. Instead, they attend the drill floor on a twenty-four-hour basis.

As I lay in my bunk at night, listening to a rig that never sleeps, I wondered how exactly CEOs or engineers might reason their way into dragging a 120-metre tower to the edge of Atlantic deep water—at a cost of roughly $20 million a year for each rig. That anyone is able to marshal such an impressive collection of equipment, engineering and expertise in such a forsaken stretch of ocean is no small measure of our faith in fossil fuels. But how is all of this economical?

Energy, more than many commodities, is defined by its proximity to market. Distant oil and gas frontiers—the untapped Alaska and Canada's High Arctic, for example—still pose serious challenges: scores of abandoned plans from the 1970s, including nuclear-powered submarine tankers to skirt the pack ice of the Arctic, testify to a long tradition of frustrated frontier exploration. By contrast, Sable's gas fields are close to some of the largest urban centres in the world. "Proximity to Atlantic Canada and the northeastern United States markets certainly gives this project special value," noted PanCan chief operating officer David Boone. Already, much of the gas from the nearby producing Sable Offshore Energy Project is headed south— along with half of all Canada's total oil production—and the *RG III* will soon help lay another subsea pipeline to move gas to anxious consumers down along the eastern seaboard.

Sable enjoys a prime location, and long-term demand for natural gas will skyrocket. "Canada is one of the few highly industrialized economies that benefits from higher world oil and other energy prices," noted the U.S. Energy Information Administration. While natural gas prices rose and fell by 60 percent on the New York Exchange during 2000–2001, the real cost of energy remained relatively high—with the likelihood of higher demand and potential power shortages on the horizon, as jurisdictions across the continent struggle to meet the demands of the world's hungriest energy market.

While prices fluctuate from month to month, expensive power over the long term is what makes this offshore rig an attractive economic proposition. When George W. Bush declared an American energy crisis in 2001—one so dire, he claimed, that international greenhouse gas agreements and energy conservation should be sidelined in favour of all-out exploration and production—he was actually addressing the effect of high prices, such as a fivefold increase in natural gas prices, more than a lack of fuels. To be sure, the electricity blackouts that washed across California during 2000–2001 were serious moments of short supply. But it was hardly a catastrophic moment that would require, as Bush seemed to imply, the rapid development of every last remaining conventional energy reservoir on the continent. Any scenario that can be vastly improved by cutting back on air conditioning is probably not a full-blown crisis. Not yet, anyway.

The truth is that our economy, rooted in natural resources and fossil consumption, exhibits a strong tolerance for expensive power. But many costs are borne by ordinary consumers, not revenue-rich producers. In 2000, for example, *The Economist* estimated that world oil prices could increase 30 percent but world GDP would only decrease less than 1 percent. In other words, we can pay ever-increasing rates for oil and gas, but the economy would not immediately collapse or hemorrhage—a common concern during the oil shortages induced by the Organization of the Petroleum Exporting Countries in the 1970s. This is especially true for Canada, where a number of economic sectors and regions thrive off high energy prices and governments collect burgeoning royalties and gas taxes.

In practical terms, expensive power means that in 2001 Canadians spent more on their cars and gasoline than on food, clothes and shoes combined. Increasingly we pay more for heating than ever before—consumer natural gas prices spiked almost 50 percent between 2000 and 2001—and high energy prices forced up costs on everything from fresh produce to airplane fares. That's the political and economic reality: regular folks usually benefit last from fossil resources owned and distributed by the planet's largest companies. Many energy expenditures are non-elective—home heating, public transport, commuting— and a core of market demand stays static whatever the price. What's amazing is that by 2001, domestic inflation rates hadn't yet boomed, despite the huge flow of unevenly distributed energy wealth. In fact, Canada's economy, some boosters trumpeted, had never looked better, despite the fact that power costs are pushing low-income Canadians and pensioners toward penury.

For the same reason, the hope that higher energy costs will spur innovation and efficiency across North America haven't yet been borne out: power-hungry conveniences such as air conditioning and large sport-utility vehicles continue to grow in number. Canada remains one of the most energy-intensive countries in the world, with a hunger for power that explains its status as the world's second-largest per capita greenhouse gas emitter in 1995.

The reality is fairly simple: there's still good money to be made exploiting energy the old-fashioned way. To be sure, huge energy profits and skyrocketing prices cannot sustain each other forever, whatever our capacity for absorbing and accommodating high energy costs. But this hasn't yet translated into a nationwide, market-driven campaign for efficiency and energy savings. That's why rigs litter the Gulf of Mexico and American governments push to exploit sensitive arctic reserves in search of conventional fuel: it's not cheap to find and extract fossil power, but it is still considerably more profitable than reducing consumption and building green alternatives.

Some regions are basking in riches—Alberta and British Columbia increasingly export energy resources to the United States—while other provinces that export manufacturing, such as Ontario, are threatened by an American economic slowdown caused by soaring energy costs. Others still, such as Nova Scotia and Newfoundland, are hoping for a fossil windfall (even though the federal government currently claws back most of their oil and gas royalties through equalization payments). It's a clear indication that, in Canada's future, economic health will have a lot to do with one's position on the energy food chain. The denizens of the *RG III* are simply ahead of their time.

And while oil and gas companies enjoy some of the largest profits in the industrialized world, the Sable gas effort will nevertheless have perceivable climatic benefits: if the thirty billion cubic metres of gas beneath the waves here can be brought to market, then the antique fleet of coal-fired power plants that pollutes the central and northeastern edge of the continent could more affordably be converted to natural gas turbines, thereby decreasing greenhouse gas emissions by roughly 20 to 30 percent. If things turn out right, the accelerated conversion of many northeastern coal plants to natural gas would be a clear environmental gain.

But in this age of climate and energy chaos, gains and losses happen concurrently. A fleet of roaring natural gas rigs is not a long-term climate solution; by the early 1990s, Norway's offshore rigs burned enough diesel and waste gas to account for a full 18 percent of the country's total greenhouse gas emissions. And if gas prices dip too low, producers will have little or no reason to expand gas supply: cheap gas is not why the *RG III* is out here drilling in the middle of hurricane season. Short supply, in turn, could sustain downward economic pressure on utilities to burn more coal in the face of high electricity prices.

What passes for normal in this world is something incredible: billions spent on exploration, prolific tax credits for oil producers and growing household income spent on energy—all to sustain a fossil fuel status quo that, according to world scientific consensus, might ultimately end in catastrophe.

ASK ANY ROUGHNECK WHY he comes out here for three weeks at a time, and chances are he'll say it's for the money. While scenery is fantastic and accommodation is top-rate, there's nowhere to hide or escape; it's a voluntary prison of a sort. After prowling the deserted top decks at midnight—still no sign of the hurricane reported to be blowing up from the south—I wondered how exactly people make themselves at home out here on the edge of things.

Up in the radio room, perched on the top floor, Bob Symes sits amid an array of computers, phones and satellite monitors. He admits that the eat-sleep-work routine isn't for everyone. "Early on, there was lots of turnover out here," he says. "A lot of guys didn't like it. They thought you had to be big, tough and mean to work the oil field—but you see the build of a lot of guys out here. They're just regular."

Despite all the physical labour, rig life demands a particular frame of mind. The isolation, the marathon shifts, the close quarters, extensive safety requirements and prohibitions on alcohol, all of these things require stamina and self-discipline. And as you walk the halls, sit for meals and prowl the drill floor, there's a notable dearth of testosterone. It is incredibly macho work, yet there's not a gorilla in sight.

"You don't need to be six foot eight and be able to carry five hundred pounds," Bob says. "But you got to realize that maybe you're not going to see your kid's graduation. Not going to see their first steps or hear their first words."

Many are unprepared for the mental strain. "We've still had people come out here and not last a week." Until 1980, Bob worked derricks, but a freak caustic soda explosion burned him badly from the waist up. "Just the same as if somebody took boiling water and threw it. Fifty gallons hit me and the next thing I knew I was in the hospital." His vision permanently damaged, he retrained as a radio operator and has stuck with rigs ever since. Compared with fishing, he says, it's still the best work around.

If you ask people what keeps them working offshore, they'll usually say it's the money—out here, a mere galley hand can earn $32,000 in a year. But the *RG III* harbours another draw: the rig literally hums with energy, almost alive in its continual creaks and shudders. This is a place where people, mostly men, can do meaningful work in an environment that's constantly changing and presenting new challenges. There's an esprit de corps that comes with working a big rig on big seas, but there's also a surprising sense of warmth that pervades the rig, something that resembles a large family.

Down in the locker room on the main floor, Darren Kolodychuck and a few others are already discussing Christmas, which is still several months away. "Usually, we put up a tree in the cafeteria," says the drill specialist from Alberta. "It's depressing to be away from your family. Last year we had a gingerbread house–baking contest."

Tony Ross, a mustachioed Harley enthusiast who attends the odd biker gathering, nods his head in agreement. "Heck, on Halloween, we even carve pumpkins."

Lest anyone think this is *Leave It to Beaver* on the North Atlantic, it doesn't take long for people to remember the suicides, head cases and personal trouble that happen offshore. One company man during the 1980s, for example, blew a mental gasket on a sister rig, the *Rowan Gorilla I,* then promptly went ashore and shot himself and his son. Another hanged himself on a transatlantic rig tow.

Sometimes, the job itself demands things you'd never imagine. Inside the derrick's control booth, G.G. Macdonald charts the progress of the emerging drill string. It's 11 P.M., a calm, moonless night. A light fog has rolled in, the floodlights glow; the humidity deadens the sound of the diesel engines that roar beneath the floor.

Later, in the drill top-floor office, Macdonald recalls the last few days he spent aboard the doomed *Rowan Gorilla I,* which sank in high seas while under tow in 1988. At the time, the identical *RG I* and *RG III* rigs were the largest in the world: with legs jacked up, they each stood 150 metres high. Cutting an easterly course south of Sable Island, the *RG I* and its tugboat crossed into deep water en route to the North Sea and hit a winter storm. The rig began to take on water when they decided to shortcut to the Azores for repairs.

About eight hundred kilometres east of Sable, the storm suddenly got worse. "I remember the tug captain calling over to say that the barometer had started dropping," Macdonald says. "We thought it might be a good thing. But it dropped bad."

Now well beyond the range of search and rescue, the twenty-six crew of the *RG I* were alone as a hurricane force storm began to tear their rig apart. "There wasn't a handrail left on the deck," Macdonald says. "But what caused the most damage was a container that had broken free and was smashing around, shearing off hatch covers and snapping posts off." One crew member swam underwater through the rig's flooded pump room to open a drain valve that would buy them some time. Others kept toiling below decks to keep engines and pumps going full bore. But they couldn't keep up with the ocean water that was likely leaking through a structural failure beneath the waterline.

Early on December 14, 1988, the tug's tow line snapped and the *RG I* was left to drift, completely at the mercy of the storm, now blowing at about 100 knots. "At about 4 A.M., I looked out the stern from the radio room—I wanted daylight to come so bad—and I could see this light above, which I thought was dawn breaking," Macdonald says. "But it was really a whitecap on top of some rogue seas. A huge, huge wave. It hit the stern and the whole rig just stopped dead in the water, shuddering."

By then, there wasn't a container left on board; drill pipes and collars were scattered across the deck like spaghetti. Seas were about twenty-four metres and there was only one lifeboat left: twenty-seven seats for twenty-six people. "We were listing pretty bad to the stern and we were scared. Scared. We radioed HQ in Houston, we asked them some questions." His voice trails off to a whisper. "But no one really responded. Probably because there wasn't much we could do." He's not saying that the company abandoned the rig—and collected some $21 million in insurance—but he's still confused as to why they were sent out into winter seas with nothing but a tugboat.

Somewhere in the middle of it all, he remembers lying down on his bunk during a lull and accepting death. "I wasn't scared any more. I just lay there. I thought, 'What a waste . . .' I was scared so long and I just accepted my fate. A peace came over me."

At this stage, the rig was going to sink. But it wouldn't just sink, it would capsize—quickly, too, probably with no warning. So the decision was made to abandon: everyone suited up and filed into the enclosed escape craft. Gale-force winds howled and moaned through the bent girders and towers of the listing platform. Two hours and twenty minutes after dropping into the ocean and steering clear, the *RG I* fell off the tug's radar. No one saw it go under. It was another twenty-six hours until seas had calmed enough to attempt a rescue—by then, a small flotilla of cargo ships and tugs had arrived. It was the longest anyone had survived in an ocean escape pod.

"The funny thing is that we all survived," says Macdonald. "But I was having problems." Several years ago, a psychiatrist diagnosed him with post-traumatic stress disorder. It's an affliction that's common to soldiers: from Vietnam vets to peace-keepers in Bosnia, PTSD is sustained damage from experiencing wartime atrocities and sustained fire. "I've had several near-death experiences—but I got sick from this."

Macdonald's glad to be back offshore, running a drill floor where every hole is a new adventure. But he's haunted, too. "You just can't witness something so terrifying. You just can't wipe it away—no human being can."

# NEW STORMS

## Sable Island

O N THE SHORT HELICOPTER TRIP between the *Rowan Gorilla III* and Sable Island, we fly over several offshore platforms, tiny gleaming islands in a sea of blue. Hurricane Gordon has veered west into the open ocean, leaving only high winds and rough seas in its wake. Down below, the growing chop looks like a series of small ripples.

Off in the distance, a long spit of white sand snakes through high surf. Soon, a patch of green appears and a whole island unfolds: a one-kilometre-wide collection of tall grass, ponds and sandy beaches. On either side of the island extends a vast, hypnotic series of breakers that crash upon the beach, a network of whitecaps that eighteenth-century sailors sometimes mistook for sandy cliffs and safe harbour. "I peered through a curtain of fog," wrote one sailor who arrived on calm seas in 1916, "which revealed the most striking landscape I had ever seen: the island appeared to be made of burnished gold and the hills, which faced me, had the angularity of waves in a storm."

From a nautical perspective, Sable is a treacherous sand trap some eighty kilometres long, shoals included. But from the air, it is a green and gold oasis, speckled with brown ponies, swaying grasses and deep blue ponds. Groups of grey seals loll about in the surf and pairs of wild horses trot across thick patches of marram grass. Though scarcely a mile wide at its apex, this idyllic scene runs about forty kilometres into the distance.

The dunes and shoals that continually change and shift have led marine geologists to wonder if the island is mobile: like a giant sandy worm, it has wiggled back and forth across the map ever since there were maps of the region—roughly twenty-six kilometres of island have disappeared and reappeared since 1766. Its outer extremities change and move on a regular basis. Up until a 1992 geographical survey, it was generally thought that Sable Island was migrating eastward, amoeba-like, in a slow-motion bid to rejoin the mainland. Only its midsection has stayed put for any length of time—but even here, roving dunes and shifting sands gobble up old houses, ponds and landmarks. Consequently, despite continual habitation since 1801, there are few fixed place names or reference points.

On an island that seems to harbour more mysteries than ship-wrecks, the feral ponies are yet another source of wonder. The horses have roamed here continuously since 1738, when Boston merchant and clergyman Andrew LeMercier unsuccessfully attempted to colonize Sable. Over the next two centuries, other settlers, scavengers, survivors and entrepreneurs would periodi-cally attempt to settle and populate the island with a veritable Noah's ark of critters: cattle, goats, sheep, pigs, dogs, cats, rats, mice and rabbits. The horses outlived and outlasted everyone, including the settlers. How they managed this, nobody knows.

Now some 350 in number, the stout ponies forage, mate and socialize much as they have since the eighteenth century. With no trees on the island to speak of, their only shelter comes from large sand dunes that deflect freezing winter rains and summer hurricanes. Every spring, scattered green patches of sandwort, marram grass or cranberry mark where fallen horses have decomposed into the ground. The ponies have survived every misfortune that Sable's fierce climate can offer—and have been deemed a valuable genetic resource for their efforts, the noble Sable breed. Subsequently, they seem to regard humans as curious but inconsequential guests on their island.

Protected by extensive environmental and marine legislation, Sable Island is actually part national park and part prison camp: you need approval to arrive, approval to leave—and don't even think about messing around while you're there, because the officer in charge commands the Coast Guard too. Aside from military and penal jurisdictions, it's some of the most highly regulated territory in North America. My permit had almost been cancelled once, I was told, because I'd requested a few days on the island for extra research. I was curious, based on initial reports, about long-distance smog—a modern-day mystery—that was afflicting the island.

On the day I arrive, after weeks of preparation, *RG III* radio operator Bob Symes receives a transmission from Gerry Forbes, the island's officer in charge. "He says he wants you off the island in forty-eight hours—*guaranteed*," says Bob, one eyebrow arched. "We've got some weather rolling through soon, so I told him, 'Gerry, you know nothing is guaranteed out here.'" Anyone familiar with Sable knows that it's common to be stuck on the island for days under thick fog or high winds. "Seems he's intent on something," says Bob. "Don't expect the welcome wagon."

Gerry is waiting at the helipad as the Sikorsky sets down. He politely shows me to the visitor quarters at the edge of the weather station, a small collection of whitewashed buildings that sit alongside a field of meteorological instruments. Looking out over the sand, grass and distant surf, I receive Sable's mandatory environmental briefing: no climbing dunes and no chasing horses. Stay out of the water—sharks, remember, eighteen varieties—and don't go walking off alone, day or night, without notifying whoever is on duty. Because it wouldn't be the first time people have gone missing.

Then he disappears into a shed. With Gerry gone, the whole compound appears deserted, save for a few mares that nibble on a nearby drift of grass. A sea breeze picks up and you can hear the ocean booming from both sides of the island; Ipswich sparrows, unique to Sable, fly overhead along the prevailing wind.

IN ANOTHER BUILDING, Pete Davis readies himself for another birdwatching attempt. After floating an early-morning weather balloon and attending the station's instrument patch, the weather technician is taking the afternoon off. The twenty-six-year-old maritimer is out here earning money to finish his commercial pilot training; his aviation background makes him handy with the meteorological equipment. Thing is, he doesn't really like birding. "Um, my brother says he'll kick my ass if I don't do it," he says, holding a massive pair of binoculars.

Some mainlanders consider Sable Island the Holy Grail of birdwatching: the roseate tern, semi-palmated plover, the red-breasted merganser, and the endangered Ipswich sparrow make up an aviary population unique on the continent.

For Pete, weather remains the big event. Atmospheric forecasts are Sable's main claim to fame. Not only is Sable's station part of the continental data network that feeds our insatiable appetite for weather reports; it also supplies leading data for European forecasts across the ocean. Twice a day, Pete sends up balloons—produced on site from Sable's tiny helium plant—that modem down data from 5,400 metres. Some 50 percent of

France's upper air forecast, for example, is determined by the Sable Island weather balloon launch.

And as we enter an uncertain millennium of weather—freak storms, climate change and transcontinental pollution—scientists are increasingly drawn to Sable's relative isolation; it is an ideal spot from which to observe global trends and transformations. With continuous weather observations since 1871, Sable provides a reliable benchmark for long-term studies. But what passes for normal keeps changing. One computer chart from the weather room plots a steady 10-percent increase in carbon dioxide readings between 1975 and 1997—a forebidding long-term trend in carbon accumulation that has been linked to worldwide climate change. These readings are similar to trends observed at Alert, Canada's military base on the northernmost tip of remote Ellesmere Island, as monitored by Environment Canada.

But what's truly unusual is a decade-long spate of bad weather across the North Atlantic that stretches from Sable's stormy banks to Britain's cold North Sea. This already troubled patch of ocean seems to be getting progressively worse, especially near Iceland, as part of an overall increase in North Atlantic storms noted by climatologists. Before 1989, no more than ten winter storms—the kind that drop like bombs—were measured during any given season. But after 1989, twelve to seventeen storms arrived each consecutive year into the mid-1990s. During the 1970s, by contrast, only six major winter storms a year were observed.

For those who study climate, this is an important trend, because major transformations in our atmosphere or oceans will occur within existing weather cycles. Climate change does not announce itself as a single, dramatic event; it speaks through the ebb and flow of existing weather systems. So if the storms of the North Atlantic are becoming more frequent and ferocious, they are an important signal.

Pete explains that weather systems are inherently connected: just as Sable's atmospheric forecasts allow French meteorologists to predict incoming weather as it crosses the Atlantic, so a series of larger, connected dynamics criss-crosses our oceans, atmosphere and polar regions. This concept of a macroclimate system—a large-scale system of atmospheric energy that connects different points across the hemisphere—has been in circulation for almost two centuries. Teleconnectivity, as it has been called, is climatic cause and effect between two widely separated points on earth.

The growing number of storms on the North Atlantic, for example, has been linked to the growing intensity of a high arctic air mass, some twenty to thirty kilometres above the North Pole. The polar vortex is an ultra-cool body of air that swirls above the pole, part of a climatic pattern scientists have described as the Arctic Oscillation, which has been growing stronger over recent years: cooler air, stronger winds, more precipitation. As cool weather systems spin off the pole into the warmer climes of the south, weather energy of the vortex is absorbed by the North Atlantic's climate, thereby fuelling a greater number of storms. Many believe that this growing temperature differential—between the pole's upper atmosphere and warming southern climates—is the source of new storms, erratic weather and changes in ocean circulation.

As the earth's climate warms at a rate not seen in a thousand years, links are being found between the storms of Sable and other symptoms: warmer and wetter than normal conditions in northern Europe, additional storms across the North Atlantic, as well as snowstorms and colder temperatures across Labrador, Newfoundland, the Maritimes and the northeastern United States. (Linked to a strong Arctic Oscillation, the North Atlantic Oscillation [NAO] is a system of atmospheric energy currently centred over Greenland that is believed to spread and amplify the climatic forces that shape the weather of the northern hemisphere, affecting everything from agricultural yields to fish stocks. Climatologists have observed NAO-related currents pushing warmer Atlantic water 20 percent farther north into the Arctic Ocean, contributing to thinning pack ice and, possibly, slowing oceanic heat circulation. One Columbia University study, for example, found that 50 percent of Turkish winter precipitation is determined by the Greenland-centred NAO, the easternmost limit of its influence.)

Until the 1990s, climate change was often discounted as the chaotic expression of natural weather patterns. But by 2001, storm tracks were hardly the sole purview of climatologists and meteorologists. Over the last half century, global economic losses from catastrophic weather events increased tenfold: from $3.9 billion (U.S.) a year in the 1950s to $40 billion in the 1990s. One of the first global industries to grasp the implications of climate change, teleconnectivity and growing storms has been, not surprisingly, the insurance sector. In February 2001, a group of private insurers working with the United Nations Environment Programme delivered a dire estimate on the growing cost of frequent tropical cyclones, rising sea levels and damage to fishing stocks, agriculture and water supplies: $304.2 billion (U.S.) by 2050.

Climate patterns across the North Atlantic, skipping like a broken record, are transmitting signals that the average observer might discount as random bad weather, even here on Sable Island. But in a place where killer storms are commonplace, you have to wonder what it all means when more clouds gather.

IN THE SAND DUNES around Sable's weather station, things appear generally as they did eighty years ago, back when there was just a single telegraph line ashore. Dunes shuffle from one side of the island to the other, horses wander on an open range of their own keeping, and the humans busy themselves with the lonely and beautiful task of living here. But from climate change to offshore rigs, the modern world is quickly encroaching on Sable's little eighteenth-century kingdom of horses. Eleven days earlier, the island was hooked up to the Internet.

And then there's the garbage. Pete and I are walking along Sable's north beach, where everything from medical waste to plastic pink flamingos is splayed across the golden sand. A total of eight tonnes of ocean-borne garbage arrives each year, borne by the swirling currents of the Atlantic.

It's like some impromptu museum of consumer culture. A single patch of sand offers the following: an empty can of Easy-Off (New, Improved), a plastic toy boat, a single running shoe and a tampon applicator. An occasional seal carcass—one of seven hundred decayed shark kill that wash up every year—serves as a reminder that we're still standing on the edge of the continental shelf.

Pete shakes his head. "This place never ceases to amaze," he says. "Over on the other side of the island is last year's wreck—a $250,000 racing yacht that grounded because the skipper was using some little map from a placemat or weather chart or something." It was the first big wreck in living memory—no lives lost—and the surf soon reduced the boat to a worthless ball of fibreglass and rope.

Over the past few years, memorable items have included mass deposits of baker's yeast boxes, vodka bottles and heroin packets. A few years ago, someone found a wooden leg sticking straight up in the sand. (Later, an owner was located: a one-legged fisherman had bought himself a new prosthesis and tossed his old one overboard.) Some of the garbage has circled the Atlantic several times and French, Nordic and Portuguese packaging is not unusual. It's all tied into the modern energy chain: refineries around the world produced the petrochemicals that form Sable's ever-changing warehouse of plastic.

But the island has always received strange little offerings. In the days before navigation technology, back when Sable claimed most of its wrecks, residents and stranded survivors scavenged whatever the ocean pushed up onto the beaches: timber from wrecks, barrels of bread and biscuits and rum. The bodies of drowned victims would often circle the island for days before washing ashore, floating counter-clockwise with the prevailing current.

As Pete and I walk along the beach, packs of grey seals scatter into the ocean. Their real enemies, sharks, lurk just beyond the breaking waves, out past where the seals must pass in order to find fish. In the meantime, they bob nearby in the blue surf— one hundred black-eyed bodies attentively watching our every move. These aren't goofy little harbour seals, but serious 180-kilogram mammals that will attack with eight-centimetre fangs during winter calving season. Their gaze never falters as we trudge past.

I ask about the nearby drill rigs. Modest amounts of drill effluent are discharged into the ocean, with the approval of government regulators, but nothing on the scale of the oil spills during the 1970s and 1980s. Recently, when one unidentified rig was testing its well on a full burn, black smoke temporarily obscured the sky. There were no official reports, curiously, but it was enough to get people talking. "One time I thought the rig was on fire—half the thing was lit up," says Pete. Air instruments on the island now monitor volatile organic compounds, the noxious by-product of an open gas flare.

The two petroleum companies out here, PanCanadian and Sable Offshore, actually help fund the island's operations. A few years back, the federal government decided it wanted to get out of the small, sandy island business and it turned operations over to the privately run Sable Island Trust, a non-profit body that oversees the station. Funding still arrives from federal and provincial governments, but the island's denizens now solicit donations and project funding to help get by. In many ways, it is an island for hire. Out here on the edge of Canadian territory, this public-private arrangement means that the island has to keep hustling for research grants and funding. Station officer Gerry Forbes jokes that they are going to set up a donation jar in front of the weather office.

So far, Gerry won't let me interview him. Nor will he help me locate Zoe Lucas, the island's second permanent resident. Stationed here since 1974, the biologist and botanist is considered the foremost living authority on Sable: it's reported that she knows every one of the island's 350 horses by name and can discourse extensively on rare island fauna that can't be found anywhere else in the world. Of the two, Gerry is considered the sociable one.

Sixteen years ago Gerry started as a labourer and has gradually worked his way to officer in charge, earning an MA and publishing several scientific papers along the way. Now he runs the whole island.

Curious, I ask Pete: "What's the most interesting thing on Sable Island?" Keep in mind that, on a glorious day like today, prancing unicorns and pixies probably wouldn't seem too far out of place.

Pete doesn't hesitate for a second: "That'd have to be Gerry."

LIKE THE STATION ITSELF, evenings on Sable Island are quiet and lean. It's 9 P.M. and a fog has rolled in. The wind blows, as ever, across the compound, pushing clouds of fog across a few spotlights. Next to the weather building, meteorological instruments rattle and spin in the darkness. Almost everyone has disappeared for the day. Gerry is out fixing a broken atmospheric instrument in the weather garden, a small laser beam that tracks the altitude of the cloud ceiling.

Pete holds down the weather room, a long rectangle banked with computers, instruments and chart tables. "It really blew me away when I first got out here—Gerry just knew everything about the island," he says. Not only that, he can fix diesel generators and program all the computers. All the weather software here is his.

The computer array is impressive. "Nine different units, each monitoring one thing—and each hooked up to phone Gerry if something goes wrong." Um, the machines *talk* to Gerry? "The computer that monitors the generator will notify Gerry on his cordless phone if it's not happy, but it's not like they chat or anything."

He admits that, yes, things do work a little differently out here. Sable's horses will walk right up to you—fifteen centimetres from your face—and stare because they're curious. They don't seem to mind the company. And if some of the humans are less than happy to see a new face, well, get used to it.

The truth is that Sable is a wild place that's always harboured wild people. Before the days of radio and air rescue, shipwreck survivors would often spend months on the island, rooting for berries and seal meat alongside a curious selection of residents that, until the 1800s, included pirates, mental patients, boat wreckers, criminals and religious hermits.

"Back when staff didn't get off the island much, people got a little kooky," says Pete. A nearby computer monitor plots the ascent of a balloon as it moves into the stratosphere, forty kilometres above. The wind continues to howl outside, rattling windows and fences. "People went nuts on a regular basis. You hear stories, like one guy who dragged around a dead gull on a string, like it was his pet."

Behind the pretty horses and idyllic grassy dunes, Sable Island has a well of darkness—not just the body count levied by its shoals, but an atmosphere of dread that pervades the island's wee hours. Tonight, for example, the windows rattle from the sheer force of the wind, a spotlight plays over the swaying grass of nearby dunes. The wind hums through the guy of the radio mast and howls around the chain-link fences that surround the station. Clouds of fog storm through the compound, broken by patches of moonlight. But this is precisely what makes Sable Island compelling: its wildness is complete and unsettling.

Pete admits that it's easy to get the creeps at night. "Your mind starts to play tricks on you—I could see how somebody could lose their marbles." Bound by fog, total darkness can envelop the island. The clatter of wind instruments and the swish of grass can play upon one's ears. Over the years, currents and sandbars have occasionally pushed up old wrecks, ghost ships that linger half submerged and then disappear in the next storm. With accounts of ghosts that stretch back to the 1600s, Sable comes with a rich folklore of lost souls and tales of dementia among the living.

The storm door opens and after hours of wrestling with meteorological instruments in the fog, Gerry, exhausted, plops himself down in a chair. He's finally in the mood to talk. "Where I grew up in northern British Columbia, you'd talk about people going 'bushy.' A lot of people find it entertaining here for the first while, but you add another couple of weeks and it's a whole other game," he says. He's seen a lot of people come and go over the years. "We've had people who've hated it from day one."

"We suspect that we might even be squirrelly already," says Gerry to Pete with a sly grin. "Some people say I was crazy even before I came out here, so what can you do?" It turns out that

Gerry is a knowledgeable source with a keen sense of humour. But he still wants me off the island in two days.

The conversation turns to weather, as it often does, and Gerry shares a nagging concern. For the last decade or so, Sable has been inundated with periodic, intense clouds of ground-level ozone. Photochemical ozone—otherwise known as smog—is a mix of fossil combustion by-products, sulphur dioxide ($SO_2$) and nitrogen oxides (NOx), forged through a ground-level reaction between ambient air pollution and sunlight. It's a stew of reacting chemicals common to large cities—but not remote islands in the ocean. Nevertheless, what Gerry has come to understand, along with several other weather experts, is that the pollution of the eastern seaboard doesn't disperse uniformly across the ocean. Instead, it often congeals into rivers of noxious smog, shaped and propelled by westerly winds that push these plumes off the edge of the continent.

Under the right circumstances, these pollution rivers touch down on Sable Island, sending ozone readings off the chart and leaving islanders to cope with acid fog, haze and occasional eye and respiratory irritations. As charted by American and Canadian authorities, ozone readings on Sable usually average 35 parts per billion (ppb), elevated but manageable. Urban health authorities usually issue air quality warnings by about 80 ppb, but several times over the last ten years, Sable has seen readings as high as 166 and 184 ppb. Gerry sketches out a formula to illustrate: "$SO_2 + NOx + H_2O$ = Acid Fog."

Scientists new to Sable mistakenly assume that the air and climate of the island are pristine, assuming that the nearest industrial source is more than three hundred kilometres away. But nothing is truly remote any more: exotic substances that scientists have found here include micro-particles of bat guano carried on long-distance winds from New Mexico.

Sable Island is still an opportune place to study global and hemispheric trends, and a series of ongoing climate studies measures baseline concentrations of carbon dioxide and the role of carbon sinks in the absorption of human-produced greenhouse gases. Air collected on Sable by remote, semi-automated samplers, periodically serviced by weather staff, is shipped to various worldwide locations (although funding cuts have limited the station's support operations).

It used to be that ocean-borne garbage and soil erosion on Sable were the things that people worried about. That's all changed. Like it or not, our environmental concerns have shifted from conservation—cultivating and protecting pristine ecosystems—to something much larger: the problems of combustion by-products, mysterious weather patterns and a challenging dearth of green energy alternatives.

Even Sable's plans to set up a wind turbine on one of North America's windiest spots—a fitting solution to the weather station's non-stop diesel generator—have been mired in logistical difficulties and financial troubles. Turbines are the fastest-growing source of renewable energy on the continent. But for a host of reasons, it's still more expedient to ship in a yearly supply of diesel from Halifax on the annual Coast Guard mission to Sable. The petroleum that burns in the generator here has taken a long journey: carbon from the exhaust stack likely came from the Middle East or South America as crude oil, tanked across the Atlantic and refined in the Maritimes. (The Maritimes and Eastern Canada still rely heavily on imported crude, worth upwards of $16 billion in annual crude imports—which eats into Canada's growing energy trade surplus.) After a trip back across the Scotian Shelf, it arrives on a heavy-duty landing craft that crawls up onto Sable's north beach each year where it is trucked to underground storage tanks lodged deep in the sand.

By 2001, the island's wind turbine proposal was still awaiting federal environmental assessment. In the meantime, Sable's weather station burns imported, emissions-heavy diesel in a place where the wind rarely stops blowing. Off in the distance, a gas platform silently pipes raw natural gas due west, directly away from the island, answering the call of continental gas markets.

A FEW KILOMETRES DOWN the north beach, another crew convenes for a day's work. Marine biologists from the Bedford Institute of Oceanography in Halifax have been coming to Sable since the 1970s to study grey seals. The island hosts the world's largest population of these mammals, some 60 percent. So twice a year, regardless of weather, scientists fly in by helicopter for several weeks of chasing large mammals with small nets. I'd already crossed paths with the team the day before as they roared down the south beach in their four-wheeled all-terrain vehicles (ATVs). They offered up an invitation to come visit— and, circumstances permitting, do some seal wrestling.

Among other things, marine mammal study offers us a unique climatic window: by tracking the progress of these impressive creatures, we can approximate the health of an entire aquatic food chain. Already, studies by Canadian scientists have found strong links between changing climate patterns and disappearing cod stocks. Over the last few decades, Labrador and Newfoundland cod began to shrink in size as changes in arctic sea ice cover and deep ocean currents began to push successive waves of colder water south along Canada's coast. ("While fishing played a major role in the decline, a decrease in the average weight of fish also contributed [to the collapse of Canada's cod fishery]. This weight reduction was due, in part, to North Atlantic Oscillation–induced environmental conditions with smaller size fish during high NAO cold, extensive ice years," notes K. F. Drinkwater in a 2000 Bedford Institute study.)

Across the deep basins of the central Scotian Shelf around Sable, fishermen also reported a dramatic decline in shark catches in 1998 shortly after a large influx of deep cold water from Labrador; it is believed that the sharks, a mainstay of Sable's marine environment, have moved out of the region

towards warmer waters. Likewise, other fish stocks have moved
south and the lobster fishery on Georges Bank, south of Sable,
has slowed with the increased cold currents because the lobster
are too chilled to climb into traps. The impact of oceanic
temperature swings on plankton, an important carbon dioxide
converter and the main pillar of the aquatic food chain, is not yet
known.

I wondered: how do seals cope amid all the aquatic garbage,
cold water, ocean-borne toxins and storm activity? In the
past, they've done surprisingly well, but things can change
quickly, such as the arrival of deep cold currents. We'd have to
catch some seals to find out more.

The Bedford HQ is the oldest house on the island, built in
1946 for the island custodian. It resembles something between a
cozy college clubhouse and a mad scientist's lair: computers and
electronic seal-homing equipment are scattered amid a quaint
selection of hand-me-down furniture, some taken directly from
the beach that lies ninety metres from their door. Jim McMillan,
a lanky sixteen-year Sable veteran, is in the kitchen doing early
prep on tonight's dinner. Debbie Austin and Tyler Schulz, grad
students, sit in the living room, fiddling with a $3,000 computer
pack that they're hoping to glue onto their next seal. The appa-
ratus measures feeding frequency, diving depths and duration,
and also transmits global positioning system signals, so that they
can track the seal as it swims about the Scotian Shelf.

Every hunt is an adventure. "Last winter, I blew a few tires
after some females chased me down and bit my wheels," says
Debbie, describing the challenge involved with driving through
a beach full of cranky seals. "It's a bit like a video game out
there." During the fall, seals are more sedate—so today's hunt
requires only four people to tackle a seal, as opposed to the
usual six or ten needed during winter.

Don Bowden, team leader and professor of marine biology
at Bedford, outlines the hunting strategy. He rides up front,

scouting the beach for seals that carry a special brand marking them for ongoing study. This can take hours. Once a seal has been located, Don quickly decides if it looks safe to pounce. If so, the team rides a special formation—a broad question mark pattern—specially designed to confuse and disorient the seal, thereby giving them several extra seconds to ditch the ATVs and tackle the seal with a net.

"We noticed that seals will look at you from one direction and as you go around behind them, they turn their heads until there's a blind spot," he says. "It takes a second or two for them to turn their heads back around—an advantage of about two body lengths. We discovered that one through trial and error."

Grey seals are intelligent and large, so the non-motorized part of the hunt—the netting and wrestling—gets a little chaotic. Sometimes, the seal has bodyguards, so you either pick a route around them or try to shove them aside like a blocker. Face to face with a 270-kilogram mass of agitated blubber and muscle, Don says, the trick is anticipating the animal's next move—will it fake left or charge forward?

"You wait until they're just about to bolt and then you pounce on them," he says. "But they can stop suddenly and rear back, so even if you get the net over, they'll throw you off."

"If you're standing in front of them, between them and the water, they'll just go for it," adds Jim. "If they're cornered, they might even hoof it over the ATVs." The team has managed to bag seven in the last week, a respectable average. Remarkably, the humans remain injury-free.

The fog storm intensifies as we ride onto the north beach, towards the end of the island, a thin sandy spit where seals usually congregate. Everyone rides in high gear and the dunes fly past. A few ponies dodge out of our path and it feels as though I've joined the coolest biker gang in the world: Sable's seal workers and their critter computers.

Up front, Don raises his hand and the team members ride

their signature manoeuvre around the edge of an unwitting seal. They stop in the surf and Jim dives off with a 2.4-metre net, chasing down the seal on foot. Don and Debbie are close behind, forming a triangle around Jim. They pounce just as the seal lunges and manage to wrangle the net underneath and around the target. It requires the brute force of three people to subdue the seal long enough to close the net and pin the catch against an ATV until Debbie can inject a tranquilizer.

Meanwhile, Tyler and I are attempting to rescue two ATVs that are disappearing into the surf. Knee-high in ocean, we hit the ignition and accelerate out of the waves, but not before we're partially submerged by surf. Dripping, we park the bikes in front of the net and do a head count. Everyone present, no injuries.

For the next two hours, we sit on the beach and the team weighs the seal; takes water, blood and tissue samples; and prepares the computer pack. We wait for the writhing seal to fall under the spell of the tranquilizer as the light falls. In an hour, it's snoring like Fred Flintstone, groggy and safe. As its soft fur dries in the sand, Debbie glues on the critter computer with marine epoxy. The computer—and all its data—will be back in the hands of the team when they return in January to re-capture the same seal. The epoxy residue will fall off when it moults its winter fur in the spring.

"We're trying to understand, among other things, how these animals make decisions about how to use the ocean," says Don, as we sit in the dark fog. "Are they making a good living? Are they thriving where they're at—or if they're looking for another supermarket?"

What they've found so far is that seals are actually a lot like people: they harbour a basic affinity for their hometown, but will travel enormous distances to earn a living. And despite all the garbage in their water, grey seals are a happy, carefree bunch whose numbers are increasing—no small thanks, perhaps, to a thinning shark population. Diving to depths of four hundred

metres in deep water, the seals commute as far as New England
or the northern Gulf of St Lawrence for food. Some never leave
Sable Island.

One thing is for sure. In an ocean environment that's seeing a
surge in storm activity and sea-level growth, the grey seal is
likely the best prepared of anyone in Canada to weather any
sudden environmental downturn. Sable won't disappear under
the waves any time soon—the Intergovernmental Panel on
Climate Change estimates a possible 88-centimetre increase
before 2100—but with increased storm erosion around the
island's many low-lying areas, it's not impossible that short-term
climate transformations will eliminate the island's natural
airstrip on the south beach (already periodically flooded) as well
as some of the island's prime grazing land. It's hard to say how
the ponies will fare. The high points on the island—the monster
dunes that reach up to twenty metres—are largely devoid of
grass and other plant life.

Back at the house waits a fabulous dinner: Jim's Sable Island
Chowder and freshly baked French bread. In the meantime,
we're stuck on the edge of the south beach until the seal wakes
up. A vast marine frontier stretches out before us—only whitecaps and the surf are visible in the twilight. "This is a place where
time becomes real again," says Jim. "You've got a morning, an
evening. We eat proper meals . . ." Debbie finishes the sentence:
"and sleep like rocks."

Along the first line of breakers, hundreds of grey seals line up
to stare at us, heads bobbing, ever watchful. If they were thinking bad thoughts, we'd never know.

# UP FROM THE UNDERGROUND

## Cape Breton

DON DELESKIE WANTS to show me something. We drive from his home in the working-class Sydney neighbourhood of Whitney Pier, past the town's closed, rusting steel foundry and into a nearby residential neighbourhood. First there's an alley, then a dirt road, and then a muddy trail into a broad field where the road stops, just before a municipal landfill project.

Here, with no fence or warning signs, are the remains of an old dumping ground. Nearby, a bright orange creek flows out of a mountain of municipal garbage. These are the headwaters of the Sydney tar ponds, a series of polluted streams that feed into Muggah Creek. Few know about this spot—and those who do know tend to avoid it. "Underneath the town dump is where they used to throw PCBs and other chemicals from the steel plant," says Deleskie, a retired steelworker turned community activist. "The dump has been around ever since I've been around and before that. The creek runs right through the coke ovens and down through the tar ponds."

Rain pours down as he scrambles down the bank and almost falls into the orange stream. Next to the creek is a large black pond with dead trees sticking out of the middle. "You gotta see the stuff. Burned the skin off my hands once." He stirs the goo, causing a rainbow of colours to wash downstream. It's all part of the largest urban chemical hazard on the continent, a coal-fired legacy of mines, foundries and failed regional development strategies that have left behind thirty-three times the amount of toxic sludge found at Love Canal.

Up a wooded embankment, less than a kilometre away, are the homes and strip malls of Sydney's commercial area. Here, inside a former K-Mart outlet, are the newly opened telemarketing facilities of Electronic Data Systems Corporation (EDS), one of the largest data and technology service companies in the world. Prince Mine, Cape Breton's last coal pit, is about to close; thousands have already lost their jobs as successive coal mines closed over the last two decades. The options for re-employment are scant: one either takes a low-income job in Sydney or simply moves away, usually to Ontario or Alberta.

Amid the ruins of failed coal mines, steel foundries and tar ponds, Cape Breton greeted the new EDS complex with considerable fanfare on September 26, 2000. After 3,700 applicants were screened earlier in the year, 450 were finally awarded jobs. I arrive at EDS on the eve of the launch, at a special Family Night gathering: newly minted employees mill about, with kids, balloons and clowns scattered throughout posh cubicles, meeting rooms and staff lounges. Electronic Data Systems has designed its telemarketing offices with mood-enhancing colours and ergonomics to buoy the spirit. There are nap rooms, a central cafeteria and several lounges. It is an office disguised as adult daycare. Passing overflowing snack trays and fresh gourmet coffee, I stroll about the indoors environment that is the very antithesis of the traditional employer in Cape Breton, the dark coal pits of a coal mine.

So distinct is this indoor world—needing only external power lines and phone jacks—that it can set up operations down the road from an open-air dump of PCBs, heavy metals and dioxins, yet everything seems perfect. A full cleanup of the coal-fired waste—some 700,000 tonnes—would create hundreds of new jobs, but government grants and tax subsidies have, instead, opened the doors for EDS and other high-tech service companies to pick and choose an army of phone workers from a large pool of local unemployed. The ponds stand idle while a growing number of Cape Bretoners manage magazine subscriptions, telemarketing campaigns and customer service queries from across Canada and the United States.

There are few places where the opposite ends of the industrial age so clearly run up against each other. It's not just the fenced-in coal mines down the road at New Waterford and Glace Bay— no nap rooms there, to be sure—nor the by-products of coal combustion that still seep into Muggah Creek, just across the highway and down the hill from EDS. Dependent on coal, ensnared in a larger system of power production, Cape Breton embraced the modern age but somehow never managed to save itself. Some blame the government. Some blame the community and the companies. Some even blame coal itself, the fossil fuel that couldn't compete with oil, uranium and natural gas.

The brutal economic fact is that Maritime coal, rich with impurities and far from today's markets, could no longer compete with above-ground strip mines that supplied better coal at lower prices. Consequently, most of Canada's coal, some 80 percent, is now produced in Alberta and British Columbia. It's not for lack of supply—Canada's coal reserves are vast—but simply that the long historical arc of the industrial age has, for the moment, passed the eastern mines by.

"THIS IS ALL PART of what was supposed to be a comeback for Cape Breton," says Steve Drake, sweeping his hand across the horizon. Before us is the Atlantic Ocean, indifferent and empty. Beneath the waves is a subsea coalfield that stretches most of the way to Newfoundland. If it had all gone according to plan, he says, miners might still be travelling to the coal face every day, eleven kilometres out, boring into what some have described as a near-endless supply of coal.

Instead, we stand next to the abandoned headframe of the Lingan mine, which was large and modern when it opened in 1974 in response to the energy crisis, and was flooded and sealed by 1992. Although we're only a few kilometres from the main street of New Waterford, a historic coal community perched on the edge of Cape Breton's eastern tip, the windswept ocean bluffs of Lingan are deserted. Hemmed in by barbed wire, the towers that lifted men into the deep are now rusting away, attended only by a roving security patrol. Nearby looms Nova Scotia Power's largest plant, twenty storeys high and showing no signs of slowing down as it ships coal-fired electricity as far south as New York. And Drake, who's the last remaining miners' union official in Cape Breton, has been watching his industry fall apart.

A few months earlier, this spot was swarming with angry coal miners, television crews and an RCMP riot squad. An illegal strike of 1,600 miners made national headlines in January 2000 when negotiations with the federal Crown corporation Cape Breton Development Corporation (Devco) broke down. Early in 1999, Devco announced it was getting out of the coal business for good, after thirty years of operation: everything, except the Prince mine in nearby Point Aconi, would be closed for good. There would be no plans to reopen mines—not even newer pits, such as the nearby Donkin, that are still flush with coal.

In short, the power blockade was the fight of people with nothing left to lose. On January 9, 2000, ten men entered the depths of the Prince mine in Point Aconi and, eighteen kilometres out, holed themselves in for a twelve-day hunger strike. They became the anonymous symbols of protest that even union leaders couldn't stop. Soon, five hundred miners swarmed the power plants and ran human blockades that cut off coal trucks. This threw the province's politicians and media into a frenzy. It was only a matter of time until the coal ran out and power shortages set in.

The focus on power was strategic: some 70 percent of Nova Scotia's electricity comes from Cape Breton's two large coal plants. "It was the dead of winter and they had only 50,000 tonnes in reserve," explains Drake, pointing towards the one-hundred-metre stacks at the Lingan plant. "So they shut down the trucks. And people in Yarmouth and Halifax never before made that connection to that light on the wall and what was going on seven miles under the ocean."

Most miners knew their jobs were gone; 1,160 people faced unemployment or early retirement. In the last moments of a 280-year-old industry, miners demanded a final compensation and pension package that would help keep their families off welfare in a regional economy that suffers 20-percent unemployment. "When you're out there twenty to twenty-five years, you're not in good shape," explains Drake. "I look okay, but I've got bad lungs, a bad neck and bad back from working underground. And everybody gets that. But when they made the announcement to close everything—and twenty-year vets didn't qualify for pensions—the miners got visibly upset."

For many, the last great coal strike was about promises that were made long ago by politicians who have long since disappeared. "We were promised a future here," says Drake, referring to Devco's original mission to wean Cape Breton off coal dependence. "Miners were promised a future here. Our communities were supposed to be rejuvenated. But it didn't work out that way. And now we're looking at economic devastation." In the end, the miners achieved a small victory: forced arbitration allowed union officials to negotiate a more inclusive severance and pension package.

Back at Lingan, twilight falls as Steve Drake looks out over the ocean. Seismic crews have been out there, he says, mapping the coalfield for potential offshore gas. Rumours of a whole new offshore industry are circulating in what many hope is the beginning of another energy boom. In a few days, Drake's brother is moving out to Alberta to seek out drill rig experience and a welder's ticket, in the hopes that he might one day return and work the rigs in the waters next to his hometown. Drake himself is running for mayor in New Waterford's upcoming municipal election; he knows that his own days in the coal business are numbered. Though his family has been involved with mines for eighty years, he's the very last union official in Cape Breton. (In 1960, the United Mine Workers boasted a membership of 6,500—by 2000, it was down to 350.)

The last union honcho hopes the offshore rigs arrive soon because there's not much else on the horizon. But like many others, he's staying put—a decision he made long ago. "When people see the headlines that say Devco sucked $1.8 billion from taxpayers, they don't know the rest of the story about how the guys like me were hired in the 1970s," he says. "They said I'd be here for life. I was going to Alberta to work and I decided to stay here. I had the ticket in my hand. I was only twenty-one. The Thursday before I was supposed to get on the plane, I got the call from Devco. It changed my life."

Twenty-five years later, Drake looks out upon an oceanic network of empty mines that, if the government has its way, will soon be sold for parts, as large corporations like EDS leverage public money for new operations. He shakes his head—as though the bad news is still sinking in—gets in his car and drives off.

Some said that it was high time that the legacy of Devco came to a close. Created in 1967 to assist Cape Breton's failing coal economy, the Crown corporation spent upwards of $1.8 billion on the island's coal operations and economic diversification efforts. "My sense is this is the best damned thing that has ever happened for the people involved," Paul Patterson told *The National Post* in the months following the Devco closure announcement. The Cape Breton business professor echoed the government opinion that clinging to coal's past was futile, an expensive exercise in economic romanticism. "For those who let go and come out into the sunshine of the New World, it's not a bad thing. It's time to move on."

IT IS DARK IN A coal mine. Veteran miner Roy Lazzarato warned me of this before I arrived at the stone portal that descends into a hillside along the Alberta edge of the Crowsnest Pass. It seemed obvious enough, but there is really no other way to convey the oblivion of an underground mine. It is total and complete. Topside darkness is usually cut with ambient light— the moon, urban glare—so the sensory deprivation down below still comes as a shock.

We walk into the darkness ahead and the temperature drops about fifteen degrees Celsius. We're only fifty metres into the front passage of an abandoned mine that Roy recently refurbished as a historical site. Along the way, our headlamps shine into dark tunnels that run upwards off the side of the main artery, old coal workings angled at thirty to forty degrees. That's where men chased the coal seam up into the rock, toiling away at impossible angles and leaving behind catacombs that make the mine seem like a beehive. In fact, the whole mine is on a sideways tilt, thanks to the peculiar lie of the Crowsnest coal seam.

Fifty years ago, Roy arrived here from Italy. Unlike other young men who travelled into the mountains of the pass looking for work, he hadn't really planned on becoming a miner. "I was in Lethbridge Christmas Day," he recalls. "Spent all my money on a party—had to work in a mine. So I work here and I like it. I meet a girl, we marry. Been here ever since. No regrets. No injuries."

Miners travelling west from Cape Breton, Scotland or Eastern Europe all followed the same path. "There used to be lots of good Cape Breton men here—but most are gone now," Roy says. "A few stayed though." Islanders kept arriving west into the 1990s to work the now-closed mines of Grande Cache and Tumbler Ridge. But when those operations closed, most islanders moved on.

Roy points up to the mine's dark ceiling. "You read things. The mine, she tells you," he says. "You see some dust falling in a place—you come back to the same place the next day and see dust, that's the rock moving. That's for old-timers to see."

Like other underground mines, Bellevue pumps out a deadly supply of methane. Known as "blowers" or "feeders," fissures in the coal strata naturally expel methane. And the larger the mine, the more gas collects. Disasters are inevitable unless fresh air is pumped in from above. A single spark can set off a chain explosion that will rip through a mine, feeding on particles of coal, oxygen and methane—an explosion so furious that it can suck the air right out of a mine.

Roy explains that this is precisely what happened a few kilometres across the valley at the old abandoned Hillcrest mine. Canada's worst-ever mine disaster began at 9:30 A.M. on June 19, 1914, with an anonymous spark deep in Hillcrest number 2. Feeding on methane that oozed off the coal face and untreated coal dust that caked the mine, a series of fireballs roared through the mine and out the side of the mountain, blowing debris, equipment and miners into the air.

Those not burned by the firestorm had to contend with structural failure. Ceilings collapsed, entombing miners. "It came upon us like a huge breath of coal dust, flying chunks and gas," recalled one miner. "There was no report I heard—just a dull rumble and a horrible black, blinding, choking hurricane, the intensity of which seemed to grow every second like a huge growling monster of destruction."

In total, 189 miners were killed, leaving four hundred children fatherless—90 percent were under the age of eight. The explosion of 1914 was but one of a score of disasters that scattered the pass with funerals.

Across the valley, inside the old Hillcrest Miners' Club, the conversation turns again to carnage in the mines. "We started at sixteen years old, driving horses," says Red McNeil. "They were bringing in horses right off the damn farm: they'd get spooked, fall down the chute and get partway stuck. So you had to wait for the fire boy to put some dynamite in and blow its head off, chop off the legs and throw it down the chute. Had to do that twice. Poor beautiful animals from the farm.

"Horses were more valuable than men back then. Bosses were company men. They didn't care if you were laying there—'You work, you bastard'—they kept it moving."

The old-timers recall, in quiet awe, how they took their first shifts back when mine accidents and death were a common occurrence. It wasn't exactly their first choice of career. "The reason we went into the mines was that it was the only work we had," says Louie, another old-timer. "In 1948 we got $5.72 a day in the mines. Some looked at that dark hole and said, No damn way I'm going in there." But for immigrants and islanders wanting to escape a claustrophobic past, it was an opportunity, however meagre. "We went back and forth from mining," says Red. "Some stayed and some got killed." The last mine on the Alberta side of the pass closed in 1982; the huge open-pit mines of Elkford and Sparwood still ship coal west to the port of Vancouver, where freighters move it across the ocean to steel forges in Japan.

Red and I leave the Miners' Club and drive up a mountainside behind the town in a tiny silver Jeep that grinds and rattles its way along. He wants to show me something. Lush green forest passes by as we bounce and heave along a black gravel road that swings back and forth across the mountain. The black trail is no accident: "Yup, it's all coal," says Red, swerving to avoid a boulder. We arrive at a lush meadow after the road levels off: long grass and wildflowers fill out a broad pasture littered with old wooden fences, cement foundations and machine parts. It could be an old, deserted settlement, but Red points out that we're actually standing in front of the old Hillcrest number 2, site of the 1914 mine disaster.

Red's parents arrived in Hillcrest from Cape Breton just in time for the disaster, after a new railway spur connected the pass to the Canadian Pacific Railway's main line in 1898. Some of his cousins were lost in the blast.

He remembers the thing he wanted to show me. We climb through the concrete archways of the mine's old wash house— its peaked frame could be mistaken for a church—and hike behind the engine house to the edge of a small bluff. Here stands a gnarled apple tree, its branches intertwined around a trunk that lurches skyward. Apple trees don't grow in the Rockies.

"Came from a miner's lunchbox," Red says, pointing to the wash house. Long ago, someone pitched an apple core that fell short of the bluff and took root on the edge. Decades later, Red found it while tending the site. "I come up here every once in a while to check on things," he says. "And pick a few apples. They're good apples, you know."

NORTH AMERICA'S FIRST commercial coal mine sits about a twenty-minute drive southeast of Lingan on an unmarked patch of land. From the highway, I follow a rough trail onto an open bluff that overlooks the North Atlantic. The site is abandoned and overgrown: only a few bare patches of coal can be found behind the grass and shrubs on windswept bluffs. Down at the water's edge, decaying steel bolts are the only clue to the extensive mine workings and pier that jutted out from the hillside, ready to fill ships bound for Boston or Halifax. This, as historical reports indicate, is where a primitive room-and-pillar mine was bored horizontally into the embankment in 1725, just above the high-water mark.

Despite its anonymous trappings, Port Morien is an important starting point: as the site of North America's first coal mine, it launched a first wave of industrialization that fuelled Canada's appetite for speed and horsepower. Before highways and the Internet, coal-fed trains steamed across Canada, compressing time and space through the nation's first network; steel foundries delivered ships, engines and skyscrapers; and coal-fired turbines and generators helped bring electricity to millions of Canadians without hydro power. Moreover, all of this was done with growing efficiency and affordability. Beginning with coal, cheap power became a social force—an incredible surge of raw energy that transformed Canada forever.

But with speed came displacement. Horrible mine disasters from Springhill to Westray across Nova Scotia once marked the toll of cheap power on coal communities—by 1967, an estimated 2,135 miners had lost their lives in the pits of Cape Breton alone. As with those who arrived in the Crowsnest Pass, thousands abandoned the island, seeking opportunity elsewhere.

Today, Port Morien and its corner store, church and community hall bear no evidence of the decline that unfolded across the island. The mines vanished a long time ago; people now work either in Sydney or on fishing boats, or are retired.

From the beginning, there was no easy profit, no golden age for Cape Breton coal. Bountiful supplies of coal in other parts of North America and high transportation costs dashed the get-rich-quick dreams of many coal entrepreneurs even during the nineteenth century. The Port Morien mine, for example, bankrupted a succession of owners and managers. It was finally sold in 1894 to the Dominion Coal Company, an international consortium that would soon control most of Cape Breton's coal production.

By the nineteenth century, a major coal operation could be planted down just about anywhere. Most Canadian mines were grafted from Britain's coal empire: state-of-the-art mining techniques, capital and experienced managers all arrived from across the Atlantic. Soon, advances in steam technology allowed bigger and deeper mines, thereby increasing the demand for workers. Professional miners were recruited from England and Scotland, as well as larger steam engines, surface railways—the complete system of British mining. (Another import was child labour, a practice that was phased out by Nova Scotia labour laws in 1923, but only after an estimated ten thousand boys had worked the pits.)

But by the late 1870s, the local coal boom faltered as American markets increased their output. And as settlers and industrial development pushed deeper inland, the coalfields of Cape Breton grew more distant from emerging coal markets. It was the island's first big economic crisis, set well before Confederation.

The solution, as proposed by Dominion, included plans to consolidate Cape Breton's mines and salvage the coal economy by shipping more coal west to Montreal. With government permission, Dominion consolidated mine ownership—aided by close ties with the Bank of Montreal and the Bank of Commerce—and gained a virtual monopoly on Cape Breton. The island has been controlled from afar ever since, following a national pattern of hinterland resource extraction and regional underdevelopment.

Headed by Boston industrialist Henry Melville Whitney, Dominion's influence over the coal community was considerable. Not only were sixteen major collieries under its control, but whole towns—company houses, company stores and doctors— came under the purview of corporate interests as far-flung as London, Montreal and Toronto (as Dominion Iron and Steel Company and, later still, British Empire Steel Corporation). Major shareholders included Canadian Pacific Railway and the Canadian Bank of Commerce. By the time it built the Sydney Steel Mill on the shores of Muggah Creek in 1900, Dominion employed more than 14,000 men in its Cape Breton mines—up from an initial 3,500 in 1894—and by 1914, the company accounted for more than 40 percent of Canada's coal output.

But the power enjoyed by the company within the coal tri-angle of Sydney, Glace Bay and New Waterford didn't go unchallenged. Strikes opposed company-imposed wage cuts, including the notorious strikes of 1909, 1920, 1924 and 1925 when police and federal military forces were deployed on behalf of the company, ultimately pressuring workers to accept wage cuts of between 20 and 40 percent.

Conditions seemed almost feudal. In 1925, Glace Bay health officials reported that 2,000 sick miners were unable to work and that their families were on "the verge of starvation." In 1922, Canada's Dominion Bureau of Statistics estimated that it cost a miner 90 percent of his earnings to pay for rent and food; workers, in fact, lost money and ran up debts.

"There are men still alive who remember children going to school dressed in flour bags, whole families sharing a bowl of soup made from potato peelings, strikers living on a few mackerel or cabbages from their gardens, trying to survive on 'relief' of 13 cents a day," noted Cape Breton writer Silver Donald Cameron of the events of 1925. "The government placed electric fences and machine-gun nests at the pitheads and brought in army units as far west as Winnipeg."

All the fighting and ideology would come to naught; Cape Breton's decline was already well under way. Early boom and bust cycles had concentrated mine ownership into the hands of a few overseers, ultimately resulting in corporate consolidation, shaky operations and public bailouts. Automation was gradually reducing the number of men in the mines. Perhaps worse, coal had been outpaced; it was a bulky fuel for large industrial engines at a time when consumers were falling in love with automobiles and the rush of petroleum's concentrated energy.

Consequently, coal markets began to shrink across North America during the 1950s, thanks to several oil booms and a postwar wave of hydro-power construction. By the 1960s, coal's share of national energy production had collapsed to its current level of 11 percent, primarily for electricity generation. It was all a far cry from the 60 percent it enjoyed at its peak during the 1940s. Although coal was still a cheap fuel, it simply did not fit into postwar patterns of expansion and consumption; even the trains that shipped Cape Breton coal were powered by diesel fuel.

By the end of the nineteenth century, a number of islanders had already resolved to try their luck elsewhere. The Canadian government was recruiting to settle its vast western territory with some three million sod-turners and fortune seekers. It advertised a western paradise, an oasis from the industrial blight of the past. And, hearing of booming coal mines hidden in the crags of the Rocky Mountains, a number of Cape Bretoners took up the challenge.

AT 7 A.M. ON A SUNDAY MORNING I meet Allan McPhee in the Tim Hortons on George Street in Sydney. This is, for the moment, the most important spot in town: hordes of old-timers and families pass through, en route to weekend outings and hockey practice. A public school principal by trade, Allan grew up watching Cape Breton unravel.

He isn't sad to see the coal mines disappear. "It's all government money. Cape Breton lives and dies by government money," he says of today's situation. The island has become a problem that's passed from one government to the next. "That's why they pump all the money in here. Otherwise the economy would fall apart."

Telemarketing and toxic waste might well be two peas in the pod of regional underdevelopment, says Allan, but first things first: Cape Bretoners aren't born with a genetic urge to shovel coal. Most islanders, in fact, would be happier working above ground, just like everyone else. "The miners I know are smashed up," he says. "There's no magical lure to go down there in that mine. It's not romantic. A lot of those guys are off with a broken leg, silicosis [black lung]. One guy I know can't go through a metal detector at the airport." So it's important not to mistake the mythology of coal mining—Canada's image of Ye Olde Cape Breton—for any local desire to keep digging.

Consequently, any new job here is usually perceived as a good job. But 20-percent unemployment, welfare dependence and other afflictions of a fallen economy aren't going to be fixed by a few new phone banks. "We have the highest percentage of young pregnancies and single mothers in the country," Allan says. "There's a lot of people that have been out of work all their lives. Many of them don't want to work; even if they go work the call centres, they make $9 an hour or $1,500 a month. If they're a single parent, they get $900 a month for assistance, plus $200 for going back to school, plus the cost of child care— there's no point in them going to work."

This is what happens when the power runs out: without a grounded local economy, the island has foundered. And few alternatives include a made-at-home solution, partly because the island has always been controlled from afar, via government funding and a long-term emphasis on extracting fossil fuels, sometimes at considerable public expense. It's a classic economic trap, explains Allan, the curse of rich natural resources that defines many Canadian communities: when the market dried up, the companies left or went broke, and the people stayed on. But there was still enough coal to keep a few mines going. And that provided a sliver of hope that another energy windfall might come along.

"If you really want to understand Cape Breton," says Allan, "you have to look at what happened with Devco and the federal government—how millions were wasted chasing energy supplies that nobody wanted."

In fact, the mines probably would have been closed long ago were it not for a federal plan to revive coal during the height of the 1970s energy crisis. When the government bought out Dominion in 1967, the original Devco plan was to close the coal industry completely by 1981. Island coal production had actually been falling since 1913, when 8.1 million tonnes were taken and sold from Nova Scotia's coalfields, bottoming out at 1.9 million by 1971.

But Devco didn't close the mines—in fact, it opened up several new pits and hired thousands of young Cape Bretoners to work in them. Then, when the Yom Kippur War broke out in October 1973, the Organization of the Petroleum Exporting Countries capitalized on the moment and racked up the price of Saudi Arabian light crude by almost double. Within a month, Canadian Energy Minister Norm Macdonald was calling on Canadians to reduce their energy consumption. On December 6, Petro-Canada was launched by the feds as a new Crown corporation, along with plans for Arctic oil exploration. By January 1974, crude prices had increased sixfold. The uninterrupted boom of increasingly cheap, plentiful energy that fuelled post-Confederation Canada had come to a shuddering halt.

Looking to capitalize on the energy shortage, Devco opened Lingan in 1974 and then Prince in 1976. When the second oil price shock hit in 1976, pushing oil prices up 160 percent, coal prices followed: Cape Breton coal that sold for eight dollars a tonne a few years earlier now sold for fifty-two dollars a tonne. Thanks to events halfway around the world, coal was king again.

The energy crunch intensified. By 1980, oil reached its record high of more than $45 a barrel, pushing the demand for coal even higher. Within a decade, Canada's oil imports had quadrupled—from $945 million in 1972 to $4.5 billion in 1979—and the Maritimes and Newfoundland, which burned imported crude exclusively in their oil-fired power plants and gas stations, paid for much of that increase.

In pursuit of cheap, available power, the government expanded its plans further, leading to a comprehensive $2 billion coal scheme in 1978. It announced several new mines and a thirty-three-year contract with Nova Scotia Power to supply coal for electricity turbines that had been recently converted from oil.

But they still needed miners. "They went to universities, technical training schools, they even went to high schools," recalls Steve Drake of his teenage years. "They said, Don't go out into the brave new world, young man—you come and work in the coal mining industry here in Cape Breton because you're going to be here for life." Some 2,000 young Cape Bretoners were hired as part of a national effort to ensure energy self-sufficiency.

For a while, it all seemed like a great idea. But when oil prices dropped, so did the demand for coal and the $2-billion plan fell apart. Cape Breton's oceanic coalfields ceased to be of strategic importance. And Devco became a liability. "So they backed away from the whole thing," says Drake. "But because they'd hired all these young Cape Bretoners to work in the mines for this megaproject, they said we weren't efficient enough. That the miners weren't productive enough."

Canada had changed, too. In the wake of the energy crisis, homes and appliances were built more efficiently, cars were downsized and designed to burn less gas. The crisis had introduced the notion of conservation to a nation that had giddily guzzled its way through most of the twentieth century. Residential energy use decreased by almost 15 percent between 1978 and 1999. We discovered the "negawatt," the Amory Lovins notion that energy saved is usually the cheapest source of power. And, in the end, it turned out that Canada had lots of power to spare.

The great untold story of Devco would be its spectacular decline after the 1970s energy crunch. It turned out that Devco had been a make-work project all along. "Every time they wanted to downsize, they'd just put a new pension package together," says Drake. Pension expenditures didn't rebuild the local economy but they did keep the coal problem at arm's length from Ottawa. "And the way they did that for thirty years was hand out pensions, almost exclusively," he says. "In Devco's history, they had about 9,000 people and they pensioned off about 7,800.

"The big decisions that cause the big problems were made far from Cape Breton," says Drake. "They were made in Ottawa. And that's where, we believed, the problem lay. They just wanted out, no matter how they had to paint it to the public in Vancouver or Toronto or Montreal. So the guys down here looked bad. But it was no one's fault.

"I was here twenty-four years and I had a good run. Devco was a good company to work for," says Drake. "But if the federal government had followed through, everything would have been okay. But it wasn't. There was mismanagement, too. But there's enough blame for everyone that was involved in this—unions included—to share."

STEVE FARRELL, FORMER DIRECTOR of mining operations at Devco, agrees. "There's enough blame to go around," he says of Devco's demise. He too thinks there's still a small but viable mine industry left in Cape Breton—and he's willing to gamble his own money to prove it.

Farrell, a soft-spoken mining veteran, is drawing diagrams of various mining techniques on a napkin for me. At one time, Prince mine had the fastest-advancing longwall operation in the world: whole city blocks of coal could be sheared off in a few hours. Computerized hydraulic jacks would advance themselves, holding up the strata as the cutters and conveyor belts ate through the coal.

North Americans still demand coal: world energy demand is projected to increase 57 percent by 2020—no small thanks to

contentious American plans to build 1,300 new power plants—
which means that coal still could have a future in Cape Breton.
But it would require a local coal operation that's free of politics
and meddling. Strikes are no longer an economic factor; in an
age of normalized labour relations, Farrell says, the last fifty
years have seen maybe one or two major strikes.

These days, he's working with a small co-operative of laid-off
miners who are looking to reopen the flooded Donkin mine—a
huge coal reserve of 1.5 billion tonnes that was built near the end
of the 1970s' energy crisis and never reached full production. The
Cape Breton Miners' Co-operative was launched a few years ago
when 37 miners committed $880,000 of their own money, earned
from Devco severance packages. But they still need more juice.
Farrell is looking for American investors and a long-term supply
contract with the coal-burning power plants on the island. Steady
work, mechanization and lean management are the only way to
keep any new mines running. "There is room for a coal industry
here: 650 could mine three to four million tonnes a year," he says.
"Twenty years ago, you'd need 3,000 men for the same job."

From the 1992 Westray coal disaster—twenty-six killed in a
privately run mine that cut corners—to the erratic Devco
legacy, it's clear to Farrell that the only sure solution is local,
especially when it comes to creating jobs and looking after
themselves. He does the math on another napkin: if they sold
directly to the power plant, Virginia coal might be cheaper per
unit, but Donkin coal would still have a twenty-five-dollar-per-
tonne advantage on transportation. Nova Scotia Power is already
importing 20 to 30 percent of its coal. And Donkin's coal is a
grade higher than most local coal, so it could probably substitute. As Lingan's power plant imports a growing percentage of
fuel, what's the sense in shipping coal to the doorstep of one of
North America's largest coalfields?

Besides investment capital, the biggest problem is the federal
government: it wants to sell Donkin for scrap, along with every

other mineworks in the Devco package. The miners' co-op didn't make it onto the government's first short list of sixty prospective buyers in 1999 and unsuccessful proposals have been launched since. After a year of talks, exclusive negotiations with an American firm, Oxbow Carbon and Minerals, fell through in March 2001, leaving the prospects for a worker co-op increasingly dim. Under the co-op the Donkin mine would have been the first locally controlled mine operation in living memory.

But the government has other interests. In 1999, the Liberals rolled through Sydney promising a new wave of high-tech initiatives—thanks to the $68-million federal and $12-million provincial funds of a joint task force, Enterprise Cape Breton. As the Donkin miners' co-operative languished, generous public subsidies were handed over to some of the world's largest telemarketing companies—EDS and the nearby ICT Group—on behalf of a "high-tech" crusade that delivered jobs paying only $8 and $15 an hour.

By 2000, $20 million had been spent on luring an EDS phone complex to Sydney, delivering 450 new positions, soon to expand to 900. Founded by Ross Perot in 1962, the company claimed $18.5 billion (U.S.) in revenue in 1999, flush with contracts from the American military to scores of blue-chip corporations.

"We are giving people the dignity of work," said Prime Minister Jean Chrétien, who arrived in Sydney in April 2000 to announce the EDS facility and defend the government's newest Atlantic subsidy program. He refused to meet with Devco miners to discuss their future. Instead, he talked about the ancillary benefits of high unemployment. "The people will not quit their job. That's one of the things about going into an area like that. When they have a job, they keep the job for their lives."

It struck some as odd that the prime minister would be touting the attractions of captive labour markets to a hometown audience. Nevertheless, EDS opened its first "Customer Interaction Centre" in Canada at Sydney, precisely because it couldn't recruit enough workers in Raleigh, North Carolina, where a remarkably low 1.5-percent unemployment rate priced workers out of its mid- to low-end wages.

The high-tech drive strikes Farrell, a former miner, as overblown. Even if the Donkin mine co-op never ships an ounce of coal, a few government-sponsored call centres aren't going to fix underdevelopment from a century of coal dependence. "Steelworking and coal mining: they're industrial jobs," says Farrell. "To think we're going to become computer buffs overnight is a stretch. Everyone talks about the new economy but the problem is that everyone here isn't included."

Besides, throwing public money at American corporations only failed before. Devco's first development strategy between 1968 and 1971 offered substantial subsidies to secondary industries from outside Cape Breton—"footloose industries" that might be persuaded to settle locally with heavy incentives. "This period was one of industrial development failure," writes David Johnson in a 1995 report. "Of nine such projects launched during these years, costing some thirty million dollars, only two survived past 1971. Most outside firms, once having exhausted their Devco funding, simply pulled up roots and departed."

A few months later, the federal high-tech plan suffered a setback: a major call centre with nine hundred jobs for Glace Bay abandoned plans to open in 2001. Stream International had been negotiating with provincial authorities about setting up shop in the former Devco headquarters. The company had already held a local job fair that attracted more than two thousand people. But it wasn't to be; Stream chose Prince George, British Columbia, for the location. "It was a business decision," said Rick Beaton, vice-president of Enterprise Cape Breton Corporation. "They like to be the largest employer in an area."

EDS is, however, clean work. Cape Breton's call centres might well be publicly subsidized salt mines of the computer age, but islanders are not going to lose their lives fielding cranky customers from Florida. As Edna Budden, chair of United Families—a Devco miners' advocacy group—told the Nova Scotia standing committee on economic development in 1999, any return to the coal face would be a mixed blessing. "When the economy is bad and jobs are hard to come by, there will always be people who would be willing to take the risk, especially if it has been ingrained in your blood," she said. "Personally, as a mother, I have a twenty-year-old son who I would not want to see go in a coal mine."

THE THING THAT OFFERS steady employment in Cape Breton is precisely the thing that governments, companies and most citizens don't want to touch: several hundred new jobs could be created easily with a comprehensive cleanup of the tar ponds.

And there's plenty of work to be done. Most of Sydney's waste came from the foundry's coking process, in which coal was metallurgically fired to produce a vital fuel for producing steel; the coke ovens operated almost continuously, twenty-four hours a day, from 1901 to 1988. All effluent and waste was dumped on site. Estimates range from $500 million to $2 billion for a complete cleanup.

From the headlands near the town dump and beyond, Muggah Creek flows through a set of old coke ovens and industrial sites, feeding into the south arm of Sydney Harbour. The site remains virtually untouched, save for a series of dams to manage water flow and an experimental incinerator that was built in 1994 and then decommissioned due to technical failure. The main ponds lie behind the chain-link fence across from the homes of Intercolonial Street. Site supervisor George Hennick stands on top of a small dam that regulates the flow of Muggah into Sydney Harbour, inspecting the dark pools that swirl below.

The amount of contaminant here is incredible. Directly below the surface lie two to four metres of toxic sludge, part of the 700,000 tonnes of contaminated sentiment within the Muggah watershed and surrounding fields. This, in turn, contains about 3,400 tonnes of polycyclic aromatic hydrocarbons (PAHS), an intensely carcinogenic collection of substances that is created through the processing and combustion of fossil fuels. High volumes of heavy metals, dioxins and PCBS are also present, along with other aromatic hydrocarbons like benzene, toluene and a series of "unidentified organic compounds" that even by 1996 scientists couldn't identify. In fact, short of radioactive waste, just about every carcinogen known to humankind is represented. That this volume of unremediated toxins lies close to homes and schools is unprecedented on the continent.

It all began in 1899 when Dominion, kingpin of the island's coal mines, turned soil on Muggah Creek for its new steel foundry and coke ovens. By 1981, after decades of unregulated air emissions and water discharges, government tests discovered elevated PAHS in lobsters, some twenty-six times greater than normal. An immediate ban on lobster fishing was launched; follow-up tests along Muggah showed the estuary to be "completely devoid of all life," with water that was "acutely toxic to test organisms." Between 1981 and 1986, provincial and federal governments reviewed cleanup options and decided on a plan to gather and incinerate the waste.

By 1988, the coke ovens were finally shut down. Similar to the beehives of brick ovens along the Crowsnest Pass, Sydney's coke firing metallurgically transformed coal into a pure fuel for steel smelting. At the time of the 1981 lobster study, the foundry released pollutants into the water at ten times the industry average. Likewise, PAHS from the coke ovens exceeded those found in other steel communities across North America, thanks to an antique metallurgical process and inefficient combustion.

As early as 1958, authorities were aware of a growing pollution problem. "A study conducted in 1958 revealed that dustfall and dry sulphate deposition were extremely high, exceeding Ontario's objectives by as much as 15 to 40 times on occasion," recounted one report by Nova Scotia Environment. By 1977, a federal health study suggested "that air pollution in Sydney may be causing impaired respiratory function in school-aged children." By 1984, the first of several studies reported elevated incidences of cancer-related death—"significantly elevated mortality"—in Sydney. Some government reports raised questions about self-induced disease—smoking, hard living—but nearby upwind communities such as Sydney Mines and Glace Bay didn't show the same elevated mortality rates.

"If there's a bigger cleanup in North America, I'm not aware of it," says George Hennick. Then he corrects himself: there's no cleanup happening here. He and a few other former steelworkers maintain the site, but the multi-million-dollar incineration facility built in 1993 has, with the exception of some test burns, lain dormant ever since. It's a sad truth and he's pained to say it—especially when fellow steelworkers and Devco refugees could have all had jobs working on a decade-long cleanup. "We've been shut down since December 13, 1994," he says with a sigh. People used to worry that a cleanup would threaten steel mill jobs, but more now see the toxins as a possible boon to local industry, spinning off hundreds of "new economy" cleanup jobs. But sadly, there's no action scheduled for at least the next several years—just more studies.

Hennick agrees to show me what's left of the one serious attempt to clean up the ponds. After clearing several security gates, we drive towards the idle steel foundry. The road runs alongside the harbour and then takes a steep turn up what appears to be a small three-storey mountain on the edge of the water. It is, in fact, an enormous pile of waste from the foundry—slag, steel scraps and who knows what else. The view from the top is spectacular. George asks that no pictures be taken of this part of the tour; they don't want to publicize that this waste hasn't yet been evaluated—and nobody really knows what lies beneath. Why? Because it's all part of the steel foundry package that the Sydney Steel Corporation is still trying to sell off to foreign investors.

We pull up to the foundry and walk behind the old red-brick powerhouse—a looming Victorian structure that once held the guts of a four-storey, coal-fired turbine. The roar of the place must have been incredible. Next to the silent powerhouse sits a futuristic-looking collection of steel beams, pipes and towers. This is the incinerator that would have burned the sludge and the toxins.

"It operated for about a year and then closed," says Hennick, as we walk around the structure. It was an innovative cogeneration plant and high-volume incinerator that recycled waste heat to fire an electricity turbine, thereby creating power to sell back to the grid or the steel foundry. But the special pipeline built to transport the sludge—far safer than open-bed trucks—didn't work. "It was pumping 80 to 90 percent water and 20 percent sludge," he says. "They looked at other companies to come in, try to pull the technology together." After the incinerator failed, it was decided that the cheapest alternative was to just bury the waste: reroute the creeks into a holding pond, cover it over with slag and put down topsoil—a $36-million encapsulation program.

"But that plan didn't go over too well—so the province threw up its hands, because it would have been $120 million to incinerate," he says. "Incinerator stayed shut down, largely because of money; when it was $30 million, it was a great idea, but $120 million was something else."

The tar ponds soon became locked in a slow-motion jurisdictional dispute between federal and provincial governments. "Seventy percent of this material is on federal property, so who's paying for it?" Hennick asks. A Joint Action working Group (JAG) was launched, with a $26-million budget to manage and study the site but no mandate to remove waste. So yet more studies were done. Some community members disavowed the process, and sporadic contamination trouble—goo seepage in basements, unidentified substances on open land—has since kept the tar ponds in local headlines. In the meantime, the cleanup cost went from $120 million to $2 billion.

Over on the other side of the foundry, steelworkers are picketing the plant's closing. Soon, it will probably all be sold for parts. The fate of the incinerator and the cleanup plan are equally uncertain.

NOBODY EVER THOUGHT THAT COAL could bring so much trouble. It used to be that people who worked in the plants and in the mines reaped the consequences of power—mines collapsed, forges exploded and unions fought management—but during the latter half of the twentieth century, a change occurred. Communities and residents began to realize that they themselves were sometimes at the losing end of the energy cycle. Especially spots without political clout or swank demographics, like Sydney's Whitney Pier and Intercolonial Street.

Across the tar ponds, outside the gates of the complex, several men in white contamination suits and rubber boots are drilling core samples. The muck at the edge of the lower pond looks forbidding—and smells like hell—but no one is wearing a mask. They report that they're working on yet another study. Behind us are the houses of Intercolonial Street.

Sharon Williams has lived on Intercolonial for twenty-three years. Airborne fumes and health warnings have turned the neighbourhood inside out. "Some days . . . you couldn't sit on the patio, couldn't go outside, couldn't do anything," she says. "But like most things stuck in front of you, you just tune it out. The neighbours do the same, they just tune it out. It's unbelievable the kind of money they put into it. Been going on fifteen years now. Still no further ahead than we were twenty years ago."

People continue to live here, despite well-established health concerns, mostly because their homes have been devalued to such a degree that they can't sell—especially when rumours of a government buyout keep circulating. So they wait.

"In the meantime, we have homes that have no value. On our street alone you couldn't give a house away—unless it was 'buy one, get one free.' We had a few owners try to sell—one had a house that would be worth eighty thousand dollars anywhere else in the city, but he couldn't even get thirty thousand dollars."

Over on the other side of the ponds is the working-class neighbourhood of Whitney Pier. On Sydney's infamous Frederick Street, about fifteen homes have already been bought out on sites in clear view of the old coking plant, just upstream from the lower ponds at Intercolonial. As before, the coal-fed waste sites—and hot spots—are all near homes and schools, and protected only by chain-link fencing. One street recently had a basement goo seepage problem, resulting in residents' being forced to leave the premises. By mid-2001, five children from the neighbourhood had tested positive for high levels of arsenic in their blood and urine.

Last year, Don Deleskie, who's fighting chronic respiratory disease, stood on the banks of one of the ponds and shovelled sludge into a barrel—his own personal cleanup effort. Two television people covering the event were overcome by fumes, collapsed and had to be taken to hospital. "Thank God it was reporters that were dropping. I don't say that 'cause it's good. But it was news then."

I'm sitting in his house in Whitney Pier, a few blocks away from the fence. He couldn't sell his house either, but he doesn't want to. He's sticking around to fight the government, which he claims has criminally neglected and mismanaged a clear public hazard.

Deleskie got into the environmental issue fifteen years ago after retiring from the steel foundry. He was born and raised in Whitney Pier, and the tar ponds stuck in his earliest memories. "I remember being a kid and having to watch what way the wind was blowing because of the orange ore dust from the pond. . . . The paint was peeling off the buildings. When you see the sky turn pure orange, well, what are you sucking down? Every window had a rainbow on it—every different colour. This was an unbelievable place."

Then a family tragedy struck. "My mother was thirty-seven years of age when she died of cancer. And I remember waiting for her on the doorstep like a dog for her to come back. I never ever want another child or family to go through that.

"And it went from there, I suppose. You hear of people dying more and more. And you start investigating." By 1993, the retiree had already gone on two hunger strikes to protest the deferred cleanup, meeting ministers and bureaucrats along the way.

While responsibilities for the cleanup are bickered back and forth between governments, new information continues to confirm the community's worst fears. One 2001 study discovered that soil and groundwater samples taken around Whitney Pier had arsenic levels up to sixty-seven times acceptable limits, as well as elevated traces of lead and benzene. "They've been studying this since 1980—studying, studying and studying," says Deleskie. "The tar ponds have been studied to death. I could go up and bring a crate down of studies. And they'll do the same studies again. Then they tell us it's okay because most of the waste is underwater. They must think we're totally brain-dead. Or totally stupid."

Later, we visit Sheila Windsor, Don's sister, who taught school in the Pier for eighteen years. "In 1960, no one had ever brought it out into the public," she says. "We didn't realize the damage that was being done to the health of the community. . . . Women just thought that it was something that happened—this miscarriage, or this child born with a deformity—and didn't realize how high it was in relation to the rest of Canada. Our rates of miscarriage are higher, so are birth defects and anomalies than other parts of Nova Scotia."

Now she watches some of her former students get sick. "Students die of cancer, others dying of childhood leukemia. . . . I'm still ashamed to see students, now in their thirties, that I taught at that time are coming down with breast cancer.

"I think a lot of people here couldn't believe that anything could be that bad. And there still is that defensiveness. And a bit of apathy, because they feel the government is going to do nothing anyway.

"A number of people my own age have died—that I went to school with or was associated with. They have been dying off: you'd almost think it was an epidemic. There's these people: fifty-seven, fifty-two, fifty—all cancer."

There is a forsaken feel to the neighbourhoods around the ponds—like some polluted nook of Eastern Europe. These are working-class people who have been abandoned by government and are now stuck in limbo. Their homes have been devalued and most can't afford to move, yet compensation and cleanup aren't forthcoming. In practical terms, they are captives; some accept the situation, while others rage against it. "The hardest part is knowing what is there and realizing that your government has almost contempt for you," says Sheila Windsor. "If they would even come out and say, 'Yes we truly have a problem. We're going to work together.' Admit the birth defects, the anomalies."

Later, I ask Allan McPhee about the ponds. "I taught some of those kids from Whitney Pier," he says. "It's an issue for some people. The waste is dangerous, no question. What's interesting is how they've spent tens of millions of dollars and they haven't taken any sludge out. The only one who's taken anything out is Deleskie."

ON MAY 16, 2001, the federal government announced that the very last coal mine in Cape Breton would be closed for good. Prince mine and its 440 workers would fall idle by the end of 2001, bringing Devco's layoffs to more than 1,500 since 1999. The mines would not be sold to anyone, including the Donkin miners' co-op, which had made an unsuccessful $20-million offer to Devco earlier that same month. In total, $1.8 billion in federal money had been spent in Cape Breton since 1967 and the island would now have to import all of its coal.

Besides retirement homes and world-class fiddlers, the only sure thing in Cape Breton any more is the Lingan power plant. It roars ahead twenty-four hours a day, generating six hundred megawatts of electricity, enough for 600,000 homes from Nova Scotia to New England. With power consumption following an ever-increasing continental trend that began in the 1940s, jobs at Lingan's plant are some of the most secure in the region.

At the heart of the plant are four furnace boilers, seventeen storeys high, that combust a non-stop stream of pulverized coal. Coal dust is air-jetted through a series of nozzles into a blast chamber to create a swirling fireball fifteen metres high that twirls above the floor of the furnace. Times have changed: tending a continuous coal-dust explosion is now one of the safest jobs a Cape Bretoner can have.

Some 1,247 tonnes of coal daily disappear into Lingan, making it the tenth-largest single source of air pollution in Canada, based on 1998 reporting data. Already 30 percent of its coal is foreign, shipped in from Pittsburgh or Venezuela, and soon all the island's coal will arrive by boat, crossing over the abandoned oceanic mines of Glace Bay and New Waterford. In 1999, 1.3 million kilograms of hydrochloric acid, 369,000 kilos of sulphuric acid and 21,700 kilos of arsenic (Canada's third-largest single source) were released as combustion from the non-stop coal burn.

The one-hundred-metre stacks that vent the combustion waste of Lingan are outfitted with scrubbers and filters to reduce fly ash and sulphur. And like most smokestacks, they are specially designed to blow emissions skyward, far away from the site—partially to avoid blanketing local residents with ash, sulphur and hydrochloric acid. But old solutions to pollution from coal-fired power—scrubbers and tall stacks—have become part of a newer set of questions.

I'm standing on the roof of Lingan, looking out over New Waterford about sixty metres below, and there's little physical trace of the noxious gases that roar out of the furnaces. Driven by heat from the 550-degree fireball, greenhouse gas emissions such as carbon dioxide, acid aerosols such as sulphur and nitrogen, as well as trace elements such as mercury, accelerate through the tower like a bullet. Under the right wind conditions, they shoot out the end of the tower at one hundred kilometres an hour and climb to four times the height of the tower. From there, prevailing winds carry emissions away from Lingan Point, usually out over the North Atlantic, circulating into the currents of the troposphere. Some might even reach the stratosphere, some forty to fifty kilometres above the earth's surface.

The stacks are an effective long-distance broadcast system for the kind of chemicals that periodically blanket Sable Island. Moreover, the stacks do little to mitigate Canada's greenhouse gas output: some 8.4 million kilograms were produced by Nova Scotia Power's generating stations in 1999, the tenth-largest source in Canada. Twenty years ago, few would have noticed if several million kilos of greenhouse gases and sulphur had gone unaccounted for. Lingan's towers addressed one problem—decreasing the rain of chemicals into the community—but created another.

What happens next is the beginning of an energy transference bigger than any earthbound force: climate, the unsettled atmospheric and oceanic balance of the planet's energy. From deep underground to the middle reaches of the atmosphere, Lingan is now just the beginning.

# THE ARCTIC VORTEX

## Iqaluit, Resolute, Eureka

IT'S A FRIDAY AFTERNOON at the Iqaluit Municipal Arena, an airplane hangar of a building in the middle of the territory's frozen capital. Iqaluit faces off against Pond Inlet. Teenage boys scramble up and down the ice, hoping to prove themselves in front of the hometown audience. The one-hundred-strong crowd, in turn, goes wild as Iqaluit scores a succession of goals. Especially the teenage Inuk girls who've come to watch their classmates. So begins the annual Baffin Island hockey tournament, several days of non-stop play. Communities that once met out on the pack ice during hunting forays now await the passing of the Zamboni ice machine together, bundled up in fur-fringed parkas and kamiks, much like any other local hockey audience in North America.

Up in the stands is Iqaluit's coach, John Donovan. A southerner who moved north years ago, he watches over his team quietly as his assistant coach, a former Inuk player who'll one day have his own team, runs the bench below. Boasting the only artificial ice surface in the territory, Iqaluit is the hub of Nunavut's hockey world. While other communities like Cape Dorset to the east and Arctic Bay to the north skate on natural ice rinks—covered with a roof to keep the winter cold out—Iqaluit enjoys modern facilities that are commonplace down south.

It used to be that the biggest concern was lack of available hockey equipment and the high cost of travel to this community two thousand kilometres north of Ottawa, but there's something else afoot. Stricken with an unusually warm December, teams across Nunavut couldn't begin their hockey season because their natural ice rinks wouldn't freeze. For long stretches around Christmas 2000, Iqaluit enjoyed curiously balmy weather with temperatures above those of southerly Canadian cities. "It's warming up all right," says Donovan. "A lot of places have trouble with their ice. Two years ago, warming in March nearly shut down a tournament in Rankin Inlet. The rink melted right in the middle of the tournament—the paint was coming through the ice."

A year earlier, in the spring of 1999, a lone news item appeared in Nunavut's weekly newspaper, the *Nunatsiaq News*. It reported that the Nunavut Territory Hockey League was having trouble holding itself together: climate change in the North has drastically cut short the playing season in locales across the region. With only one artificial rink in the territory, minor-league players from Rankin Inlet on Hudson Bay to Arctic Bay at the north end of Baffin Island were falling off the official roster because play schedules were being so disrupted by an erratic ice season. By the beginning of February 1999, only seven hundred players had registered, fewer than half the usual number.

So I called Jim Ramsay, president of Nunavut's minor hockey league, to find out more. He confirmed that the warming trend in the Arctic over the last three to four years has dramatically clipped the outdoor hockey season because the rinks keep melting. "In the Arctic, believe it or not, we have trouble with ice," he says. Until a few years ago, Rankin Inlet hockey began in late October; by 1999, it was beginning only in January. Even in Arctic Bay, site of the world's northernmost hockey league, the regular season has been shortened by two or three weeks. "We run tournaments in the spring because the freeze-up is so slow," reports recreation co-ordinator Thomas Levi.

Back at Iqaluit's artificial ice, there's little skepticism about climate change. "All ice rinks in Nunavut are natural ice," explains Jim MacDonald, president of Iqaluit hockey. "So we wait for the cold to come and the arenas to freeze. With global warming this wait is longer and longer each year." A few coaches around the tournament confirm that several communities are scrambling to build their own artificial ice rinks. They just can't trust natural ice any more.

Rising air temperatures, disappearing permafrost and unpredictable sea ice are causing concern across the Arctic. Record summer temperatures that were, in some Arctic regions, almost five degrees Celsius above normal, precipitated a record ice melt in 1998, flushing out the channels of Canada's High Arctic Islands. "This was some of the oldest in the Arctic Basin," reports Thomas Agnew, a climatologist at Environment Canada. "Clearing of sea ice was three to four weeks early and the lowest minimum sea ice in the High Canadian Arctic in the last forty-five years of sea ice was recorded." Moreover, six of the ten largest summer sea ice melts since 1953 occurred between 1990 and 1998. And High Arctic floes along Sverdrup, Nansen and Eureka channels have broken up every year since 1998, leaving behind only traces of old ice that once locked these island passages in a near-constant frozen grip.

In 1999, scientists at the University of Washington found that the thickness of the polar cap ice had decreased 40 percent since U.S. submarines first took measurements in 1958. Almost 1.4 metres had disappeared from the thickness of pack ice that covers the North Pole. Here in Iqaluit, one of the spots least affected by warming in the Arctic, freeze-up in Frobisher Bay arrived in January, over a month late.

I arrived in Iqaluit to grasp the impact and potential fate of the south, by way of the eightieth parallel. My final destination is Eureka, a remote weather station almost two thousand kilometres north on Ellesmere Island. As I travel to the northernmost civilian outpost in the world, the earth warms at a rate not seen in a thousand years. So what, exactly, is happening to the frozen parts of our planet?

Hockey players, hunters and scientists are all asking questions about ice. Inuit elders recount that today's sea ice is far more erratic, mobile and fragile than the ice of ten or twenty years ago. Polar bears have become disoriented by the change, wandering far inland at times when they're usually out prowling the floes for seals. Skies are cloudier, and thunder, previously unheard of in many areas, sometimes roars in the distance.

The North is far more than pristine wilderness impinged by the industrial south. The icy Arctic is, in fact, one of the earth's great thermostats, a fundamental counterbalance to the warming force of solar radiation that burns the equator and the atmospheric heating of the greenhouse effect. Poleward heat transport is the primal engine behind our climatic balance: what earthlings experience as weather actually begins in the thermal energy transfer between the globe's heat-laden middle latitudes and the frozen poles. And within this, the deep freeze of the Arctic regulates global climate in ways that we are now only beginning to fully understand.

IT'S MINUS THIRTY-FIVE in the winter darkness and global warming feels like a distant rumour. As I wander around in a down survival suit, Inuit hunters, sporting caribou skins and rifles roar down Iqaluit's main street on snowmobiles. Taxis and four-by-fours line up at the city's main intersection, a mini–rush hour at 4 P.M.

Around the corner from the hockey arena is the small, one-room hut of Iqaluit's Hunter and Trapper Organization (HTO). In between caribou tags, a Coleman stove and a computer, David Audlakiak is busily tracking this season's polar bear kills. "Anybody in the business of selling refrigerators would not do well today," he jokes. But only nine bears, including two defence kills, have been logged since the season opened. It's a slow start, mostly because the sea ice was slow to freeze along the bay this year, making it difficult to travel to the ever-important ice floe edge, where bears hunt seals, and seals forage for dinner. In fact, sea ice was more than six weeks late this year in parts of Frobisher Bay.

"One thinks the land to be very plain, not much to harvest, but my kin learned to exist in this hard kind of climate," David explains. "Ice is usually safe for hunting in late October but we had to wait until Christmas."

Local hunter Maquitoq has worked Frobisher Bay ever since he and David arrived back from residential school in 1968. "The weather up here has been really weird," Maquitoq says. "We would get thunderstorms and then we would get snow. Last month, the weather didn't get cold at all—it just wasn't cold."

Not everyone believes the theories of southern scientists here, but hunters are nevertheless observing change: winter ice sets in slower, springtime ice is retreating faster and thinning quicker. "For my family, it takes longer to get fresh seal in the bay," says David. "We cannot have seal unless the ice can support Inuk weight. So warming hasn't helped us any." Prime hunting season happens on either side of the winter deep freeze, when moving ice and abundant food draw out the animals. But now, irregular ice makes it more dangerous to pursue polar bears and seals and, in turn, more difficult for the bears to pursue their prey. Consequently, bears wander inland, away from traditional hunting grounds.

The link between polar bears, hunting and climate change is no accident: Arctic sea ice insulates polar oceans from the warming rays of the sun, reflecting as much as 90 percent of solar energy back into the atmosphere, whereas open water absorbs most heat.

The pivotal role of ice in global warming is what scientists call a feedback loop—the more ice that melts, the less protection there is against further warming and melting. If ice can't recover during the Arctic's dark deep freeze, the melt cycle intensifies.

Moreover, melting ice infuses the ocean with freshwater—sea ice desalinates naturally—which, in turn, changes the density of the ocean, altering its circulation.

Indeed, the water due east of Iqaluit—Baffin Bay and, south, the Labrador Sea—is considered the ground zero of a planetary network of ocean currents that serve as the primary regulators of the earth's climate.

Oceans act like a large energy battery, storing up heat and insulating the world from the extremes of atmospheric activity. A complex maze of oceanic currents circles the earth, ultimately delivering heat energy from middle latitudes to the poles. Consequently, polar oceans and sea ice are doubly important in terms of climate stability. (The heat delivery process is known as thermohaline circulation, and alterations in the variety that is dominated by the Arctic and Nordic oceans can affect global climate, particularly the climate of Europe and North America, according to a 1998 report by the Intergovernmental Panel on Climate Change [IPCC].)

Solar heating and melting freshwater, especially from the glaciated reaches of the Arctic, are feeding into Baffin Bay and the Labrador Sea, potentially delaying or suspending deep water circulation. It's a potential chain reaction that could happen within a few decades, what many believe is the cause of previous rapid climatic transformations that have been etched in Greenland ice core samples since the last ice age finished ten thousand years ago. It turns out that Arctic ice has a message for us: climate change can happen swiftly and with relatively little warning. Some scientists even argue that the climate could swing cold before heating up further, while a smaller number argue that the long-term geologic trend is a permanent cooling trend, leading to the next ice age.

It could all happen sooner: some scientists predict that summer ice over the North Pole could disappear by 2100. "Considering the amount of area the polar ice cap has, it's an impressive scenario," says Guy d'Argencourt at the Nunavut Research Institute, a long red converted trailer around the corner from the HTO.

David doesn't have much time to conjecture about potential climate catastrophe. He's too busy trying to keep local hunters in business. With the fur market damaged by animal rights activists and with the high costs of gas and living expenses, most Inuit hunters already subsist on small margins. "Sometimes it is cheaper for them to buy food from the Northmart," David says of the large grocery store in the centre of Iqualuit that's full of imported goods. "After four thousand years of surviving on the land, this is what happens."

He's angry that many Inuk, though resourceful, are faced with a dwindling set of options as they become dependent on city food, shelter and government assistance—all this at a time when disturbing levels of mercury and DDT continue to move up the Arctic food chain. It turns out that several Inuk I've talked to here are homeless—regular denizens of Iqaluit's overbooked emergency shelter. "There's not one person in this room who hasn't had to go to Social Services for help," David says. "There are contaminants being discovered in our ocean. Governments make it hard for us to hunt. What's next?"

THE SKIES OVER IQALUIT are changing. "To my memory, when you would look up into the sky during winter and spring it was beautiful blue," says Annie Shoo. "In the last decade, it's been more hazy—not true blue."

Annie and Shorty Shoo live down the street from the Nunavut Research Institute. They are both elders who have hunted across south Baffin, living as their ancestors did, until the 1960s. "Drastic changes since my time growing up," says Shorty. "In my time, there would be snow that lasted all summer and would never melt. But in the 1990s, the snow patches on the slopes near here melted away."

While rain and thunder are unusual for Iqaluit—especially during winter—the thing that strikes them, besides volatile ice floes, is the colour of the sky. One explanation is Arctic haze, frozen pollution aerosol that has been accumulating in the Arctic atmosphere for years, akin to an urban layer of smog that sometimes turns Northern skies yellow and orange. The haze derives mostly from the coal, smelting and other industrial pollution of Eurasia. It takes roughly two weeks for pollution to travel what scientists call the "Siberian Express" from northern Russia, over the Arctic Ocean to Greenland, Canada's High Arctic and the North Atlantic.

But another possibility is that the skies over south Baffin are clouded and uncertain simply because its climate is becoming considerably less stable. Indeed, says Guy d'Argencourt, the most curious thing about Iqaluit is that its wintertime temperatures have been dropping over the last several decades. Stuck between ice melts and cold winds, Iqaluit is on the cusp of a volatile thermal gradient that runs down the eastern edge of Canada's Arctic. With warmer air from Canada's central and western Arctic on one side and cooler air over Baffin Bay on the other, Iqaluit is in prime position for weird, unstable weather: hunters report spring and fall ice thinning around Iqaluit while the nearby Labrador Sea is sometimes locked with winter ice. It's a curious climatic zone sometimes called the Baffin Cold Spot, stretching to Greenland and south to Newfoundland.

Greenhouse skeptics have hailed the anomaly. But growing evidence shows that the Baffin Cold Spot is the site of a larger, more global shift. Under regular circumstances, Arctic weather affects much of the northern hemisphere by way of an ultra-cool vortex of air almost the size of Africa that hovers twenty to thirty kilometres above the polar cap. The vortex is a low-pressure hurricane that, in winter, clocks at 155 knots with regular temperatures at minus eighty-five Celsius. Bereft of solar energy and cooled by ice and ocean, the winter vortex pulls heat from the northern hemisphere as far south as the equator. Likewise, ultra-cool bodies of air break away from the swirl of the vortex and fly southward.

Over the past thirty years, polar winds have grown but scientists have, until recently, been unable to explain why. Spun off from a polar vortex that seems to be growing stronger, winds rush south, picking up moisture and heat from warm ocean currents, pulled north by oceanic circulation. This wind assault from the pole chills east Baffin but ultimately broadcasts large quantities of warm air and moisture across lower latitudes, creating warm winters in Europe, Canada and the United States. As polar oceans slowly warm from decreased ice cover, additional heat and precipitation is released into the atmosphere and carried south. This, by way of Iqaluit's uncertain weather, is how many southerners experience "global warming."

In other words, revved-up polar winds that deliver balmy winters to eastern North America and Europe also deliver extra ice, cold and all-round variability to parts of the Arctic. A strong polar vortex has also been identified as a governing force in the hemispheric weather pattern known as the North Atlantic Oscillation, which is linked to everything from Sable Island storms to Tunisian rainfall.

Our unsettled vortex appears to have its roots in greenhouse gas emissions. According to climatologist Drew Shindell of the U.S. National Aeronautics and Space Administration (NASA), the leading cause of stronger polar winds is increased quantities of carbon dioxide, methane and water vapour. ("Greenhouse gases have the biggest impact on the strengthening of the polar winds, and in turn, the warming of the Northern Hemisphere during winter months," he writes in a 2001 modelling study published by NASA's Goddard Institute for Space Studies. Solar radiation, ozone depletion and natural variability were deemed relevant but secondary causes.)

For those who study the cryosphere—the frozen parts of the

world—recent events stand as a portent. While a greenhouse-gas-laden polar vortex cools Iqaluit, the rest of the Arctic follows a warming pattern that is the largest and most rapid anywhere on earth. Eventually, even the Baffin Cold Spot is expected to succumb: local warming over Greenland is likely to be one to two times the global average, says the Intergovernmental Panel on Climate Change, setting in motion a freshwater melt that has the long-term potential to raise oceans by more than six metres worldwide.

As evidence mounts, polar ice emerges as the fulcrum of climate change. "One third of the increase in global temperatures resulting from increased carbon-dioxide are the result of direct and indirect feedbacks of a shrinking sea ice cover," notes Environment Canada's cryosphere study group. Moreover, emerging science suggests that human impacts on global climate are amplified by ice degradation in the North. As the IPCC puts it simply, "disturbances in the circumpolar Arctic climate may substantially influence global climate."

Mountain glaciers hold only enough frozen water to raise the sea level about half a metre, but if Greenland were to melt, even over several millennia, the sea level could rise by three metres or more. And changes in the West Antarctic ice sheet could raise the sea level another three metres within the next thousand years.

The message that emerges, though, is that cataclysmic ice melts don't need to happen in order to disrupt the environmental and health security of the south: even by slow attrition, the disappearance of frozen water and soil makes our climatic systems more susceptible to chaotic extremes.

IF THERE'S ANYTHING that worries hunters, it's the reports of animal deformities and sickness that have surfaced in recent years. "More and more ring seals are found with strange things on the skin of the animal," says David Audlakiak at Iqaluit's

Hunter and Trapper Organization. "Hunters cutting up a ring seal and getting sick from seeing the deformities—I hear some very gruesome scenes. Horrific scenes that they never saw ten years ago—contaminants that arrive by way of atmosphere are doing something to the land."

Up north, climate change and atmospheric toxins are closely linked: both are governed by weather energy transfers between north and south. Toxins like dioxin and mercury are transported by what is known as the "grasshopper effect": in the south, air- and water-borne toxins evaporate in the warm air and are blown to colder regions as warm air currents cycle back towards the pole. Chemicals reach the Arctic and are trapped because it's too cold for them to evaporate and float back up into the atmosphere with water vapour.

Toxins and greenhouse gases often share the same source—power plants, refineries, incinerators, garbage dumps. Energy deregulation across North America has kept an army of old coal plants in operation, leading to increasing mercury emissions. The U.S. Environmental Protection Agency estimates that between 60 and 75 percent of the development-impairing toxin in U.S. waters is from industrial pollution, and that coal-fired power plants are the largest and only unregulated source, dumping approximately 30.6 tonnes of mercury into the atmosphere each year. Over the last century, emissions from North America, Europe and Russia have found their way into seals, lichens and Inuit breast milk.

According to a 2000 survey of Baffin hunters by the Qikiqtaaluk Wildlife Board and the World Wildlife Fund, almost half of all hunters reported finding more abnormalities in recent years than before. "Perhaps one of the most interesting observations that was made in seal, walrus, and narwhal was the presence of round wounds in the skin," said the report. These were described as looking like burns or as though a circular bit of skin had been removed. "Further investigations into this condition are warranted." Encountering skinny polar bears and severely deformed seals, hunters could only speculate on the possible causes: toxic contamination, ozone depletion, overpopulation and climate change were all concerns.

Whatever the case, it's become clear that environmental toxins are one of the most pressing health issues in the Arctic. Chronic mercury exposure can cause developmental disabilities, defects and sickness. People are afraid to say it—and studies aren't complete—but pregnant women who eat traditional food are clearly at risk in many Arctic locales. The Centre for Indigenous Peoples' Nutrition and Environment at McGill University found that of 514 communities it studied, approximately 57 percent of Inuit tested and 20 percent of Dene had blood levels exceeding the Canadian mercury guideline. "[In one] Inuit community, over 50 per cent of residents had dietary exposure levels exceeding [guidelines] for mercury. High-end consumers had intake levels 6 times higher."

"We've always said that if anybody found the same levels of toxin in western beef or Maritime lobster, there'd be a panic," says Sheila Watt-Cloutier, president of Canada's Inuit Circumpolar Conference, the leading international political body for First Peoples around the Arctic Circle. "Imagine for a moment if you will the emotions we now feel as we discover food which for generations nourished us and kept us whole physically and spiritually is now poisoning us."

The conference leader has just arrived home from New York. For the last several months, she has been lobbying and negotiating around the world on the issue of Arctic toxins. And with success: in December 2000, she helped secure an international moratorium on the twelve worst chemicals, signed by 122 countries in Johannesburg, South Africa. After spending the first twelve years of her life travelling by dogsled with her family in Nunasiat (northern Quebec), she now jets across Africa, Europe and North America as Canada's leading Inuit representative.

"It's a matter of health and cultural heritage," she says. A decline in traditional food consumption usually brings increased diabetes and social problems associated with more de-cultured First Peoples to the south. "It's not just about store-bought food. It's about losing the hunting and the connection to the land—and the incredible learning and teaching that the land offers."

Most toxins outlawed by the 2000 treaty will still take upwards of fifty years to disappear, Sheila explains, even after emissions have been curtailed. Most are virulent and have been known to cause cancer, allergies, and hypersensitivity; damage to the central and peripheral nervous systems; reproductive disorders; and disruption of the immune system. Many of these health effects are also intergenerational, and can affect both adults and their children. Hydrocarbon-based toxins and heavy metals such as mercury are without regulated limits and are not covered by international treaty.

From the window of her Iqaluit home is an incredible view of Frobisher Bay. It's hard to imagine that we're sitting in the middle of a food chain troubled by power plants and insecticide sprays thousands of kilometres away. But across the bay, Iqaluit's dump is burning its garbage again. The ground is too frozen to bury the volume of refuse from the booming city, so it is incinerated in large piles. The smoke plume snakes along with the prevailing winds, out towards the end of the bay. The burning garbage inevitably provides what is likely Nunavut's first home-grown source of persistent organic pollutants (POPS).

Across the Arctic, community diesel generators introduce unknown quantities of hydrocarbon by-products and trace heavy metals into the environment, along with homegrown greenhouse gas emissions. And with the exception of small windpower experiments in three of Nunavut's twenty-six communities, the Arctic remains dependent on imported fossil fuels—some 340,000 hectolitres annually—for electricity.

Down south, there's economic and political pressure to continue expanding energy supplies, drawing heavily on conventional sources like petroleum and coal. And combustion byproducts such as mercury—a potent endocrine disrupter and blood toxicant—remain ungoverned by international treaties and many jurisdictions. The U.S. Environmental Defense Fund estimates that the 2001 Bush energy strategy could increase mercury emissions by more than 50 percent, largely through the expansion of coal-fired power. And while Canadian mercury emissions have fallen substantially since 1988—3 tonnes in 2000, down from 14.2 tonnes—mercury from domestic electricity producers has actually increased.

According to Ontario's Clean Air Alliance and Environment Canada, mercury discharges are falling sharply in almost all industries, except power generation. Ontario Power Generation (OPG), for example, accounted for nearly 20 percent of all the mercury dumped into the Ontario environment in 2000; OPG's Nanticoke facility, North America's largest coal power plant, produced 260 kilograms alone. (By comparison, it only takes about a gram of mercury to contaminate an eight-hectare lake.)

Due to the inevitability of long-distance transport, some of that mercury will find its way into Inuit food. The Arctic food question has loomed for several decades. In the late 1980s blood and fatty tissue samples taken from Inuit in southern Baffin Island and northern Quebec showed surprisingly high levels of certain POPs, especially PCBs and DDT—industrial and pesticide contaminants delivered from distant, anonymous sources. "PCB concentration in the blood of adult Inuit is 7 times higher than in other North American adults," notes the Canada Arctic Resource Council. "This is 3–5 times higher than the 'level of concern' guideline set by Health Canada for women of reproductive age." In August 2000, Canada announced a twenty-million-dollar fund to help developing countries with their own POP cleanups. But it's taken more than a decade for Canada to turn its domestic priorities around.

Despite everything, the toxin treaty of 2000 was the first Inuit step towards grappling with climate change. "It was the first international convention that recognized the Arctic. That was a great accomplishment," says Sheila. A portrait of Nelson Mandela and Sheila's negotiating team sits on her living-room table. "The climate change issue will be a lot more challenging for us," she says. "Because it's big-time industry. How much will they be willing to give up in terms of money and control?"

Nevertheless, Sheila feels that if 122 countries can agree on toxins, there's hope for climate change. But there is a sense of urgency: even as some airborne poisons slowly diminish, the health impact of climate change and long-distance toxin transport on hunting could force more Inuit off the land and away from their roots. For now, however, there will be no health advisories on traditional food.

"This is directly linked to what we do every day," Sheila says. "At any community feast or family meal, you can see the kind of energy that comes from the food. You eat the energy of the hunter, the heritage of your ancestor. I come home and it regenerates me. We become the food we eat."

THE HIGH ARCTIC SETTLEMENT of Resolute Bay speeds past as Hans Aronsen sleds me out onto the ice of the Northwest Passage. It's minus forty-three Celsius—with wind chill blowing to minus seventy-seven, and the professional polar-bear guide guns the snowmobile into the wind. Resolute disappears into the blowing snow behind us.

The previous day, I flew 1,500 kilometres north along the western edge of Baffin Island, across the Northwest Passage, to Cornwallis Island, where a community of 180, mostly Inuit, hunt and eke out a living as a way station for air traffic, summer tourists and Arctic explorers. Resolute is the northernmost stop in any regular air service, closer to Russia than to the United States. To the north are the rest of Canada's Queen Elizabeth Islands, a frozen and largely uninhabited collection of glaciers, mountains, muskox and polar bears—and the second-largest collection of ice in the hemisphere.

Out on the ice, Hans surveys the scene: the bay is smooth, snow-covered ice, while off in the open water beyond is a jumbled maze of rough first-year ice. In the past, multi-year ice prevailed during winter months and the passage was usually clear of shelves, fissures and pileups. Now, it's an obstacle course that only polar bears seem to appreciate.

Originally from Greenland, Hans has listened closely to local Inuit elders, most of whom have been watching weather here since the 1950s when the community was founded by the Canadian government. Wintertime ice openings—polynyas—are vital to the food chain, as plankton, animals and hunters converge on these tiny oases. But the scale and frequency of ice holes, thin ice and open water are now some of the greatest in living memory, especially during fall and spring—prime hunting seasons. "For the last three seasons when the ice breaks, it disappears and stays gone," Hans says. "Normally, it comes and goes. There's no more multi-year ice either."

It's one of the reasons Hans has recently taken to using an

old-fashioned dog team more often, leaving behind his heavy snowmobile. It's not just to impress American big-game hunters who arrive every spring on a twenty-thousand-dollar tour package to shoot polar bears. "A *komatik* [sled] and dogs is safer on thinning ice," Hans says. "In the fall, very thin ice. Can't even go on it." Until a few years ago, multi-year ice could support snowmobiles with no problem. Now, old-fashioned dog teams help shore up a shrinking seal- and polar-bear hunting season.

We stop at the site where Hans keeps his sled dogs, a circle of stakes and leather harnesses scattered about the ice. Piles of fur are curled up beneath the snow; as we approach, they wake and begin to howl.

As one of the world's northernmost permanent communities, Resolute is nevertheless seeing the same kind of dramatic warming symptoms that have been observed farther south. "There are floods in our rivers—very unusual," Hans says of the headlands behind Resolute. "Permafrost is thawing out deeper." (According to Environment Canada, the past twelve months had seen several major temperature spikes—mini–heat waves that were as much as ten degrees above normal—that, with increased precipitation, helped melt sensitive permafrost and temporarily aquify a landscape that's as dry as a desert.)

The dogs howl around us and minus-seventy winds continue to bite through our fur hoods, leaving icicles and frostbite on our cheeks. It's 2 P.M. and already the sun is disappearing, leaving a glorious trail of pink, orange and red twilight. We waste no time turning back to the beach as the light falls behind us.

Hans pulls out his hand-held global positioning system to check our route. We're a short distance from the shore, but the darkness and the blowing snow have closed in. Recent climatic shifts are, in fact, affecting traditional Inuit skills such as navigation and weather prediction: uncertain skies and unsteady winds in recent years can confuse even the most astute observer.

Back home, Hans's partner, Zipporah Kalluk, who grew up on the land east of here near Pond Inlet, explains why hunters are having more difficulty finding their way around the ice. The problem is that everything is happening from a different direction, she says. In the past, those who inhabited Canada's High Arctic enjoyed a certain degree of climatic stability. With average annual temperatures at Resolute clocking in at minus 16.6 degrees and the nearby super-cooled air mass of the North Pole prevailing, steady winds and weather were often the norm. "But today many can't understand what's happening because now it's different," she says.

Like most traditional Inuk, Zipporah's family has always paid close attention to weather, ice conditions and cloud formation. Every hunter was a meteorologist. "When they wake up every day, they go outside right away, looking at the clouds and wind," she says. "They can find out if it's a little bit bad before the storm—or if it will turn good in a few days. We decide our days according to the weather. When the wind is coming from a central place, maybe it'll be rough water, or they'll notice if the wind changes from one place to another." Things like wind-scoured ice and the position of multi-year ice could tell hunters a lot about their location and trajectory.

The old skills are being lost partially because of a broad-based shift and variability in Arctic weather—and partially because younger Inuk now rely on Environment Canada forecasts. "Elders are not open now because no one is listening to them. The whites say one thing. The elders say another."

We're sitting in Zipporah and Hans's cozy living room, looking out into the winter twilight. I'm staying in a sewing room down the hall. Hans lounges on the couch. "In the dark season, with no daylight, they used the stars to travel," Zipporah says. "For centuries before there were white people to tell them what the weather would be like, hunters named the stars so others could know which are pointing where. Some stars are very useful and some they just named." Before her family's forced relocation to Resolute in 1959 by the Canadian government—a gambit to affirm Canadian sovereignty of the High Arctic—she remembers living on the land, happy to play outside all day in the wintertime, warmed by the seal broth in her stomach, the cramped sod winter huts and narwhal hunts by kayak.

The uncertainty of High Arctic climate has elders concerned. "I feel that the earth has shifted," says elder David Ooingoot. He's worked the ice of the Northwest Passage since the 1940s, and now sunlight, tides and ocean temperature are all in flux. "Summers are a lot warmer then twenty years ago and sea water temperature is a lot warmer," he says. "It's brighter now than before. During the summer months for the past six years, the tide for three days was without any low or high tides. The water wasn't doing anything. Frozen, not moving, for the first time."

It's hard for him to express to a non-hunter what changes in oceans and winds mean. "The wind used to come from the north," he explains. "When it was dark season, we would follow that direction to find our way home. Now it comes from the northeast. . . . During the fall it is more difficult to guess the wind, because of the earth shifting. The clouds are still the same and the winds are usually more from the south."

Tracie Ooingoot, his daughter, translates; around us, his two young grandchildren, both two-year-old boys, wrestle with each other like bear cubs, climbing all over each other, their grandfather and me. "Summers are a lot warmer than twenty years ago and sea water temperature is a lot warmer," he says. "Most of the ice melts. It's not the same as before. And in the wintertime, there is more open water."

Has this affected hunting? "Yes. Because there isn't too much ice—difficult to go out. Have to wait."

He also can't explain a mysterious increase in ambient light during the four-month winter dark season. The skies are brighter. "Six years ago I noticed this shift, all the wind changes. In the past, I used to go out to the open water to hunt—used to be bright from 11 A.M. to 12 P.M. this time of year. Now, it's 10 A.M. to 2 P.M. That's how much the light has changed. Especially during the summertime, we have to pay more attention to the weather.

"Hunting is okay for the present," he says. "But I am worried for the future. Right now the salt water is already warm and it will get warmer. Up here there are some little ocean creatures, they die from the warmth of one's hand. If those little creatures remain okay, then I am okay with things."

Considering southern climes like Churchill, Manitoba, where emaciated polar bears roam the warm tundra, David Ooingoot hasn't seen much change in the local bear population, partly because they are better protected than before. The walrus are a different story. "I always go to this one spot to the north. Always walrus, but last year only two. But out in the open water, there aren't any. There used to be hundreds before. Only catch ten or less now. Somehow they have disappeared."

On their satellite TV is a breaking news report on California's energy crisis, unfolding thousands of kilometres to the south: power producers and industry representatives are pushing for government permission to speed up regulatory approvals and sidestep environmental protections to build new power plants. In a few more months, the Bush administration will launch its ambitious bid to expand continental fossil fuel supply, brushing aside international efforts to establish greenhouse-gas-emission targets.

Nobody mentions that today was the first official day of sunlight in Resolute, the time when the sun's disc momentarily rises above the horizon after a three-month winter night. Long twenty-four-hour days will soon blanket the pole with non-stop solar radiation. And the ice will melt once again, likely opening up new reaches of ocean to the sun.

IN SOME WAYS, GLOBAL WARMING is simply a convenient label for natural systems being pushed to new limits. Up close, there are still more questions than answers.

Wayne Davidson, Environment Canada's weather officer in Resolute for the past thirteen years, speaks Inuktituk and, until recently, thought he had a pretty good grasp of the weather. But he's been getting more and more questions. "Inuit in town call me with questions and I'm wondering why they're calling me," he says, noting that Inuk traditionally don't need help figuring out the weather. We're sitting in the Resolute weather station, a lonely collection of wooden buildings on the edge of the airstrip that's been there since the early 1950s.

"Talking to more traditional Inuit—unilingual—they say that the more it is cold, the brighter the sky." It's what David Ooingoot said to me the day before. After first hearing about Resolute's ever-changing sunsets during the fall of 1999, Wayne began measuring lightfall and noted that sundown and sunrise times don't correspond to the official computer projections of his own government. "Computer models have not been thoroughly checked—on the first day of sun, February 5, the sun was supposed to have set at 19:38, but 20:23 was the real sunset. That's forty-five minutes' difference."

Wayne theorizes that this unexplained variance may be an effective and as-yet-uninvestigated result of climate change. In other words, fluctuations in atmospheric temperature—especially a cooling stratosphere—can increase the light refraction, especially near the horizon. "It's like a giant lens," he explains. "Thanks to the optical thickness of the earth's atmosphere at the horizon, the disc peeks over the horizon, though the actual sun has already departed behind the earth." Changes in atmospheric temperature, he speculates, may have increased the amount of ambient light witnessed in Resolute.

"We live in twilight here. So I always look at first darkness. That's how people noticed." Far north, the low light is very much influenced by atmospheric refraction because of the concentrated atmosphere towards the poles. Wayne figures that by his measurements, the atmosphere around Resolute now reflects twice as much sunlight at dawn or dusk as the official astronomical record dictates.

"The last two or three years people have been saying that there's been more light," says Wayne. "But what they don't know is that we've been under a monster called the vortex—a huge stratospheric low that's calm at the centre and furious at the edges." The vortex wobbles around the pole, sometimes in an oval and sometimes broken into two pools of air. So far, the vortex has proven impossible to forecast, despite its vast influence on hemispheric weather and climate.

At the very least, the changing optics of the atmosphere could provide a unique way to measure climate change. "What we do know is that the current sunset model fails miserably. Nobody went back to say that our models don't work. People rely too much on machines; I did that too." We're sitting in one of the station's computer-filled offices, a building that used to house six staff. Automation and budget cuts eliminated all but Wayne Davidson. So he has little extra time to investigate. "These are issues for a proper study," he says. "My observations are very preliminary."

And Wayne cautions against any hasty conclusions. "The most common fault with predicting global warming is that people are too confident—it's too complicated to overgeneralize. Unless you have a way of proving it, it should be left a question."

Before I leave, he pulls out a satellite photo of the Northwest Passage. On one end is Resolute—and from Resolute extends a huge seam of chop ice and cracks in open water. Again, while smaller holes are common during the winter, this degree of disruption strikes him as strange. Thing is, it seems to intensify shortly after every full moon—right about now, actually. "There's something about the moon that causes the ice to go crazy—about two days after the ice goes nuts and breaks every-where," he says: "The moon is very close to the earth right now. It seems to have something to do with ice energy and something to do with gravity. The warmer it is, the less thick the ice and the crazier the ice goes."

He shows me a satellite animation of rolling sea ice fissures running south down the Arctic Ocean, away from the North Pole and crashing into the top of Ellesmere and Axel Heiberg islands. "Most people would say that this would be tides, but it's not. Tides are large between islands but not in wide-open areas like the Arctic Ocean.

"I don't know what it is—I tend to think it's gravitational pull, like a *petit* tsunami," he says. "Either way, when North Pole explorers come through here—we still get lots of Europeans trying to conquer the pole—I tell them to take it easy on a full moon. A few explorers got caught in this in 1999—they said it was like a continual explosion out on the ice, huge booming waves of energy. It's a megatonne displacement: the whole thing is moving." (A few months later, Japanese adventurer Hyouichi Kohno would perish in shifting polar ice two hundred kilo-metres north of Ellesmere. Canadian Forces rescue pilots specu-lated that the degenerated ice conditions might be linked to climate change, because "an [ice] shift that over the last fifteen, sixteen years would not have occurred this time of year.")

In 2001, scientists at the University of Toronto announced the results of a study that determined that the gravitational pull of Greenland's ice cap has lowered nearby sea levels despite a growing infusion of glacial meltwater into the ocean. But locals are more concerned with the commercial implications of their changing icescapes.

"We're probably going to see ships soon," says Zipporah's father, Hirodier Kalluk, of the supertankers that are expected to ply an ice-free Northwest Passage sometime in the next one hundred years. "When we noticed that the old ice didn't come around, it was strange at first. So we thought about it and talked about it and decided that perhaps the ice was melting at the North Pole." That was about two years ago, seemingly in advance of several scientific studies that confirmed historic thinning around the pole. Hirodier adds that the strange surge in ice that Wayne observed is called *piturnik,* an old lunar phenomenon that's become much more pronounced with the thinning of the ice.

With all the strange ice traffic moving through the channel, Zipporah reasons, it had to have come from the plugged island channels north. (This, says climatologist Bea Alt, is precisely what is happening: the Northwest Passage is inundated with the choppy remnants of the polar cap and the upper Arctic islands. The pole is literally flushing southward, causing an array of ice conditions, one of which is increased open water, especially during the summer. But sometimes a glut of ice arrives in spots, leaving a surplus of ice.)

The variability of the ice appears, as elsewhere, to have affected hunting. "There used to be lots of seals, but today there are fewer around," says Hirodier. "Since last year, there have been fewer polar bear come around. There used to be a lot of them. But we don't know for sure—they might come back again. Heard there were more at Pond Inlet. Bears are smart; a lot of white people come around with needles and make them sleep, so they are probably moving away from here."

Elders and scientists share a sense of uncertainty. Some climate shifts are already beyond our control, thanks to an atmosphere-ocean system that now retains more energy—0.5 watts per square metre of incoming sunlight—than is released back into space. "A consequence of this [energy] imbalance is that future warming of about 0.5°C can be expected even if atmospheric composition should remain fixed at today's amounts," writes NASA's James Hansen. "Future warming of 0.5°C is already 'in the pipeline.' It is this slow response of the climate system that complicates the issue of whether and how much greenhouse gas emissions should be restrained."

Zipporah glances over at the TV, which now shows law-enforcement footage of car chases, standoffs and arrests. American police officers run down suspects and draw their guns with impunity. Outside, the wind is still howling, blowing snow across the dark village. "We hunt for animals but when we watch white people's TV, they hunt for people," Zipporah says. "Down south they say to us, 'Don't kill animals.' But they're shooting their own peoples. Hard to understand."

SEVERAL DAYS LATER, I JOURNEY into the twenty-four-hour winter darkness of Ellesmere Island where, close to the edge of Canada's northern land mass, a posse of scientists sits atop a mountain studying the atmosphere for clues to ozone depletion and climate change. The chartered Twin Otter takes off from Resolute and flies away from the glowing southern horizon. Beneath us, in the twilight of the Arctic winter, snowfields and pack ice stretch as far as the eye can see. With ice cover larger than the province of New Brunswick, Ellesmere Island is one of the greatest collections of ice in the northern hemisphere. We're headed for the Fosheim Peninsula, a large frozen mass that juts out the eastern side of Ellesmere. Eureka, and its all-weather runway, sits on the far edge of the Fosheim.

If there is a front line in the battle to understand climate change, this is probably it. An hour's overland journey from Eureka is Environment Canada's mountaintop Astrolab. Built like a space station to withstand one-hundred-knot winds and minus-sixty temperatures, the five-million-dollar steel and aluminum box sleeps eight and houses twenty-six computers, high-altitude lasers that can cut through steel, and an impressive array of meteorological devices. Set six hundred metres above the ice near the very edge of the Fosheim Peninsula, the lab searches the sky, mostly during the dark season, collecting important data on atmospheric chemistry, temperature trends, ozone layer depletion, as well as the position and intensity of the polar vortex.

We continue to fly north into the full moon. Ellesmere's four-month-long winter night, extreme northern latitude and clear, stable conditions have made this high polar desert a prized spot for atmospheric research. Excluding myself, the seven people huddled in the chilly fuselage of the Twin Otter—we travel fully suited in heavy arctic gear—are all scientists. There's a Japanese contingent of four, led by eminent stratospheric scientist Yukio Makino, along with Astrolab manager Vivek Voora and technician Yannic Trottier.

The plane circles over Fosheim and touches down on Eureka's military-issue runway. Pickup trucks emerge from the darkness and we pile out and unload groceries, scientific gear and luggage before the wind chill freezes exposed skin. On the way back to the base, Eureka's officer in charge, Al Gaudet, briefs us on the local scene. An unremitting blizzard and unusually large quantities of snow have blocked the road up to the Astrolab—no one has been up there for days and we'll have to venture out into the squall by snowcat.

"The storm last week buried the upper road," says Gaudet. "We could try and plow it but it just gets covered up again." To describe recent weather as a "storm" might be an understatement: four consecutive days of minus-forty-five temperatures, snow and one-hundred-kilometre-an-hour winds. The drifts up the mountain reach close to two metres. And we can only hope that we don't get stuck.

The blizzards and snow are, for these parts, unusual. The Fosheim Peninsula is famously dry: this region of Nunavut receives less precipitation than parts of the Sahara—only sixty-five millimetres annually—and is officially classed as a polar desert. The huge drifts that block the road halfway up the mountain are a recent development. The Astrolab site was originally chosen because it had little snow and had reliable weather—and because it lay under the edge of the polar vortex.

The irony, as I learn over lunch at the station's cozy dining room, is that snowstorms and high polar winds are delaying efforts to understand this remote but crucial piece of atmosphere. "Conditions for study are deteriorating," says Voora, Astro's manager. "Gaps in our data, due to weather, are much more frequent." That's right; atmospheric conditions are hindering our study of the atmosphere.

"More storms, more snow, more overcast," adds Gaudet. "Possibly the result of higher temperatures." Other factors associated with climate change are present: increased atmospheric water vapor and an intensified vortex are leading causes.

But there's no way of saying for sure what's at play here. A few weeks earlier, I spoke with McGill University geologist Wayne Pollard about Eureka; he's been mapping and studying permafrost up here for decades—Fosheim has massive permafrost five hundred metres thick—and he's charting unprecedented melts. "A lot of sites have become completely unstable," he says. "Ten- to one-hundred-metre stretches of soil—five to fifteen metres thick—are melting and moving, throwing erosion scars across the land. It's a monster bite out of the landscape." In a place with an average annual temperature of minus-nineteen degrees, mudslides, mini-floods and slumping earth seem pretty unusual. He's still studying what's going on, though it's clear that there's some kind of pronounced, local climatic shift happening.

Nevertheless, those who watch the Arctic atmosphere remain perplexed by questions many thought were answered a decade ago. Back in the days when Canada acted as an international environmental leader, the groundbreaking 1987 Montreal accord set international limits on ozone-destroying chlorine compounds. The agreement was important because the thinning Arctic zone of protective gases—the ozone hole—frequently swings south, increasing uv-b readings across North America. ("uv-b levels are about 5–10 per cent higher than levels before 1980," notes Health Canada. "Over the last 15 years, the incidence of malignant melanoma, the most lethal skin cancer, has doubled.") Scientists originally predicted that the protective barrier against carcinogenic solar radiation would fully recover by 2001, but current ozone readings remain low.

In other words, they're still trying to figure out an issue everyone thought had been settled in 1987. "Ozone depletion during spring 2000 was up to 60 percent of the ozone layer," says Voora. "And what we thought would end in 2001 is at least dragging on until 2025."

In fact, the problem has become more complicated, due to the effect of climate change. "In 1997, stratospheric cold lasted a long time," says Makino, who makes an annual research trip to Eureka from Japan. At minus eighty-five, less ozone means that there's less heat retained within the upper atmosphere. Volcanic ash, naturally occurring, and industrial sulphur also help to lower upper-atmosphere temperatures. So, greenhouse gases and stratospheric cooling seem to work together to amplify each other: ozone depletion and polar winds both intensify under cooler conditions. Already, Makino fears that excess uv radiation from a wounded ozone layer may be damaging widespread plankton populations, which in turn could increase ocean temperature.

Voora and I finish lunch, board the snowcat and drive out onto the smooth first-year ice of Slidre, a protected bay that opens west onto Eureka sound and Axel Heiberg Island. Our plan is to cut across the ice and drive straight up the flat ramparts of the mountain, skirting the large drifts that block the road. All this talk of science has got Voora, a grad student and Arctic veteran from Hamilton, Ontario, thinking about the politics of climate change. "Why are we so stuck on science when the evidence for climate change is becoming clear?" he asks, hauling the snowcat through the first set of drifts. "Do corporations run things? So many people driving in big suvs [sport-utility vehicles] and General Motors gets the benefit." I brace myself on the roof to keep from flying out of my seat; it's as though we're plowing through a sea of whitecaps.

Voora recalls Canada's performance at the 2000 Hague negotiations, where Canada helped to stonewall efforts to implement the troubled Kyoto protocol, the international agreement that is expected to pave the way to global greenhouse-gas reductions and an international system of emissions trading credits. It was American-style industrial advocacy, charged a number of European non-governmental organizations—and, some asked, how could Canada even be taken seriously when its minister of the environment failed to show up at the talks? "We got petty about a 5-percent emissions credit," Voora says, referring to Canada's attempt to receive emissions credits for exporting nuclear technology and claiming its shrinking system of forests as carbon sinks. "Negotiators bickered about technology exports when we need alternatives. Look at what's happening up here—it's not abstract any more."

Canada's first national consultation on climate change in 1994 produced recommendations and improvements that, by and large, went unnoticed. "In the energy supply and production sector, which saw the largest [greenhouse gas] increase—20 per cent—since 1990, barely one-third of the recommendations had been implemented," noted the Pembina Institute, an independent energy think-tank, in a 2000 report.

Governments, already the beneficiaries of rich fuel taxes and production royalties, fared little better on regulatory issues, financial incentives and public education. "Only one-third of the package of measures recommended to federal and provincial governments over five years ago has been implemented, even though half the package consisted of voluntary, education or research measures that could have been put into place at little political cost. Governments have exhibited a breathtaking lack of leadership and interest in this issue of compelling global and national importance."

The prognosis is that Canada will increase its emissions by 20 percent, while enjoying the riches of an energy boom, by 2010. In the meantime, Canada's federal government continues to oscillate on climate change, from critic of the American backlash against Kyoto to an eager salesperson of domestic oil, gas and electricity.

Even up here on Ellesmere's high frozen plains, the quest for fossil power goes back more than a century. Iced in during a pioneering scientific mission, the Nares expedition of 1875 mined high-quality coal from surface seams on the island's forsaken northeastern edge, less than eight hundred kilometres from the North Pole. More than a hundred years later, in 1981, $2.25 million in coal exploration would follow in the footsteps of the first Arctic mine, covering 155 sites—an estimated 20 percent of Canada's coal reserves—across Ellesmere and Axel Heiberg islands.

Beneath the tracks of our snowcat lie seams of coal that reach deep into the permafrost of the Fosheim. Just south of here are several abandoned oil wells, the world's farthest north, drilled in the late 1970s during the great North American energy crisis. And, in the wake of 2001 oil and gas prices reaching some of the highest peaks since oil hit forty-five dollars a barrel in 1982, high-tech surveying and drilling expeditions now roam Canada's eastern Arctic, searching for new hydrocarbon deposits.

Blowing snow and drifts fill our floodlights. The Astrolab was built on top of this mountain following Canada's Montreal ozone treaty, back when the $5-million investment in atmospheric science reflected Canada's leading position on international environmental issues. But these days, federal priorities are different: as of 2000, Canada's Natural Sciences and Engineering Research Council spent only $3 million for the whole North, compared to $463 million spent by the United States on its polar research.

The money pinch is felt profoundly up here. In Resolute, Canada's Polar Continental Shelf Project—outfitter and clear-inghouse for Arctic researchers—is temporarily closed, await-ing the rich summertime funding dollars of American researchers. Back at Eureka station, a *Globe and Mail* clipping on the dining-room noteboard reports that Australia spends $2.30 per capita on Antarctic research and the United States spends $3.00 on Arctic science, while Canada spends 20 cents per citizen. It turns out that Environment Canada has hardly enough money to run the Astrolab properly—people like Voora are forced to cut corners in one of the world's most unforgiving environments, while multi-million-dollar tax credits continue to subsidize new fossil fuel projects in Alberta's $51-billion oil sands boom.

Up here, decisions on whether to plow the road or run repairs are often influenced by money. Voora, for example, has to be careful not to drive the snowcat too hard because break-downs are frequent and expensive. This machine actually has tires up front—a liability on snow and ice—because there wasn't enough money to purchase a larger, fully tracked model, one with such luxuries as a heated passenger cabin and flood-lights that don't conk out unexpectedly.

A snow squall sets in as we pass by an automated radio tower. As a scientist, Voora is distraught; a surprising amount of what we already know about climate change is frequently ignored by negotiators and politicians. "As far as I can see, there's still too much work going into assessing what's going on," he says. "So it's not 100-percent certain. It's like the tobacco issue: we've debated it for ages. We just need to do something about it."

We finally reach the Astrolab after nearly two hours of cold, punishing travel. The moon looms behind the temporarily aban-doned station as we pull into the garage. I think about boiling some water from snow—there's no running water up here because of a leaky toilet—and then I remember that, despite pristine appearances, the snow is likely laced with above-average levels of toxins. North of Eureka at Lake Hazen, levels of DDT and toxaphene in Arctic char are some of the highest measured in the circumpolar Arctic. So we'll have to wait for purified water from the station.

With no road, no water and too many clouds to operate the Astrolab's expensive lasers and infrared spectrometers, there's not much to do except venture outside and ponder the unset-tling wilderness of the eightieth northern parallel. Up here, in the dry, frigid air of Ellesmere, you can throw water into the air and it will never reach the ground: it vaporizes in a crackle and drifts away as ice crystal. We're too far north to see the north-ern lights. Compasses are famously unreliable because the magnetic north pole actually lies to the south. It's as though one has reached the edge of the world.

As the noon sun rises over Resolute below the horizon, a faint blue twilight dawns over Eureka, and the vast expanse of Ellesmere's high polar desert comes into view. Rock and ice stretch as far as the eye can see. Except for the wind, there is nothing but silence. Yet everything is in motion.

# AFTER THE ICE STORM

## Quebec

ON THE BACK OF CANADA's old two-dollar bill is a picture of rural Quebec, an idyllic scene of hills, trees and farmhouses. It is the Township of Val Saint-François from an earlier era, back before the arrival of highways and nationalism—a parish steeple nestled in the rolling countryside and forests. If the now-defunct two-dollar bill were brought back today, the scene would be different: a massive set of high-voltage lines cut through the countryside, a swath of technology three storeys high and twenty-four metres wide that carves up the land as it snakes around mountains, over rivers and directly through forests.

Driving southwest from Quebec City on Highway 116 these days, it's hard not to notice the high-voltage lines that run overhead. They weave across the highways, back roads and villages of Quebec's Eastern Townships, all part of North America's single largest energy network.

Like no other province in Canada, Quebec is awash in power; 32,000 kilometres of high-voltage transmission lines criss-cross the province, the tentacles of a massive grid that funnels electricity from 1,400 kilometres north near James Bay, where the Robert Bourassa station on La Grande River pumps 5,328 megawatts into the system. From the edge of James Bay, La Grande feeds seven separate 735-kilovolt lines that carry more power than the smaller towers common elsewhere.

It's certainly a different landscape from the open, icy reaches of Ellesmere Island. During a three-hour drive across the Eastern Townships, I pass beneath a series of huge transmission lines, 735- and 500-kilovolt lines with towers that reach fourteen storeys into the sky. The double lines clear-cut along rights-of-way; the towers loom over the countryside, cutting straight lines through almost anything that lies beneath. Many were rebuilt or newly constructed in the wake of Canada's greatest weather catastrophe, the 1998 Ice Storm, which claimed 35 lives and left 1.4 million people across Quebec and Ontario without power for days, weeks and even months.

The road weaves through Victoriaville, towards the Township of Val Saint-François. It's the scene that appeared on the back of the old two-dollar bill. And as I pass farmhouses and Catholic spires deep in the heart of the Townships, the persistent hum of power lines is never far away. This strikes me as odd; where I grew up in Alberta, only cities had this many high-level lines scattered about. And there's no heavy industry around here, save for mines and a few factories—certainly nothing like the power-thirsty aluminum forges of Shawinigan, Jean Chrétien's industrial hometown on the northern side of the St Lawrence. Several sets of reconstructed lines already flank either side of the St Lawrence around major consumption centres like Montreal and Quebec City—an insurance policy against the unlikely event that the 1998 storm would soon be repeated.

On the southernmost loop of Quebec's electricity grid, the line dips to within about 40 kilometres of the U.S. border. En route, it bisects Val Saint-François. From the village of Melbourne, just off Highway 55, one can view the newly built line as it snakes through the low-lying mountains of the Appalachian countryside.

The question, asks Val Saint-François resident Monique Fournier, is if this ungainly piece of technology—145 kilometres long—was the product of public necessity or a gambit to exploit the booming electricity markets of the northeastern United States.

"The project was announced while the lights were still out in Val Saint-François during the Ice Storm," she says angrily pointing to the lines above. "It was an 'emergency measure' without the public procedures required by law." The power corridor, one of the largest of its kind in North America, was built on expropriated land through swaths of heritage forest that has been largely untouched since the nineteenth century.

"Over five months in 1998, the government issued eight decrees on behalf of Hydro-Québec, eliminating all necessary environmental hearings, public hearings and confirmation with municipal regional councils," she says. "And then there's the map."

She holds up a copy of a leaked engineering diagram that shows the transmission grid of Montreal and the Eastern Townships. Existing high-voltage lines within Quebec's populated corridor along the St Lawrence largely run east-west, but on the map, four proposed lines—including the Hertel des Cantons, the line that runs through Val Saint-François—all feed south into export markets. A fifth additional line runs west into Ontario, where a power crunch is already brewing under scattered deregulation plans and a slew of public debt from half-operational nuclear reactors. Titled "New electric transmission lines under study for the export market by Hydro-Québec," the map was produced by Trans-Energie, the transmission division of the parent utility. The document was delivered to community activists by a government source in 1998.

As markets across North America deregulate, the continental electricity grid is rapidly changing to meet long-distance demands for power. And, by virtue of geography, Val Saint-François is part of this power funnel. Though officially announced as an improvement to domestic service, the Hertel des Cantons line nevertheless dips south where, as per the leaked map, another high-voltage line will branch off and run due south to the Vermont border, parallel to an existing 150-kilowatt direct-current line that already feeds power into Vermont directly from La Grande 1,600 kilometres north.

South of the border, power demand is surging. Across the United States, electricity supply grew an average of only 0.75

percent per year during the 1990s while demand for electricity almost tripled the growth rate of available power at a rate of 2.1 percent each year. Already, high-voltage interchanges at New Hampshire and Vermont import Quebec power at lucrative spot prices. While average prices seem stable, spot prices—the cost of a power at any given moment—sometimes rocket to thirty times their usual value, more than a thousand megawatts per hour. Where long-term contracts once governed the price of electricity, spot prices and short-term contracts now set the pace in deregulated markets. Power producers who can supply large amounts of electricity on demand stand to make vast profits.

If the Ice Storm was a reminder that our energy supply isn't guaranteed, the towers of Val Saint-François point towards the next energy frontier: the network. It wasn't hydro, nuclear or coal plants that fell apart during the winter of 1998; it was the lines and transformers that were beaten by nature. With governments and utilities jockeying to integrate into continental markets, it is the network, not necessarily energy itself, that serves as the fulcrum of power.

And when bureaucratic power runs up against a community like Val Saint-François, there's a profound clash of values: institutional power versus the consumer, continental markets versus local residents who've lived there for generations. Hydro-Québec was once considered a universal extension of Québécois values, a beacon of Quebec culture akin to the Catholic Church; but now, even Val Saint-François's sovereignists aren't so sure.

"When I was growing up, it was the French who were the workers and the English who were the bosses," says Monique, who no longer votes Parti Québécois. "Now we're starting to realize that this is the means for the government to make money on our backs."

THE MIX OF FARMLAND and high-voltage towers at Val Saint-François tells the story of modern Quebec: when Hydro-Québec was nationalized in 1963, it was an ambitious effort to escape the underdeveloped agricultural economy and low-income industry that dominated the province until the 1950s. Since Quebec lacked rich coal or oil reserves, an ambitious string of hydro-power projects served as the cornerstone of nationalist plans for industrial development and political independence. Quebec, the megaproject society, was born.

Now the largest producer of electricity in Canada, Hydro-Québec provides Quebec businesses and consumers with some of the cheapest electricity on the continent—New York residents pay, on average, almost four times the rate enjoyed by Quebecers—with significantly lower greenhouse gas emissions than fossil fuels. (Hydro power, on average, produces a total of 60 percent less carbon dioxide than coal-fired power plants and 18 percent less than natural gas power plants.)

These days, exporting even a small percentage of Quebec's mind-boggling 31,400 megawatts is a get-rich-quick scheme; in 2000, a spike in continental power prices created an increase of more than $1 billion in the publicly owned company's export revenues, new money in addition to the $906 million profit that Hydro-Québec logged in 1999.

But for some Quebecers, Hydro-Québec is simply a public trust that's forsaken its *nationaliste* roots. Cheap power is no substitute for accountability. "It's not just about this little village here—it's about the eight government decrees that took away my civil liberties," says Marni Thompson, an anglo resident who helped organize the Val Saint-François community group with Quebec nationalists Monique Fournier and Richard Fortier.

Marni is a feisty grandmother and a Val Saint-François Townshipper whose family moved here in the 1700s, first working as shepherds. We're all sitting together in the Thompson family home near Melbourne. It is the typical Township settlement: set on the banks of the St François River, an important tributary of the St Lawrence, it's a compact collection of *dépanneurs,* small wooden houses and roadside white crosses. Upstream are medium-scale hydro developments at Drummondville that have been feeding power since the 1950s. Locals don't see why they— or anyone else—would need a thousand megawatts flowing through the countryside. It's not as if they're forging steel or aluminum around here.

After the Ice Storm, it didn't take long for locals to realize that Hydro-Québec had sweeping plans for expansion in the midst of all its repairs. So they organized a grassroots campaign against Quebec's most powerful company. It all began on April 23, 1999, at a public meeting of three hundred residents, some of whose families had lived here for six generations. They were looking for accountability and information but the utility never showed up. Instead, a contracted engineering company represented Hydro-Québec. And it turned out that the route through Val Saint-François had already been decided.

"We were very naive. We went to our [provincial] representative—Guy Chevalier, minister of natural resources—because it was so hard to get answers," says Monique. It turned out that his deputy minister, Jean-Paul Beaulieu, was on Hydro's board of directors. Help wasn't forthcoming. "We wanted answers and what we got were government people who leaked documents to us."

Thus the Coalition des Citoyens at Citoyennes de Val Saint-François (CCVSF) was formed. It represents a range of Quebecers, ordinary folk who might have never gotten involved in politics were it not for the power grid: farmers, professionals, teachers, retirees, young parents, French and English, ex-urbanities and founding families. Some have worries about the effects of low-level electromagnetic radiation from the lines—something that has proven harmful in lab animals, though human health effects remain inconclusive, subject to ongoing scientific debate. Others simply couldn't believe that they'd be deprived of land rights and public consultations afforded to other Quebecers who've found themselves in the way of a Hydro-Québec project.

It didn't take long for the battle to escalate. Shortly after the CCVSF formed, Hydro-Québec lawyers targeted families with expropriation notices and, reportedly, made ever-decreasing compensation offers to locals who challenged the terms. A series of special orders-in-council from the Lucien Bouchard government made it legal for Hydro-Québec to proceed immediately with construction. "The government is in the legislature only six months of the year, so they govern more by decree," says Monique. "If they'd make a special law from the beginning, they would have had to discuss the issue in the Assembly. So they used emergency measures first and later invoked closure."

Lawsuits against the government were launched; the issue wasn't merely control of the land, but access to information, proper public hearings and a work stoppage on clear-cutting of forest and the steel pylons that were already being erected. Power, the community group argued, cannot be exempted from the legislative and regulatory process, especially when a taxpayer-owned public utility is involved. A second challenge addressed the Ice Storm directly: the route of Hertel des Cantons had nothing to do with the declared state of emergency, they contended, nor did it serve the long-term needs of Quebecers. In fact, using Hydro-Québec's own documents, they argued that the line was being built to subsidize American power markets. After all, taxpayers in New York wouldn't be saddled with the $100,000-per-kilometre cost of the state-of-the-art transmission corridor—in fact, they might even pay sub-market rates.

After a defeat in Sherbrooke's regional court, the community went to the Supreme Court of Quebec, where they were awarded victory in 1999. The court upheld Quebec's existing environmental, planning and agricultural land protection legislation. "The government was obliged to act in conformity with the laws," said Judge Jeannine Rousseau. "It could not use a crisis to grant itself authority to ignore them, evade them or only appear to comply with them." It was a clear victory—and the Hydro-Québec teams that were busily clear-cutting an eighty-metre swath across the Townships were forced to stop.

Prior to the judgment, Parti Québécois Premier Bouchard (1996–2001) had personally recommended that community members should take their case to court. "The summit of hypocrisy was in 1998," recalls Monique. "They'd already started to take down trees and we met with [then premier] Lucien Bouchard, who was in Sherbrooke for the Parti Québécois during a federal by-election. We went and said we wanted to meet him and since there was an election there, he couldn't say no. He said, 'It's good for you to go to court. I will respect the decision.'"

But facing defeat, the government instead passed retroactive legislation, Bill 42, that trumped the court decision and exempted the already-built portion of the transmission line from approvals as well as allowed expropriations without compliance to Quebec's Expropriation Act. The ninety-eight kilometres already built—worth ten million dollars—would not have to be dismantled and the final fifty kilometres could proceed unhindered by the courts. Moreover, Bill 42 barred further legal challenges over the legality of Hydro-Québec's actions or for damages.

The government had trumped its own courts, a constitutionally dubious action that, if anything, underlined the importance of the southbound power lines of Hertel des Cantons. After community meetings, lawsuits, public campaigns, blockades and a major legal victory, it had come down to a battle that, by all appearances, they could not win. "Let us not forget that the Hertel des Cantons line will probably be the first of a new series of high voltage power lines aiming at the exporting of energy to the U.S. Northeast," wrote the CCVSF in a February 1999 news release. "Indeed, we must stop claiming that hydroelectricity is a 'green or clean' energy, as the flooding of immense territories to form reservoirs produces greenhouse gases and the construction of transportation lines also leaves 80 metre wide scars on thousands of kilometres of land."

Tapping a well of widespread dissent against Hydro-Québec, provincial and international organizations rallied around the CCVSF's cause. The Union des Municipalités Régionales de Comté du Québec lent its support, as did a total of twenty individual Quebec municipalities. The Grand Council of the Crees and the Innu gave their support, along with First Nations in Vermont. New York's Environmental Advocates intervened, representing a powerful coalition of American environmental lobby groups, and met with Hydro-Québec president André Caillé to discuss Hertel des Cantons, threatening to oppose any new transmission corridors, lines, interconnections and upgrades on the U.S. side of the border.

Local governments, hardly radical, had long suffered under Hydro-Québec. The Ice Storm was the breaking point for many. "We never got a single call from Hydro-Québec during the crisis," said Melbourne Township manager John Barley to the provincial commission that investigated the Ice Storm in 1999. "It was if we were on another planet."

General unease about Hydro-Québec's power monopoly has continued to build years after the Ice Storm's passing; Val Saint-François isn't the only community that has come up against the province's most powerful unelected body. Les Amis d' St-Laurent is a community group that forced a high-voltage line underneath the St Lawrence—at considerable expense—partially because Hydro-Québec failed to anticipate resistance over expanding its transmission grid. The City of Hull had opposed a similar export power line to Ontario, a $356-million project, because of Hydro-Québec's plans for the route of the corridor. "In the past, it has argued such a once-in-a-century storm would have knocked out any system," noted the Montreal *Gazette* in a January 2001 editorial. "What's undeniable, however, is that Hydro's performance since the 1998 calamity has left much to be desired."

For francophones, the fight against the public utility was a difficult process: Hydro-Québec was an institution that guaranteed a promising economic future for an independent Quebec. Until Quebec's young natural resources minister René Lévesque endorsed publicly owned power in 1962, more than half of Quebec's electricity was owned by private companies, all anglo institutions with some $600 million in assets. (By contrast, many Ontario towns of three thousand people or more had their own privately owned thermal or hydroelectric plants by 1890.) Nationalization was a fight that would define the Lévesque legacy, one that gave rise to the famous slogan, "Maîtres chez nous"—roughly, "Masters of our own house."

The nationalist campaign for Quebec independence was, early on, defined by a populist surge against privately owned, for-profit power—the so-called anglo trust. "The people of Quebec *versus* the electrical trust," charged Premier Jean Lesage at a 1962 Montreal fundraising dinner. "He who is for the people of Quebec is against the trust!"

Politics has changed. Monique recalls that when the blackouts of the Ice Storm darkened the city and the countryside, the bright Hydro-Québec logo on top of its Montreal headquarters stayed lit, symbolic of the company's status. The Hydro-Québec headquarters in Montreal has become an important node within corporate power circles—even then premier Lucien Bouchard had his office in the same building. "Some of us won't vote again," says Monique. "I don't know what the political system is any more. I voted for René Lévesque because he had his heart in the right place. I am an *independentiste*—but I don't like what the government is doing."

"We've replaced priests with businessmen in Quebec," says Richard Fortier. "[Hydro-Québec president] André Caillé, Bombardier, Alcan—these are the heroes of the society and we're still strongly attached to the famous Quebec Inc."

For twenty-five days after the Ice Storm, the community went without power, enduring it like everyone else in eastern Ontario, Quebec and New Brunswick. But what they resent is that the storm was, as the court observed, used as a tool to expand Hydro-Québec's export capacity without consulting local residents. "It's like being betrayed by your own people," says Monique. "I have a dream country in mind but it became obvious that these people wouldn't give that country to me."

For its part, Hydro-Québec made conciliatory efforts by announcing a special commission in 1999 that Val Saint-François refused to participate in—but by then, the Hertel des Cantons was already well under construction. Before the court victory, Premier Bouchard brushed off the Val Saint-François hydro war as a "local issue." Hundreds of thousands of dollars had been spent on all sides, fighting what had become a grudge match over hydro. And while many Quebecers would hardly turn down U.S. currency for hydro power, many have questioned the vision of the Parti Québécois. Surely the PQ is better than the old anglo generation that ran Quebec like a colony—but how much better?

By spring 2001, Hertel des Cantons was still unfinished, mired in a series of lawsuits and hearings. Hydro-Québec was still forty-five kilometres short of its goal. Some made the point that, exports or not, no one is unbeholden to the grid. "If you want to bring electricity from one area to another, you need power lines," said Jacques Marquis of the province's electrical association. "Everyone wants electricity, but no one wants power lines in their backyard."

POWER IS EVERYWHERE, yet we so seldom notice it. Except, of course, for those rare occasions when energy disappears completely and we're left helpless. This was the drama behind the great Ice Storm of 1998: confronted with systemic break-down, many Canadians were faced with the prospect of living much as the colonial settlers had, freezing and scared in the middle of winter, yearning for the simple pleasures of light, heat and power.

Amid images of massive, crumpled electrical towers and communities shrouded in darkness, a small truth was revealed: Canada has always been a nation defined by an intense hunger for energy. And in Quebec, the quest for power has been the most intense. Even by international standards, Quebec's electricity grid is huge: half of all electricity in the province is consumed more than a thousand kilometres away from the source.

In its efforts to become an independent power nation, Quebec pioneered long-distance transmission during the 1960s. The world's first energy highway, a 735-kilovolt transmission line, was built to carry electricity generated at the Manic-Outardes complex along the eastern reaches of the St Lawrence Seaway. Perhaps by no coincidence, Quebec's first inter-provincial grid connection—and the advent of Canada's national grid—was sparked in 1965, after a massive power outage plunged much of Ontario and the eastern seaboard into the dark. Originally meant to protect power supplies, the newly built provincial and stateside interconnections would later serve as conduits for the growing export market, from distribution to transaction. And without the transmission technology—so clearly on display across Quebec—the province's richest hydro developments would have gone untapped.

But in 1998, Quebec's world-class grid became a victim of its own scale: with the concentration of huge doses of power into an electrical super-highway, problems compounded when four of the five high-voltage transmission lines that supply Montreal collapsed. The remaining link that normally carries only 1,000 megawatts of electricity failed to meet a demand of 6,000 megawatts from 1.8 million people. In a province where more than 90 percent of new residences are heated electrically, this was a crisis. The bigger-is-better ethos failed when customers needed it most. "Hydro-Québec is alone in North America in using 735 kv transmission lines," noted *Electrical Business* magazine in 1998. "That is, it is using high-voltage lines to carry more power at less cost over longer distances, where other jurisdictions use more, lower-voltage lines to carry the same volume of electricity."

With the shining new towers that slice through the Township of Val Saint-François, the Ice Storm was part of a broader reckoning within a continental power system that's grown to unwieldy, gargantuan proportions. "While I don't think that any practical power system can guarantee reliability," said Tom Adams of Toronto's Energy Probe at the time, "but a more decentralized supply network could significantly improve reliability over where we are now. If we had a system where power was produced closer to the consumer, it would be much easier to restart the system following damage to transmission and distribution."

Questions about the grid continue. In the wake of the Ice Storm, Hydro-Québec lost its thirty-year contract to supply power to Vermont, worth about half of Hydro-Québec's export revenues at the time. Vermont's utilities were not happy with how the crisis was handled, and echoing the evidence of the Nicolet Commission—the scientific panel that served as Quebec's quasi-inquiry into the Ice Storm—the utilities speculated that lax maintenance was partly to blame. "There have been significant ice storms in the last decade," charged the Vermont Joint Owners, a group of fifteen electric utilities. "Hydro-Québec weakened their maintenance program so badly that Hydro-Québec's union of professional engineers have long issued dire warnings of ever more imminent blackouts. Quebec's own

Nicolet Commission also pointed out that Hydro-Québec's spending on the maintenance of its transportation network in the Montérégie region dropped by 40 per cent between 1993 and 1998." By the end of 2000, the world's largest industrial and commercial property insurer, Factory Mutual Insurance Co, was suing Hydro-Québec for $75 million, claiming that the utility was negligent in safeguarding its power grid.

It isn't the first time that expansion-hungry Hydro-Québec has suffered setbacks. Its historic nemesis, the Cree peoples of the North, represented by Matthew Coon-Come and Billy Diamond of the Grand Council of the Crees during the 1980s and early 1990s, won the battle over traditional Cree territory. Proposed by Hydro-Québec in 1989, Great Whale was a $13-billion project that was indefinitely shelved in 1994 after an international campaign in New York, Vermont and several other states that foiled Hydro-Québec's plans for massive power contracts.

Of course, large monopolies have their benefits. In recent years, the utility has put some of its profits into green-power pilot projects, creating Canada's largest wind turbine program. In 2000, it froze prices for two years—a measure that most other North America jurisdictions could never dream of. And in the era of climate change, hydro power is by far Canada's most agreeable mass energy source—notwithstanding ongoing problems with land rights, methyl mercury poisoning, destruction of whole bioregions and the ensuing lost greenhouse gas sinks, forests and muskeg that scrub the atmosphere of its carbon.

But although Quebec seems like a Shangri-La of power production, the truth is that modern transmission and generation systems weren't designed with regular consumers first in mind. The mega-scale system primarily benefits those industrial customers that purchase incredible sums of energy, as Hydro-Québec and Ontario Hydro provide, usually at discounted rates. Traditional utilities specialize in volume, not efficiency or choice, which has created a system defined by highly centralized control and an all-encompassing reach.

From British Columbia to Quebec, large electricity systems pose major challenges: chaos over deregulation, short supplies and erratic prices that governments seem, at times, powerless to contain. By contrast, the first wave of power in Canada was defined by public ownership, from the wrestling of Canada's Niagara Falls hydro from American interests in the early 1900s to the final nationalization of Quebec power in 1963. Canada's modern high energy society was born in a flood of electric appliances, furnaces and lights during the second half of the twentieth century. Our first full century of power was focused on power consumption, not efficiency or scale, like a large circuit board that kept getting bigger. At its heart, a massive industrial structure grew, one that demanded volumes of cheap power. Utilities, publicly owned and never too far out of step with their governments, usually obliged. It was this large, inflexible and imperfect power grid that the Ice Storm brought to national attention.

Power has defined modern Quebec, building an economy dependent on industries that demand inexpensive electricity. Scholar Paul-André Lapointe noted that Quebec's aluminum production capacity more than tripled between 1980 and 1995, to about 40 percent of North America's output, no small thanks to energy "two to three times lower than that generally available in the United States. Moreover, it is the policy of Hydro-Québec to charge aluminum producers rates below [provincial] market price." In the manufacture of aluminum, the main variable cost is electricity (vast supplies of uninterrupted power are required to arc alumina and bauxite in high-voltage molten pots). The only smelter outside Quebec is at Kitimat in British Columbia, where abundant power from its privately owned Kemano station has kept Alcan's plant a top producer.

Not only has Quebec's provincial government lowered environmental regulations and sidestepped public hearings, says

Lapointe, but it actively subsidized aluminum producers yet gained only a 15-percent increase in jobs between 1980 and 1995. "Quebec could become an aluminum republic, just as certain Central American countries at one time became banana republics," he writes. "That is what happens when a province such as Quebec overemphasizes a single industry which is under foreign control and dedicated almost exclusively to export."

Electricity, though, is a poor commodity. Unlike oil or gas, which can be stockpiled, electricity from the grid is not easily stored or deferred, save for hydro producers that can often turn down water flow, delaying large surges of energy. The quicksilver nature of electricity can make it harder to sell in large quantities at a consistent price: on a continental scale, demand and supply are variables that sometimes result in shortages and price spikes.

Consequently, Canada stands to both gain and lose from the continental power market. British Columbia Hydro exported power at premium prices during California's 2001 rolling blackouts, for example, while Alberta suffered unprecedented price peaks during the early stages of its deregulation process. Quebec, which has no plans to open its domestic electricty market to competition, likely has the most to gain from anticipated power shortages across the United States—and smaller profits from other Canadian provinces, such as Ontario, whose old coal and nuclear plants pose a growing economic and environmental liability.

Shipping power south is hardly a new business. Public utilities have been quietly racking up export income since the 1970s, selling surplus power across the border: from Manitoba to Minnesota and from Quebec to New York and Vermont. Likewise, Ontario, British Columbia and Saskatchewan have all sold growing quantities of power to American states.

Of all Canadian provinces, Quebec has tried the hardest to run continentally. In 1993, Quebec's electricity exports to the

United States only amounted to about $385 million, a small fraction of what it had originally planned to generate and sell from La Grande River before the James Bay Cree defeated the expansion. Again, during the mid-1990s, Hydro-Québec pledged to export 3.5 gigawatts of electricity a year to markets in the northeastern United States by 2003. This was not to be: in 1992, the New York Power Authority cancelled a gigawatt purchase from Hydro-Québec's grid, worth about $13 billion, due to slumping energy demand caused by energy conservation and a strong pro–First Nations lobby. By 1994, Hydro-Québec had lost another $5-billion contract, due to lack of demand and mounting concerns over its Great Whale project.

Nevertheless, the push for continental integration continues. In Quebec, as in other parts of Canada, what is already big is only getting bigger: large debts that funded colossal hydro and nuclear programs—such as Hydro-Québec's $35-billion hydro debt—make exports a necessity. Large power begets large sales. Consequently, the power line through Val Saint-François was strategically important since Hydro-Québec's American exports were finally picking up, after a period of disappointment.

By 2001, Hydro-Québec was selling power to fifteen different electric utilities in the northeastern United States, Ontario and New Brunswick. Erratic peaks in natural gas and oil prices spurred electricity demand, fuelling Hydro-Québec's billion-dollar bonanza in 2000. Between 1999 and 2000, natural gas prices were up more than 100 percent, while crude oil prices rose almost 40 percent, all part of an energy boom across Canada.

With exports and imports playing a greater role in the power profile of Canadian communities, the ever-expanding transmission grid carries both opportunity and uncertainty. The lure of continental energy markets—and multi-million-dollar profits—has inspired many public and private companies to gear up for expansion just as Canada wrestles with the legacy of the high energy society: oversized networks, inefficient consumption and a growing list of environmental troubles. In other words, Canada is becoming a world-class energy nation at a time when traditional forms of power guarantee new and unforeseen consequences. The first energy squeeze of the new millennium affected all power sources—hydro and fossil alike. "The non-thermal generators, be they nuclear operators or hydro operators, benefited from the fact that other fuels put upward pressure on electricity prices," noted Thierry Vandal, Hydro-Québec's executive vice-president, as the utility marked its first billion in export revenues. Even though hydro power represents a whopping 56 percent of Canada's national electricity supply (as of 2000), it still doesn't offer protection from the unpredictable future of fossil power.

The high-voltage lines of rural Quebec, the lure of American power markets and the challenging issues of climate and sustainability are all part of an energy question that is only now being posed. In a nation that has literally built itself on the concept of continued growth of its power capacity, what happens if it turns out that the scale of the grid is horribly wrong?

Inspired by the energy rush, even several Cree communities were nevertheless discussing their own hydro projects by 2001. As Alex Roslin reported in the Montreal *Gazette,* Cree leaders from several bands were consulting with "Toronto-based Amec Inc., a large engineering and construction firm that worked on Hydro-Québec's original James Bay hydro-electric project, China's Three Gorges dam and Colombia's Urra dam." The Cree plan is less ambitious and likely less destructive than Hydro-Québec's 1997 offer to make them minority partners. The new plan, discussed with Amec, would make the Cree full owners after the project's costs are covered. Robbie Dick, who is co-ordinator of the Cree Regional Council of Elders, dissented: "It doesn't matter who owns it. I don't want to be part of it."

THE ANSWER, IF THERE IS ONE, appears to lie in locally based production and consumption of electricity: smaller, accountable and more efficient power. Depending on circumstances, small hydro, natural gas turbines, wind power and solar generation all offer alternatives to the mega-power networks first dreamed up during the 1950s. Curiously, the neighbourhood networks of the future could look a lot like the original power systems of the early 1900s.

In the hills northeast of Quebec City is the town of Saint-Ferréol-les-Neiges, an old logging community that now sits within walking distance of the Mont Sainte-Anne ski resort. Les Sept Chutes was its first claim to fame, a twenty-megawatt hydro-power plant built in 1916. It is one of Quebec's oldest hydro-power plants and came under the ownership of Hydro-Québec in 1963, as part of the province's nationalization plan. Over the decades, it was dwarfed by a string of modern hydro developments, each seemingly bigger than the last, and the plant was quietly retired in 1984.

But in 1999, Hydro-Québec decided to bring Les Sept Chutes back on line. The Ice Storm had inspired the province to reconsider smaller, diversified sources of energy. Off in the Gaspé, two separate wind farms at Matane and Cap-Chat were launched after the Ice Storm—133 turbines worth about one hundred megawatts, the largest array in Canada. On its own, Les Sept Chutes now feeds twenty megawatts—enough power for 40,000 homes—into a modern system that's been repeatedly humbled by nature. It is an antique that's been raised from the dead, renewable energy from the days before fossil fuel and nuclear became dominant.

I am standing inside the dam with Mariot Legare, general manager. Around us are dark passages that weave through the face of the thirty-metre structure as it rises from the floor of the surrounding river canyon. We're five metres down, behind a wall that holds back a modest reservoir—because the canyon is steep, the land displacement is minimal. The relatively small amount of water required to generate twenty megawatts stands as some testament to the Laurentian Power Company, which helped build the station after plans were approved in 1912.

Between the flickering fluorescent lights, the angular cement corridors that sometimes trail off into a dead end and the muted roar of the water beneath us, it all seems as though I've stumbled into the den of a mad scientist. The sub-aquatic corridors exist to maintain the dam, which was refurbished. "Hydro-Québec closed the site because the power production in Quebec was surplus," explains Mariot. That was 1984, during the first phase of La Grande—showing the degree to which engineers and politicians trusted the large-scale generation and transmission system they'd designed. Instead of a locally produced twenty megawatts, residents next to Les Sept Chutes would instead plug into the imported power of James Bay.

Since 1987, Les Sept Chutes has become a tourist attraction, drawing forty thousand visitors each year to its lush natural grounds. With the exception of the newly poured concrete of the dam, it provides a charming collection of waterfalls, cliffs, wooden houses and old industrial structures that somehow makes it all seem like more of a park than a power station. The homey, natural feel of the place probably has something to do with the employees who lived on site, as well as the close ties to neighours next door at Saint-Ferréol-les-Neiges. "It is an exceptional site because the workers lived here—we have housing for six families," Mariot says. "They had forty-five kids here at one point. The last family left in 1984."

We take a short walk down the canyon where a two-metre-wide pipe—*la conduit force*—carries water from the base of the dam to a powerhouse several hundred metres below. Inside the old generator room, where four antique turbines spin under a twelve-metre domed ceiling, a statue of Jesus looks down from the wall. Bright light spills in from the tall cathedral-like windows across the iron generators. Somewhere under the floor, beyond the roar of the machines, spent water rushes out the back of the building.

Les Sept Chutes, a living museum, shows the shortcomings of the massive electricity grid that has been built up around it. Land displacement here is minimal, thanks to the strategic deployment of natural features. The plant was built in the days before power stations were designed as engineering monuments. (The Robert Bourassa complex, boasts Hydro-Québec, is a fifty-three-storey-high dam and the world's largest powerhouse, descending 140 metres underground, "a veritable cathedral-like structure sculpted in the bedrock.") In other words, Les Sept Chutes makes efficient use of the available resource without posing long-term liabilities.

Locally distributed power such as that on display at Les Sept Chutes is now gaining economical and environmental momentum. A mix of economically competitive gas turbines and affordable renewables like wind power could open up a new grid, eventually transforming North America through a combination of efficiency measures and site-specific generation. "Electricity systems may be the most spectacularly successful technology of the twentieth century," says energy thinker Walt Patterson. "In this twenty-first century, nevertheless, traditional electricity systems are doomed. They have failed to reach two billion people—one-third of humanity—and the proportion of those without access to electricity is increasing, not decreasing. Moreover, the key technologies of traditional electricity, for large-scale generation and high-voltage transmission, all face financial, social and environmental problems that may become insuperable."

If the electrification of society were only starting now, with the technologies of today, electricity systems would look very different, Patterson argues. In fact, he says, the future could look a lot like the past. "In this model, companies will contract with customers to design, install, operate and maintain integrated local systems, generating electricity where it is to be used, and ensuring that the buildings and other end-use equipment make optimal use of the electricity to deliver the services customers actually desire—comfort, illumination, motive power, refrigeration, information handling and so on. Some major companies are already offering such contract packages; more will undoubtedly follow."

By tightening the production-consumption loop, consumers would shoulder more responsibility for power—management, planning, waste reduction—but local generation could achieve the same goals that pioneering public crusaders set out during the twentieth century. Their old slogans seem as current as ever: Ontario's "Power at Cost"—or, better yet, "Maîtres chez nous!"

WHEN HIGHWAY 138 LEADS BACK to Quebec City from Les Sept Chutes, it passes by the pilgrimage mecca of Ste-Anne-de-Beaupré, a Catholic cathedral that draws the elderly and infirm to bask in its reported healing powers. The basilica reaches into the sky, as tall as many modern-day transmission towers. While the crutches and wheelchairs that adorn the inside of the church are impressive—as is the flow of devoted pilgrims—it's the nearby Cyclorama d'Jerusalem, the world's largest panorama, that has me transfixed.

On exhibit since 1895, the Cyclorama is a 110-metre, 360-degree painting of Christ's crucifixion. In gushing signage, it reinforces the quaint assumption that we modern citizens are still at the centre of things, more or less in control of the landscape and the scope of human history. "From the observation point, you can contemplate all the city of Jerusalem and over 80 kilometres of surrounding countryside at the four cardinal points," proffers the Cyclorama. "Finding yourself again in biblical times in the heart of the Holy Land will fascinate you." From Cavalry, tomb of Jeroboam, and the tower of Antonia, the sprawl of biblical Jerusalem unfolds as the viewer stands on a five-metre platform in the very middle of the painting. Manufactured as a special effect before the advent of special effects, the Cyclorama pioneered the bigger-is-better ethos of the industrial age well before it was technologically possible. There's nothing that can't be improved or reinvented—even the crucifixion. Looming over the highway, the sign says it all: "Spectacle Continuel * Oeuvre Grandiose * Dimension Giante."

But these days, there is no cyclorama or diagram that could decipher the vast expanse of the grid. One thing is sure: if the power system was truly meant for consumers, we'd all be paying less, primarily because we'd be consuming less. Micro-generation through solar panels, wind power and small hydro could give many consumers a supplementary income against their hydro bills—as many Europeans have—but the greatest immediate gains still come from consuming less power.

In the face of rising energy costs and greenhouse gas emissions, the greatest energy technologies are those that help us reduce power consumption—from high-efficiency furnaces to industrial-scale cogeneration plants, a whole flotilla of large and small applications, devices and techniques offer the proven power savings. And in the long run, they're usually cheaper than the cost of power.

Efficiency solutions are often simple and elegant: they are small-scale, repeated frequently, from house to house and business to business. According to the Intergovernmental Panel on Climate Change, most developed countries can achieve 10- to 30-percent gains in efficiency "at little or no net cost in many parts of the world through technical conservation measures and improved management." But efficiency is easy to ignore, precisely because it doesn't have a lobby group, or an advertising campaign. One cannot sell energy efficiency the way one sells cars or gasoline. In the face of a consumption-driven market, it is more a paradigm than a technology: one produces energy by inventing myriad ways to control waste rather than merely increasing supply.

In Quebec, a province with some of the cheapest power in the world, the frontiers of energy efficiency are being explored not by large companies or governments but by low-income Quebecers. During the late 1990s, a Montreal community group, Option consommateurs, started a project to help households conserve electricity: home visits with consultants provide a raft of cheap savings, from weatherstripping on windows, plugging cold leaks around doors and inside electrical outlets, as well as thermostat management. With the help of Hydro-Québec's Energy Efficiency Agency, a $4.5-million body created in the wake of the Ice Storm, more than four thousand households have been consulted. Independent evaluations show that households will save up to 13 percent of their energy bills immediately with low-cost improvements that are readily available at most hardware stores. Based on the same study, it was estimated that, per dollar, energy efficiency projects like Option consommateurs create eighteen jobs per $1 million spent, whereas conventional power generation and transport create only half as many.

A household that switches to energy-efficient appliances and heating will immediately shave 30 percent off its power bill, says the American National Laboratory, accruing pollution savings equivalent to taking a car off the road for seven years. Other studies across North America have found similar results.

Future potential gains are significant. As Amory Lovins, American energy expert, has noted, "improvements that could pay for themselves within a few years could save upward of half of the energy used to cool and ventilate buildings in countries like the United States, a nation whose buildings use one-third of all energy produced and two-thirds of the electricity." Lovins estimates that sustainable replacements for air conditioning could displace two-fifths of all electricity generated—worth at least two hundred large power plants across North America.

Across Canada, gains have already been made. Canada's Office of Energy Efficiency, established in 1998, reported that national efficiency improved 6 percent between 1990 and 1997—an annual savings of five billion dollars each year and a greenhouse gas emissions reduction of twenty-four megatonnes. Nevertheless, larger-scale energy efficiency initiatives lag: many Canadian provinces, as of 2001, still had no guidelines or integrated programs to promote energy efficiency, while Canada's major fossil fuel–producing provinces—Alberta, British Columbia and Saskatchewan—invested in royalty breaks and tax incentives to spur non-renewable energy output.

For now, improvements can be found in the unlikeliest of places. Every year, for example, Hydro-Québec cuts the power on 35,000 defaulting low-income customers; what they've discovered through Option consommateurs is that energy-efficient households have more money to pay their power bills, thereby increasing Hydro-Québec's net revenue from customers who might otherwise have defaulted. The utility, in its wisdom, has already pledged an initial one million dollars to support the program.

Perhaps the hard energy path—so named by Amory Lovins for its unyielding devotion to adding megawatts at almost any cost—serves as some figurative *Titanic,* comfortable but nevertheless flawed technology sailing through dangerous waters. Are we awake to our own weakness? It's hard not to wonder if the Ice Storm delivered a message that we've only begun to grasp.

# THE WINDMILL AND THE REACTOR

## Toronto

"**Y**OU'RE DESTROYING OUR PARK!" someone shouts behind me. "You think you can put that thing up so it will tower over us? It'll be a scar on the land."

"We don't like the idea of it being forced on us," says someone else. "It's public land and it's for us and our children."

The topic at hand, surprisingly, is not a coal plant or a waste incinerator, but an environmentally friendly wind turbine. I'm sitting in a community meeting at Humber College, right next door to Colonel Sam Smith Park, a beautiful lakeside collection of forest and trails on the shores of Lake Ontario. The park, which juts out from Etobicoke on the western edge of Toronto, happens to be a prime wind-power site, where constant breezes blow off Lake Ontario. Wind turbines won't work inland around here, despite their tall towers, because the surface texture of the Toronto urban landscape dissipates the wind and renders it useless. Only what engineers call "clean wind" will ensure quality power; only about eleven optimum wind-power sites exist in the Greater Toronto Area. And with hardware worth $1.2 million involved, the location of a turbine is paramount.

A few people speak up in support of the project. "We need better power," says one. "We just can't sit here and wait for the government to fix things—they aren't. Look outside every summer, the muck that hangs over the city." It's true: every summer, fossil-fuelled smog kills hundreds but some locals seem more passionate about keeping a funny-looking tower off their waterfront.

It's October 1999 and it's been almost three years since the founders of Toronto Renewable Energy Cooperative (TREC) started looking for a site for Toronto's first commercial windmill. It's the first urban turbine ever proposed in North America, following the model of local production and consumption that's still on display at Les Sept Chutes in the hills beyond Quebec City. The plan itself is simple: one five-hundred-dollar "turbine unit" gives members a vote in how the co-op is run and a share of income from the energy produced. Each turbine generates enough power for 250 households.

But as Toronto swims in summertime ozone, TREC's general manager Bryan Young is seeing more paperwork than green power. It turns out that saving the planet is a bureaucratic nightmare. For example: Toronto Hydro, which currently cranks out about 600,000 bills per cycle, can't do the math that would deduct a co-op member's share of the turbine's output unless it makes close to $600,000 in software amendments to its billing system.

"The suit doesn't fit," Young says. "There have been no easy-to-follow steps. There isn't much policy to allow for green power."

Young is beginning to find out why there aren't more energy co-ops and windmills in Ontario. Even with a growing membership, influential friends and a partnership with Toronto Hydro, the system just isn't set up for something as strange as an independent, non-polluting power source, owned collectively by citizens. You'd think that adding proven, zero-emissions technology to the grid would be easy—as in Denmark, where 12 percent of all power is wind, a total expected to quadruple by 2025. But regulatory measures designed for mass power—nuclear, large hydro and coal—tend to exclude green-power sources in Canada.

In a country with only about 0.5-percent total green power—wind, geothermal, solar—you'd think that there would be an orchestrated effort to expedite renewable energy. "It's actually quite an obstacle course," says Young. "You have to impose yourself: find the levers and those brave bureaucrats who will champion your plan." There are ornithological considerations (people worry about birds getting caught in the turbine blades), political contacts, coalitions and alliance-building, as well as a whole list of approvals no one ever dreamed would be necessary.

There are three levels of government, technical and compatibility problems, city bylaws that need to be rewritten or revised, and a host of other complications. The growing list of government jurisdictions and departments requiring reports and approval is considerable—City of Toronto, Navigation Canada, Transport Canada, Toronto airport, Committee of Adjustment—and then there is the federal environmental assessment, a process that requires its own small mountain of paperwork and consultations. There's also a list of unwritten "unofficial approvals," says Young, "those wink-wink approvals you better have."

In a nation where anyone can still vent greenhouse gases with impunity—without economic penalty or prosecution—the thought of a wind turbine caught up in a federal environmental assessment seems, well, a little perverse.

According to the National Energy Board, wind could generate more than 1 percent of the country's power by 2025. With pilot projects by large utilities such as Hydro-Québec and the opening up of Alberta's market under deregulation, wind is still the fastest-growing power source in Canada. In terms of cost, wind has become much more competitive with conventional power, especially when emissions credits and environmental savings are factored in. The rest of the world has already taken note: 1999 saw the largest-ever one-year increase in worldwide wind-power use—36 percent—mostly because of new installations in Germany, Spain and the United States. Texas, the fossil capital of North America, is investing $2 billion in wind alone.

At the Etobicoke community meeting, some wondered if a few wind turbines could make an impact. Then again, there's no single project or machine big enough to solve all our energy problems. Maybe, argue green-power advocates, the trick is to employ a network of locally based alternatives, each adjusted to local needs.

It's not exactly a level playing field. According to the U.S. Energy Information Agency and Canada's commissioner of the environment, government spending and tax incentives favour well-financed non-renewable power; compared to the $55 million spent by federal and provincial governments on fossil fuel research and development in 2000, green power only garnered $12 million in federal research funds. (Although, thankfully, about $64 million has been spent annually on energy-efficiency activities since the early 1990s.) Either way, renewable power sources are faced with uncertain power markets, as well as a dearth of investment capital. Consequently, projects such as TREC take years of extensive public and private fundraising to get off the ground.

While TREC alone won't transform Canada into a green-friendly nation, its immediate goal, explains Young, is to show how citizen-run renewable power might work in a country that as yet has no comprehensive plan to install green energy nor special tax incentives that might spur a green-energy boom.

Toronto's windmill is a giant how-to project, stretched over years of planning and paperwork. The model isn't exclusive to wind power; it is possible, for example, that a co-operative bio-gas or micro-hydro co-op could do the very same thing—save money on power bills and promote sustainable energy—without waiting for lumbering governments to move. In other words, a bunch of volunteers are trying to rewire Canada's energy grid, 660 kilowatts at a time.

The direct benefits are small but worthy. By its own estimates, TREC figures that a standard-model wind turbine on

Toronto's waterfront has the capacity to displace 1.4 kilotonnes of carbon dioxide per year—equivalent to planting approximately 200,000 medium to large trees—as well as significant amounts of sulphur and nitrogen oxides at a time when Toronto's skyline is increasingly choked with smog.

THE ARRIVAL OF TREC and hundreds of other small projects across Canada comes at a time when our conventional power sources pose unprecedented health, economic and climatic risks. In the few years since Toronto's Green Energy Co-op was founded in 1997, coal power has boomed across Ontario. Power output from fossil generation more than doubled between 1995 and 1999, creating Canada's largest single source of air pollution and greenhouse gases. Of this, 80 percent of all new pollution came from coal.

Why? The province's aging nuclear plants, once heralded as an endless supply of cheap energy, could no longer supply the load. With Ontario leading the way, electricity generation became the largest greenhouse gas–producing sector in Canada during the 1990s, growing at a rate double that of the national average. With U.S. power markets beckoning and a growing domestic demand, utilities across Canada increased coal-fired generation by 31 percent during the 1990s. "About half of this was the result of nuclear shutdowns in Ontario," said Environment Canada in a 2000 report. "Coal is being used to pick up increased demand for electricity."

Now, more than ever, renewable energy has the power of math: in the age of climate and smog trouble, a shift to green solutions makes compelling long-term economic sense. And if billions can be found for nuclear plants and petroleum tax breaks, the argument goes, why not for citizen-controlled power that offers savings, flexibility and profuse social benefits? Green power itself has become more of a political and economic question than anything else—outstanding technological issues are either fast evolving or already settled. Moreover, Canada could stand to save $2.2 billion annually in human health and environmental damage by adopting measures to reduce fossil fuel consumption and greenhouse gas emissions, according to a 2000 study done for the David Suzuki Foundation; improved air quality alone would reduce agricultural crop damage (a multi-million-dollar problem in southern Ontario), decrease hospital admissions, and spur greater economic productivity through better rail and public transport. The list goes on.

So what, exactly, is keeping us from building a more diversified and sustainable power system?

It turns out that rising energy costs and a growing emissions crisis grow from the same root: a power system that is dangerously rigid, poorly capitalized and prone to spending public money on short-term plans that obsessively focus on delivering large blocks of power. And all of this comes at a time when most international talks between governments are focused on selling energy rather than fighting smog or managing greenhouse gas emissions.

Even in the middle of Canada's largest urban land mass, where air pollution and high energy prices make headlines, TREC will spend the next several years struggling to complete Canada's first energy co-op. "Next time," says Young, joking, "we'll build a coal plant."

IN THE BACKYARD OF THE HOUSE I rent in downtown Toronto is a large Japanese maple. It is a glorious tree, a rangy delicate thing that has grown well beyond its usual two-metre height. During the summer of 2000, this tree took seriously ill: its branches were dying off and its burgundy and green leaves curled up—the whole top part of the tree resembled a mass of brown claws, grasping for the sky.

A tree doctor was called and, it turns out, the branch die-off could be easily remedied by a replanting—the roots needed more room to grow. The leaves, on the other hand, could not be helped. "That's leaf burn," the tree doctor said. "Pollution settles on the leaves and burns with sun and moisture." I'd read about foliage burn before—sometimes referred to as a harbinger of more serious airborne pollution, usually found near smelters and other large industrial plants. But not in my backyard.

There's no remedy, says the arborist, unless I wanted to dust off each individual leaf on a biweekly basis. "That's why I moved my family out to Markham," a community near the edge of Toronto's growing sprawl. "If the air downtown is doing that to a tree, what do you think it's doing to everything else?"

The funny thing is that the summer of 2000 seemed quite reasonable: the heat wasn't so extreme that ground-level ozone made regular breathing difficult or uncomfortable. Nevertheless, there was my tree, sickly and gasping for air.

Unfortunately, it's all part of a well-documented trend. In June 2000, the Ontario Medical Association released a study that estimated air pollution would kill 1,900 people in the province in that year alone, costing the health-care system and economy more than $1 billion. This includes $500 million in additional hospital admissions and emergency-room visits of patients suffering from illness brought on by air pollution. At current rates, Ontario air pollution is expected to cause the "premature deaths" of 2,600 people by 2015, largely due to ozone and fine particulate matter.

Part of this health hazard has its roots in the once-great promise of nuclear power. In 1997, Ontario's public utility, Ontario Power Generation (OPG), announced that it was temporarily shutting down seven of its oldest nuclear reactors—three at Bruce and all four at Pickering-A—for, it claimed, maintenance and improvements for its full nuclear lineup. (Ontario Power Generation was one of three companies that emerged from the public divestiture of Ontario Hydro in 1999.) Stories of safety troubles, workers' errors and malfunctioning equipment surfaced, suggesting that Pickering's "lay-ups" were far from routine. It was, in fact, North America's largest-ever nuclear shutdown, depriving the provincial energy grid of five thousand megawatts—roughly 10 percent of Ontario's power—enough to supply all the homes in the city of Toronto.

By refiring its coal furnaces, OPG became the largest corporate greenhouse gas source in Canada: thirty-one megatonnes of carbon dioxide in 1998, a 30-percent increase in the wake of the 1997 nuclear layoffs. And Nanticoke, North America's largest coal plant on the shore of Lake Erie, became Canada's biggest source of smog-producing air pollution.

The problem, say Ontario's doctors, is that smog isn't just an urban problem any more—you can't escape it. "Smog builds up in both urban and rural areas, blanketing southern Ontario, from Windsor to Montreal and Quebec City, along the Lake Huron shoreline, and as far north as Sudbury and North Bay," says the Ontario Medical Association (OMA). "Smog episodes can last for days at a time." The OMA notes that during a smog alert, people lose roughly 10 to 20 percent of their lung capacity.

Smog, a stew of pollutants consisting of ozone, sulphates, nitrates, aromatic hydrocarbons and fine particles, arrives from a variety of sources. Much of southern Ontario's pollution, for example, comes from the United States. Toronto smog is estimated to be about 50 percent from across Lake Ontario—and 33 percent from American coal-fired power plants. (Although automobile and truck exhaust contributes more than half of Ontario's homegrown smog, coal power became the biggest single emissions source in the province during the late 1990s.)

But Ontario's smog travels back into the United States and is increasingly blamed for acid rain in northeastern states such as Maine and New York. It's all part of a northeasterly plume that reaches as far out as Sable Island, in which Midwest states pollute Ontario and Quebec. Canada in turn dumps on the northeastern states, and the Maritimes suffer the cumulative impact of everything vented from the west, depending on air currents.

Smog is a big question across Canada; the federal government estimates that air pollution contributes to the premature deaths of five thousand people across the nation's eleven largest cities each year. "This is a relatively large number of deaths when compared with some of the other involuntary risks that Canadians face," noted the commissioner of the environment and sustainable development in a special year 2000 report on smog. "Past improvements in air quality are slowly being eroded by increased emissions as a result of greater consumption of energy."

Estimated smog-related deaths actually exceed nationwide annual fatalities from breast cancer (4,946), prostate cancer (3,622) and motor vehicle accidents (3,064), as per 1997 statistics. The federal government estimates that about 20 million people—two-thirds of the population—are exposed to harmful levels of airborne pollutants, mostly derived from energy production and transportation.

Moreover, the effects of air pollution on public health are more endemic than previously thought. "Federal strategies on air pollution were originally based on the belief that there were lower limits at which the main pollutants of smog were safe," says the special report, published by the Office of the Auditor General of Canada. "However, recent research has been unable to identify safe levels of ozone or particulate matter."

Ten years earlier, federal authorities launched an ambitious air pollution plan that proposed to "fully resolve" Canada's ground-level ozone problem by 2005. But the plan foundered on intergovernmental wrangling: the provinces and the feds couldn't agree on terms—accountability and management. So, with no one responsible, it died, leaving a fractured network of provincial pollution standards. "Smog is a major public health issue and one that threatens the environment and Canadians," said Richard Smith, acting commissioner. "Given the seriousness of the problem, it is difficult to understand why progress has been so slow."

One big reason, besides coal power, is Canada's growing transportation sector. A major source of local smog and greenhouse gases, cars and trucks underpin much of our economy; it's a set of technologies not easily replaced. While other economic sectors managed to reduce greenhouse gas emissions during the 1990s, transportation's share increased by 20 percent—second only to the 28-percent increase from the electricity-producing sector. Together, electricity and transport are the major factors behind Canada's status as the world's second-largest per capita source of carbon dioxide in 1995.

Besides climate, fossil transport is an effective source of hazardous ground-level pollution: carbon monoxide, particulates, sulphur dioxide and a host of other combustion by-products flow from Canada's roughly twenty million vehicles. Diesel exhaust, for example, is one of the single most damaging pollutants for children: it exacerbates allergies, hurts lung function and worsens asthma.

Not only are people driving more, they're driving larger vehicles—fashionable sport-utility vehicles, in particular—despite rising gas prices. "The average fuel efficiency of the new vehicle fleet has not increased since 1990," noted Environment Canada in 2000. "Emissions from light duty trucks which include pickup trucks, Sport Utility Vehicles (SUVs) and vans have increased by 50 percent since 1990, while emissions from cars have actually decreased. This is because the vehicle fleet is growing and shifting towards light duty trucks which, on average, emit 44 per cent more greenhouse gases per kilometre than cars."

And the great promise of fuel cell technology is, according to many, decades away: the most common source of hydrogen fuel is gasoline and methanol, offering a mere 10-percent saving over conventional fossil engines. "Fuel cells offer no important advantages over other technologies," says Malcolm Weiss in a 2001 Massachusetts Institute of Technology study. "Over the next two decades, fuel cells will deliver an environmental performance only slightly better than advanced versions of the familiar internal-combustion gasoline engine." Beyond 2020, hydrogen is expected to replace high-efficiency combustion engines. In the future, hydro power may become much more important, as a green power source for hydrogen fuel.

In the meantime, the declining condition of public transit in many Canadian cities is pushing more people back into a national fleet of low-efficiency suvs and aging cars. While some provinces such as Quebec have made transit funding a priority—including a $2-billion pledge to repair Montreal's aging subway system and a $260-million provincial transit budget in 1999—other provinces, such as Ontario, continue to divest themselves of transport funding, which is now shouldered by underfunded municipalities. Before 1995, the province paid for 75 percent of all public transit capital funding; until 2001 that subsidy had dropped to nothing, when 30 percent was restored.

The famous 1940s story of Standard Oil buying up—and then dismantling—American public transit is well known among green activists, but the truth is that today's petroleum companies need not do anything to maintain their advantage; governments are, by slow attrition, dismantling public transit all on their own.

Ontario, refusing to help fund most of the $3.8 billion required to sustain Toronto's existing transit service over the next ten years, nevertheless finds money for other pursuits. While Toronto struggles to spend $750,000 on cycling infrastructure each year, Ontario's Tories delivered a $15-million grant to improve snow-mobile trails before a 1999 election victory in the cottage-country riding of Muskoka. "The scenario is insane, but if the money isn't there, what are we going to do?" said Toronto transit general manager Richard Ducharme when a transit rate hike was announced in 2001. He expects routes and services to gradually disappear to levels not seen since the 1960s. "There'd be such gridlock everywhere, I don't really know who'd be better off."

IT USED TO BE THAT Canadians could blame the United States for just about everything, from acid rain to imperialism. Things have changed.

During the summer of 2000, New York State threatened lawsuits, alleging that Canadian pollution crosses the border and contaminates Adirondack Park, where several lakes are already too acidic to sustain marine life. "The emissions from large coal-fired plants are among the largest contributors to acid precipitation in New York," charged Eliot Spitzer, New York's attorney general, to U.S. Secretary of State Madeline Albright. Ontario's coal-fired power plants are blanketing New York state with sulphur dioxide and mercury, Spitzer said. "I respectfully urge you to demand that Canada promptly address its own power plants' excessive emissions."

Ontario's environment minister later fired back at the Americans. "More than half of Ontario's air pollution comes from sources in the U.S.," said Dan Newman. "If Ontario were to shut down every domestic source of air pollution, we would still have smog because of the overwhelming amount of pollutants that are blown over the border from the U.S."

As continental energy markets boom, the smog issue remains mired in a series of disputes between power companies, provinces, governments and nations. Earlier international efforts to address ozone depletion and acid rain during the 1980s ended in successful negotiations that, while not curing atmospheric problems completely, managed to achieve considerable reductions of pollutants on both sides of the border.

The difference now with atmospheric issues is the size of the industrial footprint and the climatic scale of our environmental concerns. The worst ozone-depleting chemicals used to be restricted largely to aerosol cans and refrigerators, and it was possible to replace one chemical with another. Likewise, sulphur scrubbers in smokestacks provided immediate relief during the first campaign against acid rain. It was all a relatively straightforward technological fix (until, that is, it became apparent that several replacement chemicals were also greenhouse gases). But with climate change, our current economic system, rooted firmly in carbon production and consumption, serves as the first major hurdle. In other words, the production of large quantities of cheap power underpins much of Canada's economy—part of a brown economic tradition that has seen Ontario become the fourth-greatest polluting jurisdiction in North America, according to North American Free Trade Agreement statistics from 2001, with more air- and water-borne emissions than Texas.

Compared to one of the most coal-intensive nations in the world, Ontario does look moderate: coal-fired plants provide 56 percent of the electricity supply in the United States, and in some states, more than 80 percent. But of course, what Ontario's negotiators failed to mention was that since the mid-1990s, the province's own fossil-fired emissions have been climbing steadily; old coal plants such as Lakeview on Toronto's western edge are now being fired up during peak capacity periods—mostly during summer pollution season.

Province-wide smog emissions are returning to levels of the mid-1980s, back when acid rain was grabbing headlines and climate change was just a bad rumour.

Several weeks after the Americans complained about Canadian pollution, Toronto's Board of Health issued a scathing export that underlined how far Canada had fallen since the days of ozone and acid rain. It identified OPG's Nanticoke plant as one of the worst polluters in North America—"the largest single emitter of nitrous oxides and sulphur dioxides" in Canada—and a province-wide liability.

By April 2001, little had changed: neither the province nor the utility had accomplished significant pollution reductions. Even though the plant is more than one hundred kilometres from Toronto, Dr. Sheela Basrur, the city's medical officer of health, called for a federal environmental assessment on Nanticoke and plans to install additional stack scrubbers—a measure many decried as inadequate, short of a complete conversion to natural gas power. "Modeling results suggest that Nanticoke may contribute 15 per cent or more of the $SO_2$ [sulphur dioxide] in Toronto's air during smog episodes," said Basrur. "This is significant when one considers that Nanticoke is a single-point source and that there are many other sources of air pollution in and around Toronto." The rest of Nanticoke's emissions drift into the United States.

Either way, life without Ontario's nukes has been notably smoggier. "By ramping up its heavily polluting coal plants, OPG has already doubled its emissions of these air toxins between 1995 and 1999," reported the Ontario Clean Air Alliance, an independent air quality watchdog. Ontario's government, sole shareholder in OPG, has committed itself to a 50-percent reduction in smog emissions by 2015. Yet the alliance's research, taken from government records, indicates that further coal burning could increase emissions by 153 percent from 1995 to 2012.

The most telling change in OPG's post-nuclear lineup was the re-firing of Lakeview Generating Station, an old coal plant built in 1962 at the southern side of Mississauga at the edge of Lake Ontario. Out of commission during 1992 and 1993, Lakeview was running at 30-percent capacity by the late 1990s. It now runs right through the middle of smog season, making it the largest single source of air pollution in the Greater Toronto Area and the second-largest source of mercury. According to OPG's own numbers, Lakeview's emissions more than doubled between 1994 and 1999.

For its part, the public utility responded with a series of interim environmental measures and a public relations campaign. "While OPG is not a major contributor to southern Ontario's smog," it claimed in a September 2000 press release, "we recognize that we, like others, must do more to reduce emissions." Reminding everyone that 75 percent of OPG's electricity generation comes from nuclear and hydro-electric sources, it announced plans to spend more than a quarter of a billion dollars to reduce acid rain— and smog-causing emissions, while making no firm commitments on greenhouse gases.

Later that fall, the utility ran a series of print and broadcast ads trumpeting lower emissions: "Our fossil stations are provid-ing Ontario with just as much electricity as 16 years ago, while producing 60 per cent lower air emissions.

"We are a small part of the smog problem in Ontario," it claimed, "compared to transportation and industrial emissions from within the province and from nearby U.S. states."

All of this would be tremendous news, if it were accurate. For the vast number of readers who would never consult OPG's annual reports, the claim to a 60-percent reduction referred to the *rate* of acid emissions (the utility released 60-percent lower acid emissions per unit of electricity) rather than absolute mea-sures of pollution. The real decrease was only 9 percent.

In the midst of all this, the utility found enough extra power to sell $273-million worth of electricity to the United States during 2000—the bulk, $190 million, was sold during the spring and summer, right when fossil fuel plants in southern Ontario were burning extra coal to supplement peak electricity demand. "Over the next decade, Ontario Power Generation will continue to serve Ontario customers, while increasing its market activities in the U.S., principally in the heavily populated, highly industrialized northeast and Midwest," notes OPG on its investor Web site. "Our relatively low production costs give us a competitive advantage in these regions." Public health and environmental groups did their own math: a June 2000 report by the Ontario Clean Air Alliance charged that average daily smog-causing emissions from OPG's coal-fired electricity exports were the atmospheric equivalent to putting an extra 866,000 cars on the road.

It didn't help that between 1988 and 1998, the number of Ontario households using power-hungry air conditioners grew by almost 100 percent, making summertime the new peak power season, whereas cold winter months previously saw the greatest demand. Or that many commuters continue to drive large, single-passenger vehicles every day. Nevertheless, the failure of Pickering-A couldn't have happened at a worse time: after a golden era of nuclear megaprojects—resulting in a thirty-billion-dollar public debt—atomic power faltered right when smog and greenhouse gas issues became critical. Caught between unreliable nuclear plants, summertime increases in air conditioning, the lure of American markets and no penalties for increased greenhouse gas emissions, OPG followed the example of power producers across the United States, where utilities are burning pretty much anything to feed a hungry demand for electricity.

The political pressure to provide cheap available power—that is, coal power—remains intense on both sides of the

U.S.-Canadian border. Electricity is a staple that underpins the whole continental economy, and since California's chronic blackouts, power is something that many governments have come to fear. Ontario's government spent much of the late 1990s and the start of the new millennium attempting to launch electricity deregulation without the chaotic price spikes experienced in Alberta. Mike Harris's Tories, the government that thought it could privatize just about anything, appraised the unpredictable consequences of deregulation and repeatedly delayed the opening of Ontario's ten-billion-dollar-a-year power marketplace to new producers.

Fear of deregulation, in turn, delayed new green-power initiatives and fossil plant upgrades. Only after several years of chronic smog and persistent lobbying was the spring 2001 decision made to prohibit Toronto's Lakeview plant from burning coal completely by 2005. The conversion to natural gas will likely cost $500 million for Lakeview alone.

The Ontario government also promised $250 million to clean up its three worst coal plants, a proposal for more stringent emissions caps, as well as "an environmental SWAT team" with the highest fines and longest jail sentences in Canada for major environmental offences. Critics were quick to point out that a considerable range of pollution "crimes," including toxic dumping and greenhouse gas and atmospheric mercury emissions, are still perfectly legal under Ontario regulatory legislation. What, exactly, would the SWAT team enforce, if many of our laws are still tuned to the stale-dated environmental concerns of the 1980s? And when many of our atmospheric troubles are international, not local?

Plans to covert the rest of Ontario's coal plants to cleaner-burning natural gas—which would cost roughly $1.8 billion—had not materialized in time for the province's earliest-ever smog alert on May 4, 2001, heralding one of the worst-ever summertime smog seasons in living memory. On that day, millions of people across southern Ontario were exposed to elevated levels of noxious ozone and particulates well over a month ahead of the usual smog warning. This historic health advisory occurred, by coincidence, on World Asthma Day.

FROM THE OUTSIDE, Canada's oldest nuclear reactor looks like a series of large warehouses, like a large auto assembly plant with some funny-looking domes tacked onto the back end. The electric sign at the gates flashes a message: "Ontario Power Generation: SAFETY IS OUR FIRST PRIORITY."

It's November 2000 and I've come to see what all the fuss was about.

On the shores of Lake Ontario, Pickering-A faces out towards the water, awaiting its return to service; the four reactors that sit beneath concrete domes built in 1971 have not produced commercial power for years. Back in 1997, it was revealed that gross safety violations and employee ineptitude had compromised the safety of the plant: alleged drug use, lax regulations and toxic dumping were all cited as major concerns. Consequently, OPG closed the plant, along with three Bruce-A reactors, on August 13, 1997, as part of a "nuclear recovery plan" with no fixed date for return. (Pickering-B, a newer set of four reactors next to the original, along with the rest of Bruce, all continued to produce power uninterrupted.) Within several months, the provincial government announced plans for deregulation and the division of Ontario Hydro into three companies.

Once you're past the security checkpoints and whole-body radiation scanners—a photo booth for the atomic age—the inside of Pickering's nuclear complex is a maze of shiny hallways and chambers, like a hospital that specializes in uranium bundles and radioactive waste. It is spotlessly clean and wherever maintenance or repairs are under way a large portable sign announces the potential radioactive hazard. Double airlocks guard any entrance to the reactor mechanism and, along with periodic spot checks for guests, Geiger counters monitor radioactivity, in a continuous vigil for hot spots.

Beneath the control room in the very centre of the plant is the high-level radioactive waste facility. Through thick glass, I can see bundles of waste uranium fuel that are stacked neatly in what appears to be a converted twenty-five-metre swimming pool. The radioactive waste—still many half-lives from becoming inert lead—sits quietly on the bottom of the pool, lit by underwater lights that shimmer with the slow circulation of the water. After nearly a half century of peacetime atomic power, Canada has yet to construct an acceptable, permanent high-level waste facility—with the result that much is still stored on site.

Throughout the plant, equipment is being moved and engineers and technicians bustle about. For a facility that's not producing any power, it's hopping. Up in the control room, there's a row of monitors above the old-fashioned dials and lights of the circa-1971 control panels: inside the reactor core of number three, a robot appears to be extracting fuel rods. The surveillance camera tracks its ghostly movements as it fumbles around in a shower of invisible gamma particles that would kill any human within an hour of exposure.

It's forbidden to ask questions in the control room. So I ask the tour guide: what's all the activity about? Apparently, OPG is busily readying its Pickering nuclear plant for recommission— even though it hasn't yet received official permission from the Canadian Nuclear Safety Commission (CNSC), formerly the Atomic Energy Control Board, Canada's federal regulator.

The circumstances around Pickering-A's closure seemed a little muddy; the utility claimed that the shutdowns were voluntary and in keeping with a responsible set of atomic practices. "Our nuclear plants are definitely safe," said one OPG official at the time. "They always have been. Our goal is to increase their safety margins, so that we are an industry leader in safety. The Atomic Energy Control Board has identified a number of areas for improvement; and we're working closely with them to achieve the necessary improvements."

It's a confounding message. Ontario's public utility conveys the impression that its nukes were closed so that they could tinker with a few bugs in the system. But if Pickering's problems are so mundane, why was it necessary for OPG to shut down five thousand megawatts of nuclear power when the only available alternative was to fire up Ontario's coal power stations and become Canada's largest source of greenhouse gases and atmospheric pollution?

The cost of running and repairing Pickering-A has long ago exceeded the plant's original $716-million price tag. It has been estimated that maintaining Ontario's nuclear program will cost $1 billion a year for the next twenty years. The obvious question, one that nobody at Pickering would care to answer, is simple: if OPG's nukes are so great—and deserving of additional billions for upgrades and repairs—why do they still seem so beset with problems?

Even well before the closing, the nukes were operating poorly: while Ontario Hydro's nineteen operating reactors ran at an average capacity factor of 66 percent in 1996, Pickering-A ran at 36 percent. As Canada's first commercial nuclear plant, Pickering was still discovering new problems, some twenty-six years after the plant was built. Several months before the closure, for example, it was revealed that Ontario Hydro had dumped more than 1,000 tonnes of copper, zinc and other metals into Lake Ontario over the previous twenty years via a series of eroded brass steam condensers.

That was just the beginning. An independent safety review revealed a plethora of long-standing problems, and when Pickering-A closed in 1997, what remained was a chronology of events that read like a bad science fiction novel—from a "loss of coolant accident" that precipitated a $1-billion retubing of the station in 1983, to a 1994 heavy water leak that resulted in a huge release of the radioactive isotope tritium into Lake Ontario. ("It was the worst-ever tritium release from a CANDU reactor," notes Durham Nuclear Awareness, Pickering's citizen watchdog, "resulting in increased levels of tritium in drinking water from Whitby to Burlington.")

On December 10, 1994, Pickering's emergency core cooling system had been employed to prevent a possible meltdown, with about two hundred workers involved in the subsequent cleanup. Several months after the reactor was reopened on February 14, 1996, "drug paraphernalia" was found at an operating island within the station. "The continuing discovery of such items in the plant is both embarrassing and a threat to our recovery and survival as a business," commented a Pickering manager at the time.

Beset by stories about drug hijinks and CANDU reactor design flaws, Pickering-A helped spell the beginning of the end for Ontario Hydro. In November 1997, Ontario Energy Minister Jim Wilson launched a sweeping plan for power reform. "Hydro's business performance has faltered so significantly over the past decade that power costs have increased by 30 percent in the early 1990s and that Hydro's debt exceeds $30 billion," said Wilson, noting that it was Canada's largest corporate debt ever. Moreover, Ontario had the third-highest electricity bills in Canada—averaging almost $1,000 a year for residential users—and more than a third of most consumer hydro bills were padded with debt payments.

Plans for a competitive electricity market by the year 2000 were detailed, as well as a new market regulator (Hydro had regulated itself) and the restructuring of Hydro into several different companies, including separate companies for generation (OPG) and transmission (Hydro One). Furthermore, OPG would be responsible for divesting itself of all but 35 percent of the energy generation within a decade of the market's opening, from its previous 85-percent share. Power prices, the government claimed, "would be driven to the lowest possible level as customers exercise their new freedom to shop for the cheapest available power."

In theory, it all sounded good. But when Ontario Hydro posted a loss of $6.3 billion at the end of 1997, the biggest annual loss in Canadian corporate history at the time, analysts predicted that Hydro's cumulative 1997 debt of $31 billion would ultimately be paid by customers. (In the past, with its debt guaranteed by the government, Hydro was at liberty to keep borrowing money to fund its nuclear recovery program.) By the time of its restructuring in 1999, Hydro's debt totalled $38.1 billion.

Pickering-A is what power analysts call a "stranded asset"—it simply costs more money than can ever be recovered within a competitive market. After payments from Hydro's successor companies (OPG and Hydro One) and new taxes on municipal utilities, it is estimated that taxpayers will face a "residual stranded debt" of about $7.8 billion. This amount does not include the future cost of maintaining Ontario's nuclear reactors or the possible expense of converting Ontario's fleet of coal plants to natural gas.

So in addition to other anticipated costs, every time anyone in deregulated Ontario turns on a light, a "debt retirement charge" kicks in, totalling about $950 million annually until the debt is repaid. For the average Ontario home that is heated electrically (about 23,367 kilowatts annually), this means a nuclear debt surcharge of about $165 per year, over a decade, which was paid previously in the form of inflated hydro bills.

The other, as yet unresolved, impact on consumer power prices is radioactive waste. "Federal documentation indicates that over the next 70 years, at least $10 billion will be needed to find and implement disposal solutions for Canada's radioactive waste," noted Canada's auditor general in 1995. This would be in addition to an existing charge for radioactive waste disposal tacked onto customers' monthly bills.

Moreover, the preponderance of stranded assets across North America—other jurisdictions with large public investments, some troubled and some valuable—is sure to affect Canada's fledgling electricity markets. The continental debt is estimated to be between $130 billion and $550 billion, a long-term expense on aging coal, hydro and nuclear technology that could force market-driven electricity prices even higher.

These and a whole host of other factors could make the new power market in Ontario one of the most expensive in Canada. Even before most environmental and greenhouse upgrades are factored in, a minimum 20-percent rate increase is projected. "When the public figures out what has been done to them I think they're going to be very upset," said Tom Adams of Toronto's Energy Probe think-tank. "This electricity restructuring is morphing into an attack on consumers, taxpayers and the environment."

Back at Pickering-A, the $1-billion cost of restarting the plant is billed as an economic and environmental opportunity. "The Pickering re-start would add two thousand megawatts of what promises to be, without exception, the lowest cost energy in the province on an incremental basis," boasts the OPG in a brochure at the reactor's public info centre. My tour guide dutifully notes that Pickering's return to service will displace about thirteen million tonnes of carbon dioxide each year and help reduce the company's overall smog emission rates.

Energy Probe did its own calculations on Pickering-A and concluded that it would be cheaper to ditch the reactor and buy power from the Americans—or, better yet, invest the money in more sustainable power generation. "Hydro refurbished that station in the 1980s, and lost approximately $2-billion for its effort," noted Tom Adams and Michael Hilson in *The National Post*. "The venture makes no economic sense. Used nuclear capacity in working order is available in the United States for less than half the price OPG plans to pay to refurbish Pickering-A."

Strolling through the halls of Pickering, I pick up a safety sheet—OPG's monthly nuclear report card—and notice that, to date, the year's reportable safety incidents number thirty-seven, a fair bit over the target of nineteen. It's hard to know if that's really something to worry about, as everything here seems to be deemed "safe"—no questions asked—even if things don't seem quite right. By OPG's own records, the public radiation dose at Pickering in 1998 was almost eight times that of Bruce-A and -B—and nearly four times that of Darlington. It's a health hazard that the utility claims is still less hazardous than a chest X-ray, but Pickering's radiation rates have been cause for concern in the past.

Behind the scenes, there have been some serious safety questions. One 1991 study by the Canadian Nuclear Safety Commission, formerly the Atomic Energy Control Board, found elevated levels of childhood leukemia within twenty-five kilometres of Pickering and Bruce nuclear stations. Commission researcher Susanna Fraser discounted the 40-percent increase in leukemia as statistically insignificant ("in fact, most likely due to chance"). But in a 1999 affidavit, Dr. David Hoel, distinguished professor of medical science and former research director of the U.S. National Institutes of Health, testified that Canada's atomic regulator set its thresholds unduly high, thereby "denying a statistically significant increased risk." Childhood cancer is generally understood to be a telltale disease for elevated levels of ionizing radiation, a harbinger of overall public safety.

The professor of epidemiology, biostatistics and radiological risk assessment argued that the results had been buried within the report's research methodology. "In my view, the study clearly indicates an excess of mortality among children 0–14 years of age." By 2000, the federal regulator had established a comprehensive cancer surveillance system, but insisted that its leukemia findings were "correctly interpreted" and "not significantly elevated."

Questions about health and safety continue to float around the aging reactor, as experts debate statistics and safety standards. The community itself voted 87 percent in favour of a full environmental assessment by the province on the future of the Pickering-A station in a 1997 municipal referendum. The investigation never happened. Demands for a federal environmental assessment intensified early in 2001 when Pickering's application for restart came before the Canadian Nuclear Safety Commission. In the end, the regulator decided that the old reactor "is not likely to cause significant adverse environmental effects" and therefore a full environmental assessment was unnecessary.

Critics pointed at the 2001 auditor general's report, published only a few days before Pickering's approval, that expressed concern over the regulator's lack of an objective rating system to assess reactor safety. Decisions are made based on "an intuitive approach, relying on the judgement and expertise of staff," many of whom previously worked for the nuclear industry. The commission countered: "The Commission rejects any suggestion of a lack of impartiality."

In an earlier 2000 report, the auditor general noted: "CNSC's compliance and enforcement system is not yet complete. As a result, it cannot adequately demonstrate that it is achieving its safety objectives for the regulation of power reactors."

None of this detracts from OPG's official messages on Pickering-A. On the bus back from the powerhouse, I press the tour guide for details about the closing down of the reactors in 1997.

"We were never ordered to shut down by the regulator," she says defensively, noting that unless the Canadian Nuclear Safety Commission says otherwise, OPG reactors are officially safe. "But," she says, eyes lowering, "if we hadn't shut ourselves down, the regulator would have probably had to close us anyway."

DOWN THE ROAD FROM PICKERING, the Toronto Renewable Energy Cooperative is still waiting to gain approval for its first windmill on Toronto's waterfront. A promising site has been located near Ashbridges Bay Water Treatment Plant on the east side of the city's lakeshore.

It's been a long process. "The crux here is that people are not paying the true cost of their hydro bill," explains Joyce McLean, Toronto Hydro's TREC partner and manager of green energy services. "Green power, with no hidden costs, is far from being more expensive. But that's confusing to the average person."

It's November 2000 at Toronto's first-ever Green Power Trade Show and McLean addresses the crowd. There's a sense of frustration here; the staggered, uncertain process of deregulation— governed by political fears about an energy price backlash—has left independent power producers, for-profit and non-profit alike, in the lurch. "You can't have consumer choice if there's no clear process for people to put up projects," says McLean. "The onus lies on the green producer to shoulder costs of certification, disclosure, education and consultation. Without a clear set of policy rules and favourable taxes, those costs are currently being carried by the people supporting green power." Even with utilities like Toronto Hydro that offer green electricity packages to residential consumers—a blend of solar, wind, landfill gas, anaerobic gas and small hydro—the net effect is that independent organizations like TREC subsidize the status quo.

Things are improving. Within a month, TREC will be granted approval from the federal Environmental Assessment Agency— a level of scrutiny that the Canadian Nuclear Safety Commission deemed unnecessary for Canada's oldest nuclear reactor. And, in a stroke of good fortune, the province of Ontario decided that it would excuse TREC from a provincial environmental assessment, a vote of support directly from the cabinet of Mike Harris. "Based on the merits of the proposed wind turbine, such as reducing emissions of climate-change-causing greenhouse gases and smog, we felt the project deserved the green light," said environment minister Dan Newman in the provincial parliament. "This demonstrates once and for all that when partisan differences are set aside, the environment benefits."

But that doesn't stop people from wondering why it took nearly four years, thousands of volunteer hours and thousands of extra dollars to put up a single windmill. "It was essentially the same process that Pickering is having to do to get its licence back, which strikes me as wrong," says Joyce McLean.

Sooner or later, the real cost of power catches up with everyone, be it nuclear debt or health problems from poor air quality. The pervasiveness of power, the near universality of our energy system, demands a broader calculus: in the process of creating wealth, it seems that we are still impoverishing ourselves in other ways. Building the true cost of energy into the economy— something not reflected in current fossil power revenues reaped by corporations and public utilities—will be one of the great struggles of the new millennium: who should pay the economic cost of unhealthy air? Can we deliver a fair and effective emissions trading system without limits on greenhouse gases?

In March 2001, when the Ontario government announced plans for cleaning up Lakeview and several other coal plants, it hinted that residential power rates would rise accordingly, a built-in environment tax from the government that promised no new taxes. Ontario rightly figured that, since consumers were already paying a discreet surcharge to help pay down the province's nuclear debt, a green tax probably wouldn't matter, especially with growing numbers of voters polling high on air quality.

It wasn't clear whether consumers of green power—such as TREC members and others who have bought into renewables—would be exempted from the coal surcharge. Green consumers already pay the nuclear tax built into transmission fees, perhaps some indication of how much work remains to be done to level the economic playing field.

Perhaps to its credit, Ontario had begun to think big about economics: why should coal-fired electricity come without social cost? Much has been written about the environmental benefits of power pricing that reflects the true cost of the energy cycle, be it wind, oil or nuclear. But high energy prices and market forces don't always inspire innovation and efficiency.

For example: during the first real energy crunch of the twentieth century—the Organization of the Petroleum Exporting Countries' embargo that followed the Yom Kippur War of 1973—prices soared and plunged for the better part of a decade. Consequently, green power came into its own: there were how-to books, tiny companies starting up and magazine articles championing smart energy alternatives. But the movement stalled; governments took to building nuclear power stations and consumers enjoyed plunging energy prices, enough to maintain the cars, homes and appliances of the high energy society built up during the 1950s and 1960s. Moreover, fossil power bounced back for parts of the 1970s, with Cape Breton opening new mines and domestic oil companies discovering new reserves, as well as the founding of Syncrude Canada Ltd. in

Alberta, now the world's largest oil sands operation. In addition to inspiring many to conserve power, the energy shortage launched a fossil fuel–burning legacy that's still with us today.

At the time, Ontario's energy crisis solutions included building economic-environmental liabilities like Pickering-A. A total of more than 150 nuclear power plants were built across North America, all of them ordered before 1974 (including Ontario's Darlington reactor, which, in 1993, became the last plant completed in Canada). Atomic power changed the face of the North American electricity grid, promising endless supplies of cheap power from facilities that would, in many instances, eventually cost ratepayers additional billions. Thus the legacy of the 1970s energy crisis is mixed: efficiency standards improved as Canadians mobilized to reduce expenses—but the drive to provide large amounts of cheap energy delivered something much less.

AS CANADA MOVES INTO A CENTURY sure to be defined by energy, it's not clear who is advocating for citizens and consumers—and it's even less clear who is ultimately accountable for air quality and greenhouse gas emissions.

At the turn of the millennium, the lack of clear limits—and consequences—between multiple jurisdictions allowed many utilities and companies to invent their own environmental standards.

So it was big news when Ontario's government launched its own proposal for a smog emissions trading system for OPG's fossil plants in 2001. The U.S. Environmental Protection Agency was quick to criticize the plan—and not because the agency was against emissions trading: Ontario had failed to establish pollution limits for non-energy sectors, which could make any emissions trade next to worthless, because a business that can pollute for free has no real reason to purchase emissions credits, apart from environmental goodwill and public relations gains.

It's actually an international problem, one that the Kyoto protocol agreement might not fix: free emissions in one sector or jurisdiction only undermine more stringent standards elsewhere. The system only works if there's a reward for those who have converted to green and efficient energy, something that has real currency on the open market. And if there aren't consistent economic or legal consequences for exceeding agreed-upon targets, emissions trading loses the discipline of the market—pollution ceases to be a commodity—and the whole exercise crumbles into something that resembles Canada's state of affairs, circa 2002: insufficient limits on smog-producing emissions, no limits for greenhouse gases or heavy metals, and plenty of bickering between governments as to who is ultimately responsible for the whole mess.

Voluntary emissions reporting and enforcement, the current standard in Canada, can only take us so far. It's too easy to chase small goals that, over the long term, prove ineffectual. "The problem with the Kyoto target is that it's too little," says energy consultant Ralph Torrie. "With a goal of 50-percent reductions you get a level of engagement, but if you choose 5 percent, all the wrong choices get defined—incremental nonsense about planting trees in Third World countries."

There's no lack of ambitious alternatives possible. Wind energy, for example, could provide at least 10 percent of all the electricity needed in Canada—a country with more wind resources than California or Denmark, both world leaders in wind power. (California has seventeen thousand wind turbines worth 1,600 megawatts; until 2001 OPG received power from only one wind turbine worth 0.6 MW.)

Solar power, though more costly, has the distinct advantage of maximizing output during the summer smog season, the hot daylight hours when ozone bakes and the city's peak seasonal demand for electricity is reached. "Given the present technology, about two-thirds of Toronto's surface area would be required to satisfy all of our present electricity requirements through photo-voltaic (PV) systems alone," says the 1999 Solar Strategy for Toronto. "If Toronto were to combine PV with other renewable energy sources and if energy efficiency were to increase, the city could be entirely reliant on green energy within 25 years."

Perhaps the most practical and innovative project is deep water cooling, a thermal network that could rid much of Toronto's business core of air conditioning by pumping ultra-cool water from Lake Ontario through high-rises. Championed by City Councillor Jack Layton, the proposal sprang from the city's vibrant green economic community, one that helped inspire the City of Toronto to deliver a double-digit reduction of its own greenhouse gas emissions.

Whatever the power source, reducing energy demand is still paramount. In the midst of all this talk about generation, green and brown, it's easy to get focused on building things. As Wayne Roberts, co-author of *Get a Life,* points out later, it's part of our culture to assume that production is always part of the solution. The cheapest, greenest power supply still flows from reducing energy demand.

"We will look back on the way we made electricity and shake our heads—everyone missed noticing the demand side trend during the 1970s," says Ralph Torrie. "In 1973, domestic consumption was 51-percent oil—but by 1998, it had dropped by 26 percent." In other words, energy efficiency has given Canada more power than all the new gas, wood, hydro and nuclear sources together.

Efficiency is the guerrilla campaign of the high energy society—high-concept, low-budget. Toronto hosts a plethora of local solutions. The Better Buildings Partnership, for example, promotes energy and water retrofits. "Over 100 buildings from the private and public sector are involved in the upgrades, and it is expected to save building owners $3 million annually, create

430 person years of employment, and reduce carbon dioxide emissions by approximately 40,000 tonnes a year," says the Toronto Atmospheric Fund, a foundation set up by the City of Toronto to help meet its ambitious climate goals. If municipal buildings undergo energy efficiency upgrades, for example, Toronto could save more than $7.5 million on $30 million in energy expenses. (Another residential program, Green$avers, determines a house's heat budget: the number of BTUs it wastes through unnecessary drafts, as well as targets and improvements. A Green$avers visit inspired my own household, for example, to install new weatherstripping, a higher-efficiency furnace and indoor heat reflectors—all of which will pay for themselves within the course of a decade or so.)

The future remains uncertain. Leaked federal cabinet documents in 2001 outlined plans to cut transportation-related smog emissions by 88 percent starting in 2004; "MPs should expect some political challenges," the notes warn. Environment Minister David Anderson also targeted high sulphur gas and Ontario's coal fleet as prime concerns. Greenhouse emissions weren't addressed.

For its part, Ontario Power Generation plans to invest $50 million in green energy to increase its green energy capacity to 500 megawatts—including twenty-two potential non-invasive, small hydroelectric projects and a biomass (landfill gas–fuelled) energy project in Waterloo. By the summer of 2001, OPG had erected one of North America's largest wind turbines right next to Pickering-A, well before TREC's windmill met with government approvals. "This demonstrates our commitment to the production of more green energy over the next few years," said an OPG spokesperson.

But 500 megawatts isn't much when the National Energy Board predicts that Canada's domestic energy demand will increase almost 50 percent by 2025. And Ontario itself will need to replace up to 85 percent of its existing generating capacity by

2020—upwards of 20,000 megawatts—all aging nuclear and coal plants that could cost fifty billion dollars to replace.

How that money is spent—and who pays for it—remains an open question that will define the future. If decisions were purely economic, nuclear power would likely be phased out and more money would be invested in energy efficiency conversions, natural gas retrofits and community-based micro-generation. Likewise, public policy would reflect stronger national environmental standards, international greenhouse gas treaties and enhanced green energy investment.

Solutions are not to be found by marching everyone onto communes or launching new energy megaprojects, but by ensuring that viable choices are available. It is mainly a question of leadership, not technology or even ideology, because as time passes, the only sure thing is that the status quo will become prohibitively expensive. Public transit and green power production, for example, provide that strategic choice, especially when they are properly financed.

After a long hiatus, power is now becoming an essential matter of public interest: will the inertia of our brown economy—the fossil-fuelled power sources of the past—eclipse the dire need for smog reduction, climate change mitigation and sustainable alternatives? The old energy game was based on a structure of command and control. The new energy game is about trying to find long-term solutions that are both irresistible and fair.

# TWILIGHT ON FISSION AVENUE

## Uranium City

NAMED AFTER CANADA's homegrown nuclear reactor, Candu High looks much like any other school—except this one seems to have been bombed. Trees and bush grow across the front of broken windows. Scattered about under the snow are piles of refuse—drywall, bricks and a few mangled desks. I pull out a flashlight and walk over a threshold of glass and metal scattered across the entrance; the front doors hang against the building, ripped off their hinges. Local teens and fun seekers have taken apart what wasn't already demolished by two decades of parties on the rooftop.

In front of me is a long main hall; classrooms and offices branch off each side. It looks as if it was once a fair-sized school, maybe five hundred or six hundred kids tops. The darkness is cut by light from exterior windows, all broken. Twenty years after the fact, the remains of textbooks and lessons are still scattered about. A pile of absentee slips lies next to what appears to have been the principal's office. November 4, 1980: someone named Pouchain missed one period of biology; someone else missed a class of English.

By chance my flashlight comes across a handwritten assignment, half rotted and faded. It's from the day of the closing announcement. A student, looks like a girl's writing, has made an inventory of her uncertain future. "I will be affected because my family may break up," she writes. "My parents and the kids may move to Stoney Rapids and from there my dad will work for Rabbit Lake [mine]. . . . I feel they are quite worried because my father has been working here since I was born."

Upstairs, amid bricks and ceiling tiles, a catalogue of the last few months of the school unfolds. Outside it's snowing, but inside I'm reading tatters of someone's social studies lesson from 1981.

With its deserted suburban neighbourhoods and abandoned mines, Uranium City has almost fallen off the map. As the epicentre of Canada's biggest-ever uranium boom, this north-west Saskatchewan community of 180 still hangs on to its elementary school, a regional hospital and a post office. Everything else, from the town's recreation centre to the movie theatre, has either closed or been demolished. Houses, if they are still standing, now sell for about a dollar—the nice ones, fixed up and running, go for about seven hundred dollars.

The quiet, rugged landscape that surrounds Uranium City harbours an unintended legacy: a network of radioactive waste sites scattered across subarctic rock and forest, some fifty-odd uranium mines and refineries within a fifteen-kilometre radius of the town. For almost thirty years, through the height of the Cold War, Uranium City shipped atomic fuel for bombs and nuclear reactors around the world—and piles of tailings and refinery waste piled up before the advent of protective legisla-tion. Consequently, "the potential for harm from exposure to uranium released from uranium mines and mills is widespread," noted one Environment Canada report in 1999.

Here, a community of five thousand prospered within the rugged Shield country north of Lake Athabasca until the market-place declined—once in 1962, when the Americans suspended demand, and finally in 1982, when the last mine closed. Now a mix of southerners, Métis and Natives live amid the abandoned homes of the ghost town and nearby radioactive tailings. Most mines were private operations that folded when the market collapsed; the owners just packed up one day and never returned, leaving equipment, headframes, vehicles and, most important, piles of tailings and waste rock. Health guidelines for radiation exposure were only instituted in 1968 and environmental controls didn't exist until 1979, so publicly available records are spotty at best. Of all of the mines, only one has been cleaned up; work on Beaverlodge, Eldorado's main mine in the area, began in 1982 and is still being carried out today.

Canada's atomic age actually began in 1926, when Eldorado Gold Mines Limited founded and began operations that would dig Canada's first radium and uranium mines into the shores of Great Bear Lake. Later, as a Crown corporation, Eldorado Nuclear Limited struck mines in northern Saskatchewan and the Northwest Territories, shipping partially processed ore south by airplane and barge to Port Hope, Ontario, where it would be refined for weapons-grade applications and nuclear fuel. As the first country to mine uranium on a large scale, Canada pioneered a national network of mines, processing plants and transportation that would make it a leading exporter of uranium for most of the twentieth century, a steady supplier of atomic fuel in the heady decades immediately following the bombing of Hiroshima and Nagasaki.

Retracing the uranium trail, I have flown north to Uranium City on the weekly grocery flight from Fort McMurray, Alberta—on a single-engine Cessna packed with fresh milk, bread and heads of lettuce. To a southerner, Uranium City might seem like a long way from anywhere. Yet I've flown over the northeast corner of Alberta, where $51 billion in oil sands developments are reshaping the landscape and, to the south, over Saskatchewan's Cluff Lake uranium mine, where radium from 2.5-million tonnes of tailings were found leaking into the nearby lake system by the federal government.

Canada remains stuck on the messy end of the nuclear business. Even after initial cleanups, the country still has more than ninety thousand tonnes of tailings, one of the world's largest inventories of low-level radioactive waste, scattered across sites from Uranium City and Great Bear Lake to communities farther south such as Elliot Lake, Port Hope and Deloro in Ontario. "To date, no uranium mining operation in northern Saskatchewan has been completely decommissioned," noted a special joint federal-provincial panel on uranium mining in 1997. "The Governments of Canada and Saskatchewan have approved an increase in uranium production from which both will accrue substantial benefits. It would, therefore, be appropriate for the federal and provincial governments to address the environmental legacy." This recommendation, like so many others, has faded into obscurity.

The $550-million-a-year uranium industry in Canada—the world's largest exporter—is based exclusively in Saskatchewan. For the moment, it is laying off employees and slowing mine operations, still hopeful that climate change and rising power demand will deliver a future for radioactive ore. But none of today's advocates for atomic power, including the federal government, seems dampened by the tailings that dot Canada's hinterlands or by evidence that ongoing attempts to contain the nuclear fuel cycle remain unsuccessful. As some predict a nuclear renaissance, Canada's archipelago of radioactive waste offers up another question: why does a country that claims to be a world-class nuclear power continue to neglect uranium dumps that, after almost fifty years, remain a clear public and environmental hazard?

THE URANIUM CITY GROCERY FLIGHT passes over Gunnar, a large abandoned mine site nestled on a long arm of rock and soil that juts out into Lake Athabasca. Built around an underground uranium ore pillar 135 metres wide and 300 metres deep, Gunnar was one of the largest operations in the region; it opened in 1955 during the first uranium boom and closed in 1964 when the market collapsed. From above, the site seems only recently deserted: offices, workshops and bunkhouses for four hundred people stand exactly as they were left almost forty years ago. The ghostly view echoes a 1981 newspaper report—by then-rookie journalist Edward Greenspon—that detailed Gunnar's dilapidated bowling alley and gymnasium, whose scoreboards still post numbers from the last game played in 1964.

The pilot pipes up over the headphones: "A few guys from the States chartered a flight into Gunnar last summer. Came with Geiger counters for fun, said it was pretty hot down there—their counters were jumping all over the place."

Gunnar's contamination came to the attention of Environment Canada around 1978, when studies first showed elevated radiation levels in whitefish, sediment and lake water. A man-made dam that held back tailings from Lake Athabasca leaked radium and arsenic into the lake, turning a nearby bay into a tailings delta, exceeding the Saskatchewan water standard for radium. "All observed plants showed high uptake of radio-nuclides," noted one 1988 Environment Canada study. While existing studies were inconclusive as to the degree of contamination within greater Lake Athabasca—pike, for example, were less radioactive than the whitefish—a common conclusion was often reached: further study is necessary.

The call for "further study" has become a familiar refrain. Empirical surveys and risk assessments have been curiously selective over the decades and bureaucrats are predictably circumspect when I call to gather information. It's not something many people are keen to talk about; after all, this was ground zero for the world's first big uranium boom, well before the advent of environmental regulation. The expense alone of a cleanup—one that, notably, offers few political gains—would likely be in the hundreds of millions, as might potential civil lawsuits stemming from decades of inaction. Consequently, anyone digging for information in uranium country is likely to come up with more questions than answers.

What we do know is that radioactive isotopes within tailings disintegrate for more than a thousand years before reaching stable lead. In the meantime, other by-products, like carcinogenic radon gas, are produced continuously. And while much of Canada's tailings waste remains untouched, environmental and human health standards have changed significantly: as of 2000, Canada's maximum recommended radiation dose for the general public (one millisievert per year) is one-fifth of what it was previously, in keeping finally with the 1991 recommendations of the International Commission on Radiological Protection, an independent body that has set international safety standards since the 1920s. The fivefold decrease was based on strong empirical evidence taken from Hiroshima A-bomb survivors that low-level radiation was far more carcinogenic than previously thought. Yet it took Canada almost a decade to adopt the new standard.

What this all means, as we make our final approach over Uranium City's runway, skimming over tailings sites left behind by Eldorado's extensive underground workings, is that a single unit of radiation is officially considered five times more hazardous now than it was a few years ago. Moreover, Canada's ongoing neglect of historic radioactive waste from orphaned mines and Crown corporations is disturbingly out of sync with its current national safety standards.

The plane touches down and my ride into town, the Bougie family, arrive to pick up their groceries. Boxes of food and supplies are loaded onto the back of the truck. I squeeze into the front and we drive through the decommissioned Eldorado mine that sits next to the airstrip, a few kilometres from town.

Looking at piles of gravel that bury old bunkhouses and mess halls, I remember a historical tidbit: here, militant unions and socialists within Tommy Douglas's Co-operative Commonwealth Federation government championed an industry that would, in part, arm U.S. missiles trained on fellow socialists in Russia. Why? They thought that uranium—fuel of the future—could pay for medicare.

AFTER CHECKING INTO HOLLAND'S MOTEL and U-drive, Uranium City's best and only accommodation, I step outside to survey a city that's been largely deserted for the past twenty years. From the corner of Uranium Road and First Street, the remnants of a once-bustling downtown are scattered about, much of it built during the 1950s: the Rexall Pharmacy, the Roxy Theatre, the *Uranium City Times,* the Ben McIntyre Shoe Store—all abandoned, boarded up. Piles of rubble mark out where buildings have either collapsed or were demolished: the Uranium City Hotel, the Thorium Theatre and the Bay.

The streets of Uranium City echo the spirit of Canada's atomic age: from my trailer at the motel, I walk along an abandoned stretch of Uranium Road, turning onto Fission Avenue towards the main drag on First Street. Next to the abandoned Legion Hall, a metal shell punched full of holes and dotted with graffiti, is the Bougie general store. It's in the ground floor of what used to be the town's huge liquor store. There is no sign out front and locals come and go, visiting for a while and pausing over a bowl of caribou soup and bannock. Just more than half the town is Métis or Aboriginal, compared to pre-closure, when it was basically a southern neighbourhood with southern amenities: a full library, several schools, a large recreation centre with a curling rink, as well as a radio station, large cemetery and outdoor swimming pool. When the closure announcement came in 1981, local businesses were still expanding and several blocks of new housing had just been built. But soon after, most of the residents sold off whatever they could and returned south.

"This was a great place until you white people showed up," jokes Denise Bougie. "Then you all left and now we're stuck running the town." It's true: it's just as expensive to run sewage and water for 180 as for 5,000. The recreation centre closed just a few years ago, despite a popular curling league. And the regional hospital just announced that it was moving operations down the lake, stealing several jobs and some steady income

with it. "They all ran too fast from here," she says of the southerners that left. "They were scared, but there were so many
possibilities—could have been a northern outlet with all its
infrastructure. I mean, until just recently, all these other
communities around Athabasca didn't have running water. We
could have had a prison up here—where are they going to run?"

Anyway, Denise has had her hands full since a fire gutted the
Bougies' upstairs café and store—a few weeks ago, her brother
and a friend were wrestling in the café and knocked over the
deep fryer, which caught fire and burned out most of the building. Kids now use the hollowed-out store for an endless succession of floor hockey games. Groceries are now sold, part-time,
from their walk-in basement.

"If it smells like smoke, then it's half-price," says Denise's
daughter, Claudette, who's moving to Fort McMurray next year
to attend high school. She sells me a copy of her *Uranium City
News*—price: one dollar—published at the town's last school.
The recent Halloween party, reports the paper, was a huge
success and kids roamed the town trick-or-treating their way
into a month's worth of candy.

The Bougies encourage me to go out and explore the mines.
"Decommissioning? Well, they went and burned down a bunch
of buildings." Denise worked on the Eldorado takedown with
her dad—"depressing and boring"—after another family business had gone under due to the closure announcement. "They
just all took off when the money ran out," she says of the succession of mining companies. "They rape the North and don't stick
around for the long term.

"Didn't do a good enough cleanup—and we don't know how
to pay for it. Rules are good, you know, but it's politics."

It's true: historic sites like Uranium City represent the not-
so-rosy past of an ever-globalizing industry now trying to
regain its footing. Corporations that dominate the Athabasca
basin—COGEMA (France) and Cameco (Canada), largest and

second-largest uranium companies in the world, respectively—
now promote uranium as the wonder fuel of the future, a solution
to the carbon economy.

I've journeyed to Uranium City at a prescient time: with the
introduction of the 2001 Bush energy plan, calling for an
unprecedented increase in power output, the United States finds
itself considering nuclear power again, after a two-decade
hiatus. "By renewing and expanding existing nuclear facilities,"
President George W. Bush told business leaders in May 2001,
"we can generate tens of thousands of megawatts of electricity at
a reasonable cost without pumping a gram of greenhouse gas
into the atmosphere."

Canada's own nuclear industry, troubled by low uranium
prices and sluggish reactor sales abroad, is gearing up for what
could be its biggest business opportunity since the energy crisis
of the 1970s. Federal negotiators championed unpopular provisions at the 2000 Hague climate change talks that would allow
Canada to collect greenhouse gas credits through the international sale of nuclear technology. Canada would eventually drop
this demand during last-minute negotiations at the 2001 Kyoto
protocol agreement reached in Bonn, but the national nuclear
vendor, Atomic Energy Canada Limited (AECL), continues to
target developing nations. It's all part of a renewed sales drive
that could eventually deliver billions of dollars to federal coffers
for CANDU reactors that would otherwise be collecting dust.

Most North American jurisdictions still can't afford new
reactors—various deregulation measures have unofficially
heralded the end of state-sponsored megaprojects. Many, in
fact, have been planning to retire their nukes in favour of gas
turbines or coal power, based on decades of nuclear cost over-
runs and safety concerns. Consequently, the uranium of
northern Saskatchewan continues to end up in developing
countries—China, Korea and India—where nuclear technology has been sold hard and fast by AECL, a Crown corporation

that has been implicated in international kickback and bribery scandals, itself not having sold a reactor since 1996. During the 1990s, 88 percent of refined Canadian uranium was exported to international customers.

Denise hands me the keys to one of her trucks and I drive out of the downtown core towards the sprawling suburbs. Most residents live scattered about in this older part of town, built in the early 1950s. Here, electricity and sewage have been maintained, although many homes stand empty. All-terrain vehicles, snowmobiles and trucks roll through the main street on a periodic basis, but mostly things are silent. The local hot spot, the Athabasca Bar, opens up occasionally on weekends—but it's locked tight most of the time.

Along Nuclear Road, I spot a few people out chopping wood, the smoke from their stoves curling upwards into the still air. I drive west. After passing the post office, a converted bungalow that marks the edge of the inhabited part of town, I traverse the crest of a small hill and before me sprawl whole city blocks of abandoned houses, seemingly as far as the eye can see. I stop the truck and wonder at it all.

Some houses are intact, except for windows long since broken. Others have been torn apart for lumber and appliances—"Beaver Lumber is always just down the street," says Bill Holland, my host at the motel. Still others have collapsed upon themselves, as though deflated by nuclear attack. Most are bungalows with picket fences and garages—modern homes with three bedrooms and a rumpus room downstairs.

I wander through the first few blocks. Some of the garages still have cars sitting in them, late 1960s models. Overgrown backyards show the remnants of vegetable gardens and dog kennels. In the middle of one living room is a large sofa, ruined by the elements. Light from a huge hole in the wall shines across a pile of posters and a discarded record collection: album covers from Pablo Cruise and Trooper are scattered about. Down the hall, in one of the bedrooms festooned with Playboy bunny symbols and peace signs, a message scrawled on the wall screams out a tribute to someone named Bill, now long-departed: he "is THE MAN. All the LADIES love him."

DOWN THE ROAD FROM URANIUM CITY is the Cinch Lake mine, one of twenty-three known sites within a twelve-kilometre radius of the town. Like many lakes in the area, Cinch feeds into Beaverlodge Lake, about forty-eight square kilometres of water that lap at the edge of the old Eldorado mine site west of Uranium City and empty into Lake Athabasca on its southern-most flank. A 1991 aquatic study done for Cameco Corporation found that uranium levels in Beaverlodge exceeded Canadian Drinking Water Guidelines; lake trout and whitefish likewise showed elevated levels of radionuclides.

I'd read about high uranium levels in Beaverlodge Lake, but documents I'd obtained from the Saskatchewan government were missing tables that would have provided specific numbers. A 2000 survey by Environment Canada did not, however, fail to include the data: surprisingly, Beaverlodge levels registered 31 times the maximum amount of uranium found in regular

Saskatchewan water. Marie Lake, now a tailings pond nine kilometres from Uranium City, has uranium concentrations measured
at 364 times natural levels, possibly the highest in Canada. The
threat from water-borne uranium is potentially toxic as well as
radiological: kidney disease, nephritis, is common to uranium-
rich water, as is radon gas in lesser concentrations. The
Beaverlodge data were collected sometime during the late 1970s
or early 1980s because, explains the report, "only a few sites
have been sampled since decommissioning in the mid-1980s."

With tailings that drain directly into the Beaverlodge watershed, Cinch was a medium-sized mine operation that started up
during the first uranium rush of 1948–49 and closed in 1960. Its
eighty-five employees pulled pitchblende ore out of six levels of
tunnels along a three-hundred-metre shaft. With a number of
other mines, it sits on the thirty-kilometre Black Bay fault, a
geologic rupture rich with radium and uranium. Today, it is a
collection of mountains of waste rock, cement foundations—its
buildings were pulled down during the late 1980s—and scattered piles of ore. Nothing grows on the tailings piles since
they're too acidic, likely laced with leaching agents such as
hydrochloric acid that would kill off foliage and trace metals
such as arsenic, as well as radionuclides such as uranium,
thorium-230, radium-226 and potassium-210.

While exploring around a pile of waste, I almost step into
what appears to be a large hole. It turns out that I'm standing on
top of an unmarked mine shaft—the steel grate that had been
installed ten years earlier during Saskatchewan's "remedial
action" program had somehow shifted off its perch and opened
up the three-hundred-metre pit to whomever might stroll along.
I carefully back down off the pile, noticing bits of orange ribbon
scattered around the base. It could have been weeks before
anyone found me, if ever.

Open mine shafts in a remote corner of Saskatchewan probably wouldn't much matter if the site wasn't an active source of

low-level radiation. Out here, you don't know if you are absorbing too much gamma radiation or radon gas, because both are invisible and deliver no sensation to the recipient. The question of public safety seems abstract, at best. Yet that's the issue: after almost fifty years of uranium mining on the northern edge of Saskatchewan, unmitigated waste still circulates freely—waste tracked by occasional studies that acknowledge contamination but never bring together the government parties to cumulatively assess the radiological threat and take remedial action. Even in urban communities such as Port Hope, Ontario, where uranium waste has been only partially decommissioned, many residents rail against governments unwilling to act on a hazard that, by definition, remains largely invisible.

The following day, I explore a little farther out of town, turning off several kilometres after Cinch onto an unmarked road that rides up and over a rocky outcrop. Soon I arrive at a clearing, which opens up to reveal what seems to be a solid kilometre of reddish-gold sand. But it's no beach resort—these are the tailings of Lorado, a former uranium mill and mine site that has been bereft of vegetation for the past forty years. Set on the shores of Nero Lake, the waste from Lorado's uranium processing mill was discharged into a small lake next to Nero—and over the course of Lorado's three years of operation at the height of the uranium boom, the lake disappeared under the tailings, save for a small frozen pond. Consequently, 305,000 tonnes of untreated tailings overflowed into Nero and the Beaverlodge watershed.

I hike through the site, noting rusted barrels and the wooden remnants of discharge pipes. Up the hill are the concrete foundations of a uranium mill that custom-processed ore for thirty-one different mines and operators in the area, including Cinch Lake. The mill buildings and discharge pipes were demolished in 1990 by the landowner, Conwest Exploration—a company that, in turn, was bought in 1996 by the Alberta Energy Company, one of Canada's largest domestic oil and gas corporations. Most of Lorado's tailings are actually on adjacent Crown land and remain as they were left when Lorado closed in 1960.

The bits of yellow sulphur that litter the ground at the top of the site, along with a pervasive sulphur smell—even in a brisk wind—were likely part of a leaching process that employed sulphuric acid to help break down the ore into yellowcake, a concentrated powder that's 90-percent pure uranium. Milling is an important part of the uranium fuel process, since only a very small percentage of ore is pure uranium, between 0.2 and 0.17 percent on the northern edge of the Athabasca—and upwards of 20 percent at the newer mines to the south. Producers were loath to barge tonnes of raw ore down to Fort McMurray, so local chemical processing was done.

Lorado's tailings, the waste rock and effluent, were discharged as a fine sand that now covers the landscape and runs underwater. The tailings are highly acidic, about pH 1.7 to 2.0, as noted by a Saskatchewan government memo, which is some-where between the pH of battery acid and lemon juice. Feeding into Beaverlodge, Nero is a dead lake, completely devoid of fish. Its saline, acidic water supports only phytoplankton. The disap-pearance of fish, notes another report, has the unanticipated benefit of stopping radioactive transfers up the food chain.

In addition to freeing up contaminants for dispersion in sand or sludge, tailings piles brew up their own ingredients, a geochemical disequilibrium, wherein various chemicals are still reacting with each other. Sulphur oxides—there are some 3.3-million kilos of sulphur at Lorado—are likely dissolving additional heavy metals from the waste rock, thereby increasing toxicity. This would explain the extreme acidity of the pile.

The real trouble with tailings is that they retain most of the rock's original radionuclides, up to 85 percent of the ore's original radioactive energy. What I'm walking across, as I traverse the sandy barrens towards the lake, is a concentrated mass of radium.

Uranium isn't the real concern here: what's left behind is the problem, residual radionuclides exposed to air and water—a concentration of radium far in excess of what is normally found in terrestrial environments. About a month later, safely home in Toronto, I obtain a copy of a 1989 survey commissioned by the Saskatchewan government: it estimated the total dose at Lorado to be 208 millisievert per year, all things considered—208 times Canada's current public exposure limit. A separate statistical calculation, based on the volume of tailings at Lorado, estimated a high-end dose of 629 millisievert. Either way, it's a pretty sizable hit. Based on data from the study, done by Beak Consultants of Brampton, Ontario, one would probably exceed safe public limits for annual radiation exposure at Lorado in about half a day. Luckily for me, during my visit the tailings were mostly frozen, so there was probably less radon flowing into the air than at other times of the year.

Radon gas, a decay product of radium, poses a kind of hazard different from standard gamma radiation—otherwise known as groundshine. Released from decaying isotopes, gamma rays penetrate flesh, organs and bone, not unlike a high-calibre bullet—but they cannot shine far from their source. Radon is a much more pervasive carcinogen. In fact, a series of international studies increasingly points to a broad public health hazard from radon gas, one that isn't limited to waste sites and traditional sources of ionizing radiation. In the late 1990s, the U.S. Environmental Protection Agency (EPA) launched a major public campaign to address the public health hazard of radon gas. According to a major 1998 study commissioned by the U.S. National Research Council, "about 1 in 10 or 1 in 7 of all lung-cancer deaths—amounting to central estimates of about 15,400 or 21,800 per year in the United States—can be attributed to radon," often naturally occurring in basements and enclosed spaces from nearby ground deposits. And from Uranium City to Port Hope, wherever uranium has been mined and processed, radon often lurks in significant quantities, due to inadvertent public dumping and contamination.

As radium slowly decays, it emits alpha particles that form radon. Radon, in turn, has a half-life of about 3.8 days and can ably move through soil, water and air. In that short period of decay, it emits its own alpha particles, extremely energetic but poorly penetrating radiation that can be drawn into a person's lungs when carried by dust, smoke and other small particles. Once inside the lungs, alpha particles literally bombard healthy cells with ionizing energy. Although high levels of outdoor radon can pose a risk, it is radon in enclosed spaces that serves as the most proven cancer source.

An obvious question presents itself: given that the on-site gamma and radon dose at Lorado is roughly 208 times the Canadian standard, is this part of a larger public health hazard? As the crow flies, Uranium City sits only six kilometres away from Lorado. A plethora of other mines, including the ongoing decommissioning of Eldorado's Beaverlodge mine and mill, have already made the lake water unfit to drink. In my survey of available literature, the only mention of a health assessment and cleanup was a reported radon scare during the late 1970s, when it was realized that town buildings and residences were built with fill from tailings and waste rock. Consequently, houses were re-dug and retrofitted in order to reduce high levels of radon gas.

For at least one Saskatchewan ministry, Lorado is a serious problem—period. "It is the firm position of Saskatchewan Environment and Public Safety that this site must be cleaned up and made environmentally secure as soon as possible," concluded one internal government briefing paper. "To that end the department has initiated discussions with the Atomic Energy

Control Board to identify the necessary resources, develop closeout criteria and initiate reclamation and decommissioning."

That was almost ten years ago. And nothing has happened since.

FOR WHATEVER REASON, loping around Lorado has given me a nosebleed; the wind is blowing sand and dust off the tailings and I'm suddenly gripped by the realization that I have absolutely no idea what I'm doing here. I'm in over my head; even if I had a Geiger counter to monitor the gamma, I'm still breathing in radon gas.

Even though radon occurs naturally, radon levels on a tailings pile can fluctuate wildly, anywhere from relatively benign levels, just under the U.S. EPA health standard, to spikes oozing out from a buried radon concentration of more than 2,300 times the EPA standard, as previously measured at Lorado.

For all its wealth of uranium, Canadian health standards on radionuclides are surprisingly less stringent than those of the United States and Britain. Consequently, the general public is subject to a higher threshold of risk from radioactive waste—dose for dose—than any other controlled or toxic substance in Canada.

For example, Canada's public action level on radon gas—the official threshold at which a substance is considered a serious threat—is five times greater than the American standard set by the EPA and four times greater than that of Britain's environment ministry and the European Commission. "Radon is one of the most extensively investigated human carcinogens," noted the U.S. National Research Council in a 1998 study. "This indicates a public-health problem and makes indoor radon the second leading cause of lung cancer after cigarette-smoking."

The irony is that stringent American standards are based partially on studies of Canadian uranium miners. Miners from Uranium City, for example, were the focus of a thirty-year study published in 1986 that found the lung cancer mortality rate of some 8,487 workers between 1950 and 1980 was double that of the general population. These rates generally compare to those for miners studied at Port Radium and Elliot Lake.

Back at the motel, Bill Holland is skeptical about the prospect of a local health hazard. "Everyone's been born with two eyes here, right?" His two young kids peek out from behind a door. He doesn't want to be anywhere else. "I moved away from here when I was five—but if I knew what I was missing, I would have never left."

He moved back north six years ago, bought the family business back and settled in. "Up here it's just freedom," he says. We're lounging in my motel room, which is cozily furnished with a wide selection of second-hand furniture. "I can go clean my rifle in the middle of the road if I want—or take off on a snowmobile anywhere. We can speed out over the ice to Fort Chip on quads."

There's a wildness to this place that Bill finds compelling. "They say about the northern lights that if you tease them, they'll eat you up." It's true; stories about ghosts, native lore about the aurora borealis—it all seems plausible up here, amid the craggy hills and endless trees and lakes. And if you get stuck out on the ice or stranded at a mine site, you're on your own here. No cellphones or police, no search parties.

"I was on a snowmobile in the middle of January, across Lake Athabasca from Fond du Lac. Seen a shape up ahead on the side of the trail: it was a man standing behind a Ski-Doo holding a helmet. I passed and stopped twenty feet afterward. I turned around to look back and it was gone. Not a track there. I was having a good time, not worried or scared. But I find out later that seven years ago a guy died out there, frozen behind his Ski-Doo. Must have hit his kill switch and it never started again. So he curled up behind the Ski-Doo."

A CRISIS OF ACCOUNTABILITY SIMMERS within Canada's atomic legacy: environmental health science has evolved over the decades, advocating more stringent standards, while government regulations have lagged. Based on available evidence, the pattern of neglect goes like this: Environment Canada, whose data are the most extensive, will assess risk for plants and animals only; Health Canada, though concerned with human health, doesn't venture often into radiological contamination, presumably because another federal agency, the Canadian Nuclear Safety Commission, is charged with atomic safety. Yet the commission concerns itself mainly with core operating issues for active mines, research facilities and nuclear reactors— and anything outside the fence, be it historic waste or childhood leukemia, somehow merits less scrutiny.

It was only at the urging of Canada's auditor general in 1995 that the safety commission (then the Atomic Energy Control Board) assumed responsibility to monitor uranium mine sites for health and safety hazards. Mine waste and tailings from Saskatchewan to Ontario "were never subject to AECB's current regulatory regime," chided the auditor general. "Consequently, the AECB does not formally inspect or otherwise monitor these sites to assess their impact on the environment or to ensure that there are no undue risks to health and safety."

The total cost for decommissioning uranium tailings across Canada could exceed four hundred million dollars, noted the auditor general, but this was no excuse to ignore low-level radioactive waste. "Uranium tailings need to be properly contained and controlled," said the 1995 report. "Until these unlicensed sites are brought under its regulatory control, the AECB cannot assure the public that the pre-1976 sites are being safely maintained." The federal government replied to the report, pledging "to bring these tailings under AECB regulatory control."

For decades, scientists and nuclear officials worked to protect us from big doses at nuclear reactors and high-level reactor waste. Yet now the lower reaches of the waste chain have come into question at a time when open uranium tailings and waste rock still litter a surprising number of Canadian communities. In 2000, Saskatchewan pledged $250,000 for a cleanup of Lorado and Gunnar. But there's no timeline for action and it may be years before tailings are removed; according to one government estimate, it would still cost between ten and fifteen million dollars to eliminate the immediate hazard posed by the two mines.

As for why many of Canada's worst radioactive waste sites remain abandoned—including tailings in Port Hope and Deloro in Ontario—the explanation now seems fairly simple: for decades, Canada's federal government ran uranium production, regulation and marketing operations. For a period of three decades, the federal government ran the regulator (AECB), the uranium mining business (Eldorado), as well as the reactor business (Atomic Energy Canada Limited). Early on, several people held directorships and positions on all three organizations, a pattern that reflected an insider culture that flagged only recently with the sagging fortunes of the nuclear business. Only in 1988 when it sold Eldorado nuclear to Cameco Corporation, a Canadian uranium company, did the government require uranium producers to file decommissioning plans that would address long-term tailings and contamination.

In other words, the federal government and its Crown corporations stood in a long-standing conflict of interest supported by generous public funding and a lack of political scrutiny. Numbers, taken from Canada's auditor general and the environment commissioner, speak for themselves: since 1946, the federal government has spent $6 billion on nuclear technology, including mining, processing and distribution of uranium fuel. (Factoring in subsidies to Atomic Energy Canada Limited, as well as international development grants to export nukes, activists claim that $16.6 billion has been spent since 1953.) Yet by 1995, Natural Resources Canada, researching long-term solutions for uranium tailings, had spent only $10 million.

I VENTURE OUT AGAIN into the deserted part of Uranium City. The sheer size of the decaying suburb is impressive: I estimate twelve city blocks of homes, abandoned and skeletal. Some still show signs of the former tenants: a crucifix on a kitchen wall, a crayon drawing on peeling wallpaper, lawn chairs scattered across a front yard. There's even a tricycle buried under the snow of a ditch. Overall, the effect is unsettling—plastic vapour barrier and aluminum siding hang from ripped-out walls and rattle in the wind; a suburban cul-de-sac is ringed by five identical bungalows, all maimed in different ways—missing walls, blown-out doors, sagging roofs.

I pass by a decayed condo development, built shortly before the closing. Modern cedar units that no one ever lived in stand in rows, with garage doors that have fallen from their hinges and bathroom tiles and kitchen counters that remain mysteriously spotless.

Just up the road is the CANDU High School, a two-storey facility built only four years before Eldorado's demise. I'd already driven by it several times before I pulled into the driveway. Marilee Shott was there for the last day of CANDU. "It's a little hard going by there," she says. "There's only ten or so of us left in town." She remembers when the decision to close Eldorado was made public. "They came into the gym when they announced it. Kids scattered, lots of hugging and crying." She seldom goes back, even though it's just down the road.

Dean Claussen was in the last graduating class of CANDU. He's the only one left around here. We're sitting in his house, surrounded by his three kids. He runs the same fuel business his dad founded and does decommissioning work for Eldorado on the side. He says there're a few hot spots at Eldorado, but he's tested his home for radon and feels his kids are safe. Back in the late 1970s there was a radon gas scare in town: builders had used waste rock in housing materials and foundations, so many homes and buildings—including parts of CANDU High School—had to either be retrofitted with vents or partially rebuilt.

"Remediation is for those who still own property and have the money to do it. With the smaller ones, the only one was Lorado, where the owners made a deal to clear out the mill—but the rest was a disaster. Highly acidic rock that leaches. It's okay as long as you don't disturb it. You see high levels of radon and acid during high water levels—mixes up in the creek beds."

The decommissioning business is expensive: one recent project for the Eldorado mine cost $100,000 to cap a mine shaft with cement. Dean shows me a videotape of the Lorado site in the summertime. Lorado's tailings pile is vivid reddish-orange, while over at the other end of Nero Lake, tailings and sand are seeping into Beaverlodge Lake. "Nothing is in Nero. It's dead," he says. "Though they say fishing is still good in Beaverlodge."

Dean shows me another video clip, this one an archival collection of CBC reports from the 1950s. It's a document of unbridled optimism. "In an uninhabited wilderness, useless for farming, citizens are staking their claim on their growing town and surrounding mining properties," intones the narrator. Onscreen, cheerful workers drill core samples and test rocks with handheld Geiger counters. Back then, hot spots were what they were looking for.

I ask about the radon. Dean says it's no secret among town alumni. "All the old miners died from lack of ventilation—they died a little bit earlier, mainly from lung cancer, the usual thing." Today's uranium mines employ complicated systems to minimize radon exposure after high mortality rates were linked to poor air supplies underground. "You keep contact with people—one friend, his dad died of lung cancer a couple of years ago."

He's not sure about incidental radon exposure around town. Concentrations can range widely from house to house, area to area. The clouds of radon that fly off Lorado, for example, could dissipate before reaching the town. Or not—it's impossible to know for sure. "We had a guy from AECL and he said there's radon everywhere."

An EPA risk assessment for an individual living next to some of the inactive tailings piles showed a lifetime lung-cancer risk of 40 chances in 1,000—an elevated hazard, to be sure, though not an epidemic. Radon gas from American tailings is expected to cause anywhere from 170 to 500 additional lung-cancer deaths per century, all within the immediate vicinity of the site.

In one of the buildings along the main street, in an old pinball arcade, one of two local stores operates, signless and with metal grilles over the windows. The woman inside runs the same grocery store that her mom did. She doesn't really want to talk, though. And I don't ask her about the cancer in her family, something Bill Holland told me about, because I didn't travel all this way to run an ad hoc medical investigation. But it wouldn't be the last mention of sickness; though he says it has nothing to do with the waste, Bill's dad has been fighting Crohn's disease down south.

In the absence of information, there's politics. Back in 1981, Greenpeace came to town, just before the Eldorado closure announcement, to champion its anti-nukes campaign. It was part fact-finding mission, part media stunt. Predictably, most locals were not amused. "You are not welcome in our community for the fact that this is what we are all about—uranium mining," Mayor Rose Waslenka told activist Patrick Moore when he came calling. The mayor (who moved away from this area years ago) said at the time, "We're working for the betterment of the people of Canada and the world." Moore and several other Greenpeacers walked around town and the tailings sites with a gamma Geiger counter and, reported the *Northland News*, "they were alarmed by their findings which they said indicated people here were exposed to between three and five times more radiation than the average Canadian population." John Rogers, Eldorado's manager, questioned Greenpeace's "covert and unorthodox methods," plus the possibility that they didn't know how to read a Geiger counter properly.

"A lot of those anti-nuclear protesters don't know a damn thing," says James Auger, a Métis whose family originally came from Camsell Portage, about thirty kilometres west on Lake Athabasca. He worked at Gunnar mine for six years and now lives semi-retired in Uranium City, still venturing north into the barrens of Nunavut to hunt caribou. Like other trappers and hunters across the North, he takes a pretty dim view of southern environmentalists, largely because the anti-fur lobby helped push the trapping business into oblivion. But he admits the radioactive waste at Gunnar and Lorado bothers him.

"There's a place for Greenpeacers. The thing is, the uranium industry employs a lot of people. Our kids work there. We've been around it all of our lives and we haven't seen it hurt people that bad. Back in the 1950s, nobody protected the environment. If this had all happened in the 1990s, a lot of that stuff at Gunnar wouldn't be laying around right now.

"Back in my childhood days, there was no industry, so people had to live off the land," he says. "And it was a damn good living—one didn't have more than the others and when a moose was killed, everybody got some."

When he moved to Uranium City after Gunnar closed, the town was booming. With twenty-nine mines working right next door, twenty thousand people flooded the town. "You could throw a rock around at all the mines half-mile around town." Northerners could pick up a steady job, just as traditional professions like trapping were falling off.

"Trappin' is a dying thing," he says. "Who's going to go out and do all that work for nothing? It's the young people in the mines—good company benefits, RSP plan, all that kind of stuff." Eldorado pitched in for good facilities, discounted flights down south and a host of other incentives.

"It was still a hell of a community. That's why we couldn't leave," he says. "A lot of people who left here died unhappy, not satisfied."

He's right. It is truly beautiful up here—a primeval landscape that, among other things, fed uranium to U.S. and British weapons programs until 1966 and 1972, respectively. The postwar military application of Canadian ore was decried by many, but it's simply a fact of the market: there's no guarantee where radionuclides will end up once we pull them out of the ground.

# THE OIL PATCH WAR

# Alberta

"**D**O YOU THINK THE ECO-TERRORISM made a difference?" Wiebo Ludwig asks me point-blank. We stand in a spartan farmhouse south of Edmonton, the temporary head-quarters of the Ludwig clan during their three-month trial in 2000 for oil patch vandalism and attempted extortion. It's a Saturday morning in March, one week before the end of the trial. And Ludwig, who claims he's on a mission from God, is wondering what it all means.

His chilling question would haunt me for months. Did the bombings really change anything? Did the terrorized and divided community of Beaverlodge suffer for naught?

Linked to a long series of oil patch bombings and the 1998 killing of sixteen-year-old Karman Willis, Wiebo Ludwig and his clan tapped into the fears of many rural Albertans. Like other parts of the province, Ludwig's home turf near Beaverlodge and Grande Prairie presents itself as a collection of truck stops, farms, untamed bush and gas flares. It's the flares that newcomers remember: six- and nine-metre towers that burn off the noxious waste of natural gas wells, roaring geysers that tap hidden gases a kilometre below the earth's surface.

During the late 1990s, concerns about the health effects of sour gas wells spewing hydrogen sulphide—and Alberta's 5,300 flaring wells—grew as ranchers and farmers launched their own challenges against oil patch pollution and land use policies that many of them alleged heavily favoured energy companies. The profusion of hydrogen sulphide, a powerful neurotoxin with cyanide-like qualities, in communities across Alberta inspired a wave of protest that would extend well beyond the confines of Ludwig's Trickle Creek farm. (Sulphur in its solid inert state is relatively safe, but airborne emissions like hydrogen sulphide are deadly, even at low concentrations, and sulphur dioxide is a common combustion by-product.)

Before sour gas flared near their home, the Ludwigs were known as reclusive religious eccentrics. Then they started reporting animal disfigurations and respiratory illness. Letters were written to the appropriate authorities, but Ludwig was unsatisfied with what he described as a criminal lack of action. After Abel Ryan Ludwig, Weibo's grandson, came into the world stillborn and disfigured in 1998, a Suncor well was bombed near Hinton, two hours south of Beaverlodge. It would be the Hinton evidence that would convict Ludwig. In the interim, people across northwestern Alberta rightfully feared for their safety: an exploded sour gas well could spew a deadly cloud of sulphur dioxide across several kilometres of countryside.

Gas flares are the mark of prosperity in Alberta, a valuable hydrocarbon resource that fuelled $7.5 billion in profits in 2000. The Alberta Energy Company, Ludwig's corporate nemesis (and target of several bombs) itself posted net earnings of almost $1 billion in 2000, a 428-percent increase over its previous year. The continental energy bonanza that drives offshore gas exploration at Sable Island has its apotheosis in the Alberta gas market; natural gas prices, though erratic, played a significant role in raising the value of Canadian energy exports from $30 billion in 1999 to an unprecedented $50 billion in 2001.

On the ground, it's been a different story: farmers and ranchers, beset by the often meagre economics of agriculture, still don't own the mineral rights to their own properties, nor can they easily prevent companies from drilling and flaring just about anywhere—even within spitting distance of barns and homes. While Ludwig's trial made sensational headlines across

Canada, a much quieter war continued, as a province-wide collection of ranchers and farmers went to environmental impact hearings, launched lawsuits and, sometimes, waged violence against energy companies whose wells, they argue, caused family sickness, cattle die-offs and toxic contamination of their land.

A crucial question emerged: where was the Alberta government? Responsible for oil and gas regulation, environmental auditing—not to mention prosecution of criminal acts—the province was notably absent on many important fronts. For example: funding for the provincial oil and gas regulator, the Energy and Utilities Regulation Board (EUB), was cut by 28 percent between 1992 and 1998, despite a fourfold increase in the number of drilled wells. Under Premier Ralph Klein, "the 'Alberta Advantage' meant getting government out of the way of business, regardless of collateral environmental or social costs," charged the Pembina Institute think-tank in a February 1999 report. "As a result, the government has lost its capacity to provide a meaningful level of auditing and inspection coverage for oil and gas activities."

Power is politics. And there are few places that distill this more clearly than Alberta, Canada's energy province. Here, gas accounts for 27 percent of all provincial revenue, compared to 23 percent from income taxes. Government ministers invest openly and freely in the petroleum companies their government is sworn to regulate. And, for all the affluence Alberta holds, some rural residents find themselves saving up for their own electronic equipment to monitor air quality because the province is short on resources. "They are living not merely in a company town, but in a company province," noted *The National Post*'s Christie Blatchford after her first several days at Ludwig's trial: "Oil runs the show in Alberta."

Back at the Ludwig camp south of Edmonton, Wiebo is pondering his future just a few weeks before Judge Sterling

Sanderman sends him to prison to serve two years for vandalism and mischief. As a fundamentalist preacher, a would-be candidate for the ultra-conservative Social Credit leadership and a suspected party to a murder, Ludwig seems an unlikely environmental messenger. But to many Albertans who've struggled with leaking gas wells or who watch nearby flares from their kitchen windows, Ludwig was the one who brought their rural issue into the newsrooms and courtrooms of Calgary, Edmonton and Toronto. Just down the road lives the retired rig worker and farmer who loaned the Edmonton farm to the Ludwig clan, free of charge; he drops by to show photos of contamination, a pit of sludge left behind by a drill crew. Most everyone, it seems, has a story.

"This was war," Ludwig explains, eyes on fire, standing close to make his point. "Things happen. It was a question of providence."

I'm not so sure myself. Depending on whom you talk to, Wiebo Ludwig and his co-defendant, Richard Boonstra, are either messianic heroes or Bible-thumping sociopaths. The only certainty is that wherever they go, difficult questions follow.

A FEW DAYS LATER, I arrive at the temporary residence of Alberta couple Violet and Edward Holmes. They moved into this summer cottage on a small prairie lake near Rimbey in 1998, leaving behind their acreage outside Olds, an hour south, because Violet was afflicted with seizures and tremors that forced her to quit her job as a teacher's aide. It was a mysterious neurological disorder that doctors associated with a sour gas well that had been drilled four hundred metres from their doorstep two years earlier.

First their animals became sick—not long after the Canadian 88 company finished drilling a well in October of 1996—explains Ed, a masonry contractor. "You could smell the oil," he says. On some days, their eyes watered and burned from the odour. "They more than gladly paid the four hundred dollars in vet bills and didn't want to hear from us any more."

A month after the first well was completed, another well was drilled nearby for a total of twenty within an eight-kilometre radius. Then the company ran tests to determine flow rate, a process that involves burning the wells, full bore, for several days. "The ground was shaking, it was daylight at night, like a jet," recalls Violet. "A sixty- to seventy-foot flare."

Other times, the wells would run a smaller burn, an automated release of waste gases that would come and go without warning. "We'd get a horrible, horrible stink," she says, trembling slightly. "You could see liquid coming off the flare stack." Canadian 88, she says, claimed it didn't know what was wrong with its well.

It was before broad public awareness about flaring, and a number of companies, including Canadian 88, weren't exactly quick to address concerns. Nevertheless, during the late 1990s, 2.5-billion cubic metres of waste gases were flared across Alberta annually by the industry—enough gas to heat 150,000 homes for a month. And while not all gas wells run sour—30 to 40 percent spew hydrogen sulphide—flares nevertheless emit upwards of 250 different compounds, including a number of known potent carcinogens such as benzene and several heavy metals.

By January 1997, Amoco had bought the two problem wells and soon fixed what appeared to be a malfunction that was causing an incomplete—and unhealthy—combustion of gases. "They said it took about ten minutes to fix," says Ed. "There were fewer problems and the smell was better." The flares continued to operate, but less raw gas seemed to be escaping the burn. No burn is 100-percent efficient anyway, says Ed, though they still thought their sour gas problem was over.

But later that year, Violet's health turned. First, she became quivery and fatigued. A few months later, in November 1997, the whole right side of her face seized up and contorted. Hospitals in Sundre and Calgary couldn't determine a cause. By

March 1998, Violet was suffering full seizures and couldn't function at work from what had become chronic shaking and trembling. Soon, she was being rushed back to Calgary by ambulance, where a team of specialists stabilized her condition and looked for answers.

Epilepsy and a host of other conventional afflictions were ruled out. "The doctor told us it was very, very possible that the cause was petrochemical because nothing else in our lives had changed," says Violet. Though there was no diagnosis, it was suggested that she move away from their Olds acreage for a month. "No seizures for a month—back home, it was sometimes twelve to fourteen times a day."

When Violet returned home a month later, it took four days before the seizures came back, fourteen in a single day. "The doctor explained that the environment affected my central nervous system, so that solvents—even perfume—can set it off," she says. "I never went back to Olds and we sold the house. Doctors still don't know what it is."

Mobil, which purchased the wells, tested the air quality one day and didn't find any high readings. But the trouble with sour gas is that it doesn't afflict individuals consistently, nor is it emitted in a steady stream: flares can deliver considerable wallops of gas unpredictably, then turn benign. Even for co-operative companies looking to rectify a troubled situation, the confusion of factors can be frustrating.

The Holmeses have taken their case to civil court and are seeking $600,000 in damages from the two companies. "Our daughter was diagnosed with a rare tumour on her spine in 1999 and our son is never well—he's anemic and asthmatic," says Ed, who was unable to work while Violet was sick. "We had intended to retire there—the land had been in the family for eighty years. We had a nice acreage. Vi had a job she loved."

Along the way, they've met others with sour gas sensitivity, both residents and company people. "At one EUB hearing, one

Mobil rep told us he had the same symptoms," says Ed. "Whenever he passes a sour gas well, he can just tell."

The provincial regulator ran tests but said it couldn't find anything; the Holmeses never saw the results themselves. "The companies own the environmental inspectors anyway," Ed says. "The trees all around one well died in a sixty- or seventy-foot radius—the neigbours reported symptoms and irritations. The province and the companies need to admit that people are getting sick."

If you asked who was responsible for ensuring public health when a sour gas well goes bad, the real answer would be everyone and no one: government departments—from Health to Environment—know the problem but are often hobbled in their ability to take action. Lacking power to criminally prosecute, regulators like Alberta's EUB serve a quasi-judicial function without guaranteeing justice. Consequently, an ever-expanding eco-bureaucracy gets pushed beyond its depth and ability—resulting in flaring and contamination disputes that increasingly spill over into the courts. It hasn't helped that Alberta's standards were low from the beginning. A 1996 provincial study measured combustion efficiency, ranging from 66 to 84 percent; by contrast, flares in Texas must burn off at least 98 percent of gas emissions.

A series of reforms in 2000 and 2001 may improve things, but Violet and Edward Holmes have had enough of consultations and hearings. After several years already, they're prepared for a legal battle, this time with lawyers. "If they are waiting for me to die, I'm not going to let up," says Violet, eyes watering, body shaking from the strain. "I don't care if it takes six or ten years, as long as I'm alive I'm going to fight this thing and stay around."

BACK ON THE ROAD, I drive south towards Olds, passing a farm landscape that my own ancestors—easterners and Icelandic immigrants—tried to settle at the end of the nineteenth century. They would be driven off the land, temporarily, during the Depression.

This is the economic breadbasket of Alberta, prime agricultural land that covers the Western Canada Sedimentary Basin, a broad geologic formation running parallel to the Rocky Mountains that provides nearly one-quarter of North American natural gas supplies. And since the early 1990s, as established gas reservoirs have dwindled, a marathon of drilling has taken place; there is now a record number of wells, increasingly sour, and pushing ever closer to farms, cities and towns in an effort to drain old gas pools or better exploit newer, smaller ones. In 2001, some companies actually ran out of derricks, so heavy was the demand to drill.

This web of production includes no fewer than 60 major gas processing plants—where sulphur and other impurities are removed, partly through flaring—and 266,000 kilometres of underground pipeline that moves gas to processing plants and, ultimately, to export markets in Canada and the United States. It's also a web that's often broken: a total of 750 pipelines failed in 1997—more than two per day—leaking natural gas, sour gas, crude oil and contaminated water across various parts of rural Alberta. In the past, uncoated pipes, vulnerable to rust and erosion, have been standard because they are the cheapest.

Wayne and Ila Johnston, ranchers near Olds, point to where a pipeline burst on their land in 1994 and has leaked frequently since. "Amoco's pipelines kept caving in two feet at a time," says Wayne. Ila actually fell into the hole once, after the initial break spewed contaminated water and hydrocarbons on their land. "There's no consistent disease pattern," says Wayne of his cattle, "more signs of general immune system suppression." After a large Amoco flare in 1995, a hundred head of their cattle went blind, while others simply toppled over dead. For a rancher to watch animals wither and die is a double tragedy: lost livelihood and a greater sense of loss within an agricultural tradition that prides itself on knowing one's animals. "What got me was the way the cows behaved during the pipeline break: how maternal cows walked away from their babies; bulls would try and mate with other bulls," Wayne recalls.

"Our health hasn't been great. We get gassed every day," says Ila, who was recently diagnosed with respiratory disease, something they attribute to the five wells that dot their land. "It's not just one or two people, it's everyone in Alberta. We're food producers and they keep screwing up our water and our air. It's the cumulative effect. Who knows what's going to happen later on?"

They don't really trust anyone any more. "I've had the oil industry tell me a lot of things that aren't true," says Wayne. "And when there are good studies done, the industry goes out of their way to stop them."

In the past, rural Albertans were some of the most enthusiastic supporters of the conservative, pro-development style of provincial government that followed the great Leduc oil discovery of 1947. From Bible Bill Aberhart, founder of Social Credit in Alberta, to Ralph Klein's Progressive Conservatives, Alberta's rural vote has served as the foundation for two of the longest-lived political dynasties in Canadian history. But now the provincial Tories, the sole owner of all mineral rights (except those beneath Indian reserves) find themselves under attack within their own political heartland. Powerful urban interests, centred within the head-office mecca of Calgary, have changed the political balance. Though many benefit from right-of-way fees, compensation and other sorts of oil and gas income, farmers and ranchers seem to have lost status in a province that increasingly caters to continent-wide energy markets.

Not all disputes end quietly. In October 1998, Wayne Roberts was charged with the execution-style murder of Calgary oil executive Patrick Kent of KB Resources after a two-year dispute over a contaminated well site next to his family's home near Rimbey. Gene Roberts, his wife, still lives on the acreage. While her husband sits in the Calgary Remand Centre, awaiting trial, she tries to make preparations with their lawyer. She invites me in for tea but won't comment on the trial. "It's been so hard, you know," she says. "For years, company after company ignored the well—and one day Wayne lost patience. Just like that. We had finished building this house."

The crime scene, a wellhead that reportedly leaked benzene and xylene, is less than fifty metres from the home. It sits in the very centre of their property. Kent, vice-president owner of a small company that had bought the troubled well from a bankrupt company, was making small margins of money on a well that was on its last legs. While visiting the site, Kent got into an argument with Roberts, who went back into the house and grabbed a handgun. By the time it was all over, there were no bullets left and Roberts, who has twenty years' experience in various oil patch jobs, would later be sent to prison on a murder conviction.

While I am having tea, Roberts calls his wife from the Calgary jail. She puts me on the phone. "I'm looking at being here for a long time," Roberts says flatly. "It just got to be too much. Way too much."

GIVEN THE EVENTS of the last several years, you have to wonder: is Alberta's government too close to its oil patch? Has the corporate largesse of the energy sector skewed the public priorities of Ralph Klein's government?

It's no secret that oil and gas royalties frequently account for upwards of one-third of all provincial revenues—or that energy companies are generous campaign donors to Klein's Tories. It's also no secret that the board of the Alberta Energy Company is peppered with several distinguished Tory supporters who occasionally serve as personal advisers to Premier Klein. But who would have ever thought that Tory MLAs would operate their own oil wells, right alongside the very same companies they are sworn to regulate?

At the time of the Ludwig trial, several Alberta elected members were together running their own small investment venture within the oil patch while conducting the business of government. Code-named Tory Oil, the numbered energy company was incorporated in 1995 by then Justice Minister Jon Havelock with six other Tory MLAS, including two other cabinet ministers, Clint Dunford and Lyle Oberg. By 1997, Tory Oil had bought into five wells. Five MLAS remained active partners in the venture, as of 2001.

Havelock, a former Amoco lawyer who retired from politics in 2001, has been a founding partner in several Tory MLA–owned oil companies since 1995: Tory Oil, a second numbered company with former cabinet minister Butch Fischer and assorted campaign donors, and Jeslor Inc., Havelock's own energy operation. For a number of years, Alberta boasted the only solicitor general in the country who was also the president of his own oil company.

It's the Alberta Advantage, Part Two: as the government continues to slash royalty rates for oil and gas producers, various Tory members directly benefited from policies set by themselves and fellow MLAS, despite a slew of unresolved ethical questions.

Concerns about Tory conflict of interest are real. In December 1999, for example, the Canadian Association of Petroleum Producers (CAPP) made a public presentation to Alberta's Standing Committee on Economic Sustainability. Among other things, the association lobbied for a "one-stop shopping" approach to oil and gas regulation in Alberta. "Oil and gas is the foundation of the Alberta Advantage," argued CAPP in its presentation, noting that the industry will deliver four billion dollars to the provincial economy each year. Of course, CAPP wasn't talking just to public officials, but fellow oil producers and investors. Committee members included Jon Havelock, then minister of economic development, and Tory Oil backbencher Judy Gordon.

The top-shelf committee was charged with planning the province's economic future. At the time, members included Premier Ralph Klein, Energy Minister Steve West, former oil consultant Murray Smith and current Alberta Energy Company investor Peter Trynchy. And while other Alberta MLAs place any questionable assets in blind trusts, no fewer than six current Tory cabinet ministers had active financial interests in oil securities or energy companies as Ludwig sat in court—including Gary Mar, then minister of the environment.

It's a mess of ethical and political issues that begin to make Wiebo Ludwig's paranoid theories about Alberta seem a little more plausible. In fact, the overlap of Alberta's Tory government and the energy sector runs well beyond the confines of Tory Oil.

As Ludwig stood trial, one could traverse a broad circle of business dealings and corporate directorships from Jon Havelock to a Nevada mineral company, to several high-profile Alberta executives, then to a B.C. fishing lodge and back to Premier Ralph Klein, Havelock's long-time associate from Calgary City Council. Here's how it worked: Jon Havelock's father, a retired oil executive, was a director in a Reno subsidiary of Beau Canada. Beau Canada, now amalgamated, was a Calgary-based oil company whose chair, president and CEO is Thomas Bugg, a long-time Tory supporter and generous donor who helped fund Klein's 1993 leadership campaign.

Thomas Bugg, in turn, stood as a director at Prism Petroleum, whose CEO is Scobey Hartley, communications director of the Progressive Conservative Party of Alberta and core member of Ralph Klein's kitchen cabinet advisory group. Hartley was also a donor to Klein's first leadership campaign. Prism boasted successful Edmonton entrepreneur—and Alberta Energy Company board member—Mathew Baldwin as corporate director.

In turn, several directors from Prism Petroleum, including Hartley and Bugg, co-own an exclusive B.C. fishing lodge worth one million dollars with Premier Klein. Eagle Pointe was purchased in 1998 with Alberta business luminaries and campaign donors J. R. Shaw and Douglas Church.

From Tory Oil to Eagle Pointe, Alberta's conflict-of-interest legislation affords considerable latitude to elected officials in pursuit of personal gain. Tory Oil was cleared by Alberta's ethics commissioner Bob Clark in 1997—but only after a controversy in which the commissioner first questioned the ethical decorum of Tory Oil and then quickly apologized for ever having raised the issue after a vehement public attack from Havelock. It was a surprising turn of events: the ethics commissioner had been cowed by his own justice minister. "I was trying to show the media that I was being proactive here," Clark said, backing down. "On this occasion, I shouldn't have done that."

What Clark never mentioned was that the former justice minister had received financing assistance from campaign donors. In 1996, Jon Havelock accepted loan guarantees from Acanthus Resources Ltd., corporate donor to Havelock's 1993 election campaign, for the oil company he owned with MLA Butch Fischer. As public documents show, the president of Acanthus was also a partner in the company and a personal Havelock donor.

As many Albertans suffered through years of health and education cutbacks, energy companies enjoyed the lowest royalty rates in three decades. As Edmonton's progressive think-tank the Parkland Institute noted in a November 1999 report, oil and gas revenues collected by the Klein government have been, on average, less than half those of former premier Peter Lougheed. In effect, the report argued, historically low resource rents constitute a major private-sector subsidy.

Environmentalists and industry working together on Alberta's Clean Air Strategic Alliance did make early progress on the issue of gas flaring—including a 15-percent reduction in flares during 1999—largely accomplished without government. (A total 25-percent reduction is expected by the end of 2001.)

But some of the largest reforms in the oil patch during the late 1990s were law enforcement—measures that served to protect the property and production capacity of energy companies. In November 1998, Alberta's then Justice Minister Jon Havelock launched an eight-million-dollar anti-crime crackdown by way of a new agency to fight eco-terrorism and organized gangs. "We are supportive of any efforts to try and get at what's going on in northwestern Alberta," said Chris Peirce, spokesperson for the Canadian Association of Petroleum Producers.

The blurring of energy and government in Ralph Klein's Alberta has sometimes been substantial. And at some point, Ludwig concluded that polite letters and phone calls weren't good enough. "Will the government tell me the truth, so it can kick itself in its hind end with it?" he asked in a 1999 CBC interview.

"There's going to be some casualties, very likely," Ludwig predicted, rather ominously. "When the government throws seven and a half million at increasing the security rather than solving the problems people are complaining about, they're only upping the ante.

"So up and up we go."

AT A TIME OF RECORD-HIGH oil prices, you'd think that the inner sanctum of the 2000 World Petroleum Congress would be one big party. But it turns out that 3,100 of the world's top oil and gas executives are a sedate bunch.

Within the heavily guarded and fenced-off downtown core of Calgary, the only constant is the murmur of business deals, networking and technical lectures. As the champagne flows on the floor of the trade show, there's nary a discouraging word. This is a world unto itself: one could eat, sleep and do business without ever having to leave a compound that covers almost ten square blocks. In a place where there are sometimes more police than civilians, you can jaywalk with impunity. Outside the gates, three hundred protesters face off with a contingent from the more than three hundred riot police recruited from Calgary, Edmonton and Saskatoon.

For Calgary, Canada's fossil headquarters, hosting the petroleum congress is a major coup. "For the oil and gas world, it compares to having landed the Olympics," says Pierre Alvarez, president of the Canadian Association of Petroleum Producers. It's no accident: Canada is the fourth-largest world producer, pumping out 4.3 million barrels of oil equivalent a day.

The power represented here is incredible: delegates, representing all of the world's major corporations and oil-producing nations, collectively account for 89 percent of the world's oil production—a strategic position that puts the congress in control of a significant portion of the global economy. And each nation has its own energy kingdom: Canada's oil and gas industry, reports a congress briefing, is the country's single largest private-sector capital investor, with spending in the range of sixteen to twenty billion dollars each year. It employs 463,000 people directly and indirectly, a considerable force in a nation still dependent on consuming and exporting its vast energy resources.

When the 2001 Bush energy plan called for a continental energy strategy, for example, CAPP was already in Ottawa, pushing business and investment incentives that included corporate tax cuts, a more streamlined regulatory process and continued open border trade. Three Liberal cabinet ministers heard the wish list and, according to the lobbyist, gave CAPP an encouraging reception. "It's pretty clear that they're paying more attention to oil and gas issues," said CAPP vice-president David MacInnis to *The Globe and Mail*. "To have such a growing number of ministers interested and showing some knowledge of our issues—it's been a while and it's great."

But it's not as though the fossil fuel sector has fallen by the wayside. "Since 1970, the federal government has written off $2.8 billion of its investments and loans for energy projects in the non-renewable sector," reports Canada's commissioner of the environment and sustainable development in a 2000 report. This generous figure, notes the report, still doesn't include federal tax incentives for Alberta's oil sands, Canada's hottest energy property, which could cost taxpayers as much as $2 billion, according to year 2000 projections. Prime Minister Jean Chrétien himself arrived in person at the World Petroleum Congress gathering to meet and greet executives.

Behind the wall of urban commandos, there is talk of the outside world. Congress chair Jim Gray notes that almost 30 percent of the conference's programming is related to sustainability or the environment. Gray, known for his charity work around Calgary and for his maverick 1998 campaign against the Klein government on gambling, sets an example for corporate executives wherever he goes. I'm told that the environmental focus, replete with a climate change seminar, was his idea.

Not everyone is quite so interested in saving the planet. For every mention of the environment, there are several other arguments for business as usual. It is possible, for example, to hear a presentation on energy sustainability and then listen to ambitious plans for oil exploration and pipeline construction across Tibet's sensitive northern grasslands.

In fact, major differences surface within the first day of the conference. On one side are European executives who have read the literature on climate change, energy and air pollution and generally agree with their own governments about the importance of taking corrective action. On the other side are North Americans, many of whom, it would seem, still believe that most of the continent's energy resources were created for their benefit—and that climate change is a bad rumour meant to sabotage hard-earned profits.

The climate change question is a prickly one, given that congress-goers are beneficiaries of an economic epoch that, if predictions prove correct, could eventually destabilize natural and industrial systems. Moreover, if Kyoto greenhouse gas reductions became a reality, fifteen to thirty million barrels a day would disappear from world demand, leaving many oil companies very much in the lurch.

A few companies have already wrestled with this possibility. British Petroleum's Sir John Browne spearheaded a reorganization of one of world's largest corporations into "BP"—a more diversified energy company that's branching out into renewables and promoting climate change solutions. "If you want my judgement, we will leave behind this form of the hydrocarbon phase of human development," said Chris Gibson-Smith, BP policy director, in 1999, "and we will be able to look back and see trillions of barrels still in the ground, in much the same way that we are exiting from coal, knowing that there is more coal in the ground than we have taken out." Browne's high-concept "BP: beyond petroleum" message grates against Canadian heavies like Talisman's Jim Buckee and J. C. Anderson, who openly deny climate change, chalking it all up to "bad science."

(Activists outside the barricades of the petroleum congress rightly point out that the repackaged BP remains, at its core, the world's largest petroleum company: the bulk of the company's $12.5-billion investments are oil and gas development, as of

2001, with only 1.25 percent allocated to renewable energy spending.)

Divergent opinions on air quality surface in a joint press conference with Imperial Oil's Bob Peterson, Alberta Energy Minister Steve West and Jurgen Hubbert of Daimler Chrysler. While European industry leaders such as Hubbert work towards upgrading oil refineries to produce ultra-clean, sulphur-free gas, thereby making great gains in reducing smog and acidification emissions, Canadian leaders seem quick to blame everyone but themselves for such pollution. And nowhere is the issue of high-sulphur gas more current than in Canada, where an old fleet of refineries churns out dirty gas containing heavy doses of the acidifying and smog-contributing aerosol that is released into the atmosphere through one's own tailpipe. It was only the previous year that Canada's federal government announced mandatory reductions in gasoline sulphur content that equal those of the most stringent American states, effective 2005.

Steve West claims ominously that consumers will soon bear the cost of these environmental upgrades. "They say it's going to cost billions of dollars to retrofit the [oil] refineries," says West, a former veterinarian whose ill-conceived deregulation strategy saddled Canada's energy province with some of the highest power prices in the country. "Well, it's time to tell people that they're going to pay for it in their personal lives because you can't have your cake and eat it too."

In the past, sulphur was either added or not removed to increase the heat energy of gasoline. But Canada's high sulphur levels have, to date, blocked the import of several high-efficiency hybrid cars that can't burn dirty gas. Moreover, high sulphur also tends to disable a car's catalytic converter, a basic anti-pollution device that scrubs exhaust.

Imperial's Bob Peterson defends the unsteady but rising price of retail gasoline as the healthy outcome of a transparent marketplace; price spikes before long weekends, a long-time source of suspicion among consumers who complain of price gouging, are not explained. And as to why Canada hasn't advanced further in reducing greenhouse gas emissions and air pollution, who's to blame?

Not the companies, says Peterson. "What we can do is respond to customer demand," he says. "There is nothing we can do about that."

What Peterson doesn't mention is that during the late 1990s, his company refined and sold the dirtiest gas in Canada. In the middle of a growing air-quality crisis, Imperial's aging Sarnia refinery produced gasoline that surpassed Canada's new standard for sulphur (effective 2005) by as much as twenty-seven times— 810 parts per million. The gasoline was sold through Imperial's Esso stations across southern Ontario. (By comparison, Shell's Sarnia gas was 700 ppm, while Sunoco, a division of Suncor, was around 200 ppm.) And in 1999, Imperial, Petro-Canada, Shell, Sunoco and two other companies unsuccessfully tried to block the public's access to information on sulphur content in federal court. In their documents, the companies cited "the high potential for boycotts" if the numbers were available to the public. Journalists were being told that this was an issue of intellectual property and competitive advantage. "We say sulphur content is proprietary information," said Imperial Oil spokesperson Richard O'Farrell to *The Edmonton Journal* at the time. "It gets overly complicated. What does the public need to know?"

In a private interview later, I ask West why it is, if consumers must pay for environmental advances, that companies can still afford to spend vast sums of money on exploration projects that frequently never pan out. It's estimated that some $25 to $30 billion is spent on attempts to discover new oil and gas around the world each year. A considerable portion of that money disappears into unsuccessful exploration gambits.

Corporations sell themselves to investors on the basis of the size of their oil holdings, explains West, so exploration drives company worth in a sector that's heavily governed by investment capital. And in order to stabilize business, new discoveries are crucial: steady expansion is precisely what keeps traditional oil and gas giants alive. "The concern has been the volatility of this industry," he says. "But I think there will be a steady investment in exploration and development." It's a common theme here at the World Petroleum Congress, despite all the high-flown talk of sustainability. This message comes, no less, from a minister of government. Growth is good.

Later, Sir John Browne delivers a plenary address that looks to the future and sees green alternatives and healthy profits going hand in hand. The vision of an ever-expanding marketplace—the notion that there's no ceiling to human production and consumption—is never far off. "Over the last decade, this industry added almost 900 million actual new customers worldwide," says the top CEO, "and produced enhanced returns for investors."

Browne's well-publicized dialogue with Greenpeace in Britain doesn't impress everyone, least of all several Greenpeace organizers who helped organize the protests. Right in the middle of the plenary address, two activists from the Canada Tibet Committee—John Hocevar of New York and Freya Putt of Victoria, who both managed to sneak in as fully paid delegates—stand up with a banner and shout "BP-Amoco Out of Tibet." The smooth Sir John goes stonily silent while some of the assembled crowd of 1,500 hurl insults and heckle the sign-wavers: "Boring!" "Useless!" "Shut up!" The buttoned-down congress crowd gets bloodthirsty mighty quick.

(Browne's company bailed out PetroChina in 1999 from a near-disastrous initial showing on the New York Stock Exchange and invested $580 million in the Chinese oil company. At the time, it was argued that BP-Amoco's investment would help fuel PetroChina's ambitious expansion into Tibet.)

After the protesters are led out and temporarily arrested— despite the fact that they each paid a thousand dollars to attend—Browne gets back down to business. "Well, I think I shall start where I left off," he says with James Bond nonchalance. The crowd goes wild with applause. Amazingly, he continues on a green theme, pledging that "we shouldn't ignore or dismiss the real concerns about the impact of human activity on the natural environment."

Later, in a news conference, Browne explains that the global oil industry is pro-democratic and pro-human rights, but the industry reserves the right to do whatever it wants. "We welcome debate," he argues, "but the congress is a private meeting, not a public one, designated by a specific agenda." There are other venues, he says, such as shareholder meetings and gatherings of non-governmental organizations.

Browne's "private meeting" has actually claimed the downtown core of a major Canadian city. That's what's amazing about this event: they've emptied public space—streets where free, democratic assembly is usually legal—for a high-level business meeting.

It doesn't prove to be Sir John's day. After his news conference, Toronto activist Tooker Gomberg, who somehow sneaked into the congress past two levels of armed security, confronts the departing Browne and challenges him on his environmental credentials. Despite its entry into the renewable power business, BP still sells more oil than almost any other company in the world—the equivalent of twice the national output of Canada. "It's not BP, it's BS," accuses Gomberg. "Follow the money: they're putting billions into new oil but only a fraction into alternatives." Browne bolts for the door, handlers in tow.

The World Petroleum Congress, with its walled city and paramilitary patrols, shows how far away we are from having meaningful debates about energy. Here in Calgary there are lectures, presentations and trade-show booths, but the discussion is uneventful; the real transactions happen at invitation-only events. Even behind the barricades, very little happens in plain view that isn't scripted.

In peeling back the many layers of an energy state—corporate campaign contributions, conflicts of interest, business gatherings—there's a pattern: Canada's oil and gas resources have largely been left to the control of a relatively small number of people.

IN A PROVINCE INFUSED with vested interests, both public and private, it's only a matter of time before governments and companies start to confuse each other. It is an inversion of roles: a public sector hungry for new revenue and a corporate sector somehow managing to claim new powers of sovereignty.

This political identity crisis was on clear display at the Edmonton Ludwig trial. By only day three of the court proceedings, it was learned that the Alberta Energy Company had authored part of the RCMP investigation—including a plan to blow up one of its own wells—offered donations to police and paid for travel expenses incurred by police informants. The blurred line between government, law enforcement and the oil business—and the bungling that ensued from the confusion of these responsibilities—became a major theme in the trial.

After Ludwig's conviction for blowing up a gas well near Hinton and cementing another near his home at Trickle Creek, it's still not clear why things were allowed to spin so badly out of control in northern Alberta. How did a "clandestine and brazen" campaign, as Judge Sterling Sanderman put it, manage to bomb and terrorize a whole region—not for several months, but for several years?

Indeed, a growing body of evidence points towards the fact that government authority, from the RCMP to Alberta's energy regulator, failed to take responsibility at early, crucial junctures. During the first year of vandalism, locals in Hythe and Beaverlodge were often left to fend for themselves in a heated situation that eventually degenerated into guerrilla warfare. And in the process of ignoring the problem—and in underestimating the eco-terrorists—authorities continually managed to sabotage their own efforts to entrap, prosecute and jail the bombers.

From the very beginning, the Ludwig threat was ignored. It started in December 1996, the time of the first attempted bombing. The Beaverlodge RCMP detachment, then headed by Sergeant Robert Bilodeau, reported to senior officers that serious trouble was brewing in the region. Bilodeau, who served with the United Nations in former Yugoslavia and now suffers from post-traumatic stress disorder, found in Ludwig something that chilled him deeply: someone who was not afraid of war.

"He is not afraid to sacrifice his own family members to the cause and appears to have little regard for anyone that stands in the way of his objective," wrote Sgt. Bilodeau on January 9, 1997, in an RCMP briefing.

But the briefing was never followed up. Nor was the Peace River criminal investigation unit, the department responsible for serious crimes, brought in. Leaked documents show that

RCMP brass willingly ignored trouble at Trickle Creek for more than a year, leaving the small Beaverlodge detachment to cope with an escalating eco-war. As Commanding Officer D. N. McDermid admitted in an internal memo on April 7, 1997, "it seems apparent somebody dropped the ball (if they ever had it)."

More bombings and vandalism followed. Lacking sufficient resources, the local detachment borrowed video cameras and other resources from Security Management Consulting, the private security force employed by Alberta Energy Company at a cost of five thousand dollars per day. Later, the RCMP would defer to the AEC on investigation strategy, allow handouts to be laundered through an Alberta Justice community program and share confidential information with Security Management officials, who themselves were former high-ranking RCMP officers.

Essentially, the AEC—a company worth $8.5 billion—was performing RCMP duties in a situation that was only getting worse. Ludwig was in dispute with a company that was also running its own police force, leaving no one to mediate what eventually became a guerrilla war. AEC soon launched its own public relations offensive: on September 14, 1988, president and CEO Gwyn Morgan called upon provincial and federal governments for tougher legislation and broader investigative powers against those who would bomb company operations and workers. Industrial terrorism, he implored, is "a creeping sickness that must be eradicated." By November, Alberta had launched its $8-million anti-crime crackdown.

But by the time Operation Kabriole was approved September 29, 1997, the battle of northeastern Alberta was well under way. Sour gas emissions in the region had improved, but the provincial regulator was, nevertheless, still nowhere to be found. Health statistics began to emerge: between 1991 and 1993, the Mistahia Health Region, centred in Grande Prairie, reported a higher rate of birth defects—fourteen congenital heart anomalies per thousand births—roughly twice the provincial average.

The pattern of neglect is even more perplexing when the role of the AEC is considered. The company, for its part, followed provincial pollution standards and attempted to negotiate with the Ludwigs on a settlement that later fell though. Among oil companies, the AEC is considered royalty: vastly wealthy with strong political ties to Alberta's provincial government. With its private security force, the company acted as a benevolent but immensely powerful organization in northern Alberta; it was, in some ways, a government unto itself.

This is probably why paid informant Robert Wraight went to the AEC before he ever contacted police. On September 2, 1998, Wraight called Ed McGillivary of AEC West to enlist in the battle against Ludwig, and the two immediately cut a deal on the phone: the AEC would purchase Wraight's property at a generous rate if Wraight would assist the RCMP. "All right, number-one rule," promised McGillivary, seemingly on behalf of the RCMP, "your family will be looked after." (The deal was eventually scrapped, on the advice of the AEC's lawyers.)

But the largesse of the AEC—and its crisp, $100,000 reward—only complicated the situation. Wraight was later deemed "tainted" in the eyes of the court, partly because he had attempted to cut a deal with the company. In turn, the shaken credibility of the Crown's star witness helped undermine the most serious charge against Ludwig—attempted extortion— that was thrown out of court before the end of trial. The lure of energy money seemed to affect the investigation in ways that the RCMP and the Crown prosecutors never imagined possible.

But it's not as though the Alberta Energy Company ran the RCMP, as Ludwig alleged. There was no conspiracy here. In fact, the RCMP and the AEC feuded over Ludwig for months. The truth is that Ludwig would probably have faced more jail time were it not for his enemies: the dysfunctional mix of AEC's private police, the RCMP assumption that affluent companies could take care of themselves, and the assumption that Ludwig was a passing nuisance that could be handled by an underfunded local detachment.

For some unknown reason, incriminating evidence that might have convicted Ludwig of attempted extortion was never included in the trial. In a December 1996 meeting between the Ludwig clan and top AEC executives Ken Woldrum and Ed McGillivary, Wiebo Ludwig laid down an ultimatum: either the AEC buy him out for $500,000 or he was "going to declare war on the oil and gas industry," according to RCMP reports from that period.

Sgt. Bilodeau, who was invited to the meeting by Ludwig, recalls that it was probably the most blatant threat he'd heard. Basically, it was an extortion attempt that might have actually stood up in court.

As late as March 2000, Crown prosecutor George Combe, as noted in an RCMP memo, did not "see this information as being relevant to the proceedings before the court." Whether this is a cover-up or pure coincidence, we may never know. This part of the story will probably never be addressed in court. The people of Beaverlodge will never know the full truth, nor will the Ludwig clan have the satisfaction of having these issues settled.

IN JULY 2000, I DRIVE up to the remote mountain community of Grande Cache, north of Jasper, where Wiebo Ludwig sits in federal prison. It's a long trip from Calgary, where sour gas wells are now coming under greater official scrutiny.

Things have improved: in 2000, the EUB tightened its guidelines on gas wells, requiring more documentation from companies, emergency plans and safety procedures. "Significant and meaningful public consultation must take place between the applicant and residents/landowners," the EUB warned. The regulator even denied approvals for several large gas projects, applications that, several years earlier, probably would have gone ahead without question.

But as natural gas prices peaked at double their historic levels, there was a growing confrontation between producers and regulators over efforts to control sour gas. "Officials from the premier on down have said they want to get projects through the Energy and Utilities Board and Alberta Environmental Protection more quickly," noted *The Edmonton Journal* in June 2001.

On my drive to the prison, I think about Ludwig's earlier question—did the eco-terrorism make a difference? Certainly, Ludwig's crusade raised environmental awareness about hydrogen sulphide and sour gas flaring. But after millions were spent trying to catch, prosecute and jail Ludwig—not to mention the tragic loss of Karman Willis, the local girl shot in Ludwig's own front yard after a late-night prank went horribly awry—it all seems like a pretty high price to pay for common sense: people, farms and toxins don't always mix.

Indeed, as the Crown prosecutor argued at the Ludwig trial opening, it was all about money: an underfunded RCMP, the inevitable influence of a rich oil company—and the reluctance of Alberta's government to change a troubled status quo. Of course, Ludwig himself was no altruist: his demands against the AEC escalated from $500,000 to $800,000 before negotiations broke down.

Canada's 2001 auditor general's report noted that underfunding at the RCMP endangers public safety; Beaverlodge was certainly no exception. If public authorities had been doing their jobs—community-based policing and environmental enforcement—private corporations might not have filled the vacuum. And as Bilodeau admitted, "We dug a hole that kept on getting bigger and then we buried a sixteen-year-old girl in it."

As I meet Ludwig in a windowless visitation room at the Grande Cache Correctional Institution, it's clear that he originally had no idea that it would all end like this. "I was prepared to defend my family, but the path took some turns," he says. "I've been humbled—not by government, but by Himself. The Lord has chastened me for being proud, as I sit here, but what happened were acts of necessity."

Ludwig, the convict, will be denied early parole. So he walks the halls of the Grande Cache institution, reads the Bible and waits for news from his clan at Trickle Creek. He has managed to charm almost everyone working here, except for the dour guards at the door, who smile for nobody. Even though he almost sold the farm to AEC during negotiations, there are no plans to move anywhere else when he's finally released from prison.

"We aren't going on exodus—we stood our ground," he says. "Nobody on this earth really can say if it was right or just. That judgment comes later."

# ANOTHER NATION

## Stoney Nakoda, Samson Cree

THERE'S A PECULIAR STORY floating around Calgary's oil patch. It goes like this: an Indian band was informed by Indian Affairs that it had been shortchanged by a major oil company on its royalties. The claim, the band was told, was probably worth millions. But it would have to get the money back itself—the government wasn't about to go commando on a big corporation and get itself mixed up in a series of messy lawsuits.

So the Indian band—the Stoney Nakoda—took the company to court and won an award of $6.2 million. But the company refused to pay and appealed the decision. The government, as Indian trustee, was nowhere to be found. (Lawyers who represent the victorious Stoney don't miss the irony. "If the government started chasing after oil and gas companies, they'd admit their trustee position," the Indian Act obligation to protect Aboriginal interests, says one.)

The Stoney decided to play hardball and sent provincial court bailiffs into the posh downtown lobby of the company to seize assets. Expensive artwork, tasteful furniture and desks were all tagged by court officers to be carted off, in lieu of payment.

Within about an hour, steaming but acquiescent executives agreed to meet their obligations. Payment of $6.2 million was made to court. And, after distancing themselves from the dispute, the federal government arrived on the scene and claimed the money as Aboriginal trustee.

This is a national story that has yet to be fully told. Natives across Canada are claiming natural resources, as per treaties and unsettled land disputes—and usually fighting governments and companies along the way. Essentially, many of Canada's Indian treaties are being reopened, the cutting edge of a fight that will potentially cover the vast natural resource wealth of all of Canada's treatied provinces: Alberta, Saskatchewan, Manitoba, Ontario, Quebec and the Maritimes. Already, more than $190 billion in outstanding mineral claims and land lawsuits have been filed and could go before the courts over the next several decades. The main focus of these suits will be Saskatchewan and Alberta.

But on the few Indian reserves that have already enjoyed access to abundant resources, oil and gas wealth has often poisoned communities: death, corruption and political dysfunction have plagued rich reserves with an intensity that's often shocked outsiders. Indian bands who can afford good lawyers still can't seem to pull themselves together enough to address suicide epidemics and alcoholism. The question behind the headlines is whether the cash windfall of past resource wealth—and future lawsuits—will make conditions better or worse. Untapped power can be a curse, something that's the same for any resource-rich nation, white or Aboriginal.

IT BEGINS IN A SMALL RURAL COURTROOM, in the aftermath of a crime. Ernest Vernon Hunter, a Stoney Indian, stands before the judge and pleads guilty. The room is largely empty, save for a few spectators. Hunter looks down, staring at nothing in particular.

He can hardly remember what happened. In an alcoholic rage, Hunter, forty-two, beat his wife nearly unconscious during the first few hours of 1997. It was at a friend's New Year's Eve party on the Stoney Nakoda nation, an Aboriginal community sixty kilometres west of Calgary. An argument had broken out—nobody can recall what it was about. And then things got ugly. Once she fell to the floor, he started kicking her. Rondi

Lefthand, now estranged from her common-law husband, suffered permanent nerve damage.

It was Hunter's worst offence in a lengthy criminal record that stretched back to 1974. And were it not for Lefthand's willingness to co-operate with the Crown prosecutor, it would have all been forgotten, like so many other beatings and tragedies on the oil-rich reserve. Hunter and his wife were both Stoney Indians. They were sometimes a hard-living people whose oil and gas royalties—millions since the late 1960s—had evaporated into a series of social assistance plans, personal bonuses and accusations of fraud. After decades of royalties, it was hard to say whether the money had made things better or worse. For a period during the late 1990s, for example, there wasn't a month when the Cochrane courtroom didn't see at least one serious domestic assault from the reserve. Sometimes two. Drugs and alcohol were almost always involved.

Two years earlier, Hunter was living off-reserve in Calgary and had already completed an alcohol treatment program. Despite his Grade 10–level education, he had sporadic employment. And he wasn't drinking. But after job prospects dwindled, the couple moved back to the rez, living on the $239 monthly cheques each received for social assistance. Conditions at Stoney had deteriorated while they were away: social programs were being cut and there was political turmoil, not to mention a welfare dependence rate of about 70 percent.

After years of abstinence, Hunter began drinking again. He became violent and angry. Small incidents occurred: fights, outbursts. Never against his wife. Hunter sought out help, though hardly any was available on the reserve. He enrolled in an anger-management program back in Calgary, one requiring that he live off-reserve by himself in a low-budget motel. In 1996, he stayed alone for three weeks, attending counselling and holing up in the motel room.

But then, mysteriously, the tribal funding that had been

providing his off-reserve accommodation was suddenly cut off. He had become a casualty of an apparent financial crisis: despite the band's vast mineral resources and federal funding, there just wasn't enough money to cover the most nominal treatment expenses. Hunter was short of the $264 that he needed to complete his program. Penniless, he returned to the reserve and began drinking again.

*Guilty*. Rondi Lefthand sits in the Cochrane courtroom and watches her ex-husband throw himself on the mercy of the court. It is May 1997. One side of her face still feels numb from the beating. But she doesn't want her ex to go to jail. What Ernest Hunter needs, she had told the Crown prosecutor, is help, not prison time. Later the prosecutor pushes for a jail sentence, despite a report that recommended Hunter be put under community supervision.

The presiding judge, John Reilly, had seen these cases for years, ever since his transfer to the Cochrane-Canmore circuit court in 1996. Beatings, murders, assaults. The full gamut of human misfortune has clogged his courtroom. The provincial court at Cochrane sat only once a week, but over 75 percent of all cases came from the Stoney reserve. Nearby non-Aboriginal communities hardly saw murder, let alone serious domestic violence. This has been the case since the early 1970s, shortly after the Stoney became one of Canada's wealthiest reserves with the discovery of significant natural gas deposits beneath its lands. Instead of blossoming, the reserve proceeded to fall apart, in slow motion, for the next three decades.

This should have been a simple case. In almost any other court, Hunter's guilty plea would have brought an automatic sentence of eighteen months in prison. Another Stoney added to the local jail population.

Instead, Judge John Reilly returned to the courtroom on June 26, 1997, and turned everything upside down. In an explosive twelve-page decision, Reilly deferred Hunter's sentencing and, instead, ordered a Crown investigation into the reserve's troubled social and financial circumstances. The Stoney reserve was a "prison without bars and a welfare ghetto" replete with "allegations of political corruption that one would associate with the dictatorship of a banana republic." It all came down to the internal politics of a gas- and oil-rich Indian reserve.

For the judge, the missing $264 was the last straw in an epic tale that few Canadians knew anything about. As he read his decision to the stunned courtroom, Reilly painted a nightmare picture of reserve life—of "fear, intimidation and violence" and of the tremendous "powerlessness that results in weak people dominating weaker people.

"For many years," he said, "I have been asking why it is that this reserve which should be so prosperous has so many poor people, has such a low level of education, has such horrendous social problems, and has such an apparent lack of programs."

Long-time Stoney Chief John Snow, in particular, was singled out as a reason why someone like Ernest Hunter couldn't get help. "I am told that the misappropriation of funds by Aboriginal Chiefs and Councils is accepted practice on many reserves," said Reilly. "I am told by Stoney people that the way government works on the reserve is that the candidate with the most relatives wins and then he and his family share the spoils."

Moreover, Reilly wondered about governments that condoned dysfunction on the reserve: "I am told that the director of Indian Affairs will do nothing about it because it is an internal matter."

Hunter's conviction would have to wait until the Crown inquiry produced some solid facts about the Stoney reserve. In the meantime, Reilly's decision began to make headlines across the country. It produced a firestorm. Chief John Snow called the judge "false, inappropriate and racist." Several colleagues advised Reilly to transfer all his personal assets to his wife's name, for fear of impending lawsuits. Several Aboriginal leaders from other Alberta reserves praised Reilly for his honesty. In broaching the internal affairs of an oil and gas reserve, the judge had set off a bomb.

"It's a hidden mafia system that we live under," said former Siksika (Blackfoot) chief Roy Little Chief. "[Reilly's decision] is unique—it's full of revolution that may straighten out our lives under the wicked system we live under."

ABOUT EVERY TEN YEARS OR SO, the Stoney Nakoda nation implodes. Like clockwork.

Everyone has a theory as to why this happens. But what's become clear is that the federal government wants out of the Indian business, despite its Treaty 7 and Indian Act obligations. At some point, the Crown decided to cut its losses and phase itself out of the whole mess. This is the path to self-government— full of denials, covert agendas, power struggles—and it inspires fear, suspicion and hope. Many Stoney long for the day when Indian Affairs is gone, but fear what the feds might leave behind in its place.

Meanwhile, the ten-year cycle of Stoney scandal proceeds right on schedule. In 1976, armed activists from the American Indian Movement (AIM) occupied Stoney administration offices in Morley, Alberta, and demanded that the band's leadership be held accountable for its finances. It was alleged that chiefs were receiving $100,000 salaries. The band's administrator at the time, Jeff Perkins, was sitting in the tribal boardroom when AIM took the building. A rifle was held to his head.

Nearly twenty-five years later, what strikes Perkins as odd is how Indian Affairs would deliver royalty cheques for one million dollars—pure energy money—to a band that clearly had trouble managing its own affairs. The money often disappeared. "Payments were made under legitimate budget items," he said in 1998, as we lounged in the latte-and-biscotti world of a Starbucks outlet inside a Chapters bookstore, about twenty minutes down the road from Stoney. "The expectation is that the chief will pay the people. And he will get elected that way. And that hasn't changed."

The second Stoney implosion happened in 1986 when a senior Indian Affairs official held his own news conference to decry corruption on the reserve and federal mismanagement. As regional director of Indian Affairs for Alberta, Robert Laboucain knew that something was going terribly wrong at Stoney. "I worked with all the reserves in southern Alberta," he recalls. "It seemed kind of strange to me that between 1974 and 1984, the Stoney First Nation had received about $300 million through resource revenues. How did that happen? How can you have $300 million go through a reserve of 2,500 people and really not have anything to show for it?"

Laboucain asked questions of his superiors that weren't answered, then took his concerns to the media and was promptly fired. The Métis troublemaker was later reinstated by a court order but soon resigned "out of disgust."

"What I was attempting to initiate was severely squashed," he says. "It took a provincial judge to get the attention of Indian Affairs, bring them to the attention of the public, bring political pressure to bear and generate some action."

The 1990s instalment of the Stoney scandal actually began in 1995, prior to Judge John Reilly's Crown investigation, when outlaw logging nearly devastated reserve timber holdings. Over the course of a few months, trees worth about $40 million were cut down illegally by Stoney and white loggers and sold to mills in Alberta and British Columbia. At the time, several environmental activists and Stoney councillors appealed to Indian Affairs to take action. The timber that had been disappearing was actually an Indian asset that the federal government had a special trust responsibility to protect. For months, nothing was done. Finally, Indian Affairs called in the RCMP and a major lawsuit was launched against the federal government by Stoney council for $51 million in lost assets and damages.

There are plenty of problems that can't be fixed by legal battles. The reserve has no real economy of its own, save for natural gas and timber revenues. And while criminal trials occur on a weekly basis and Stoneys fill the local jail, there's never once been any fraud or white collar–crime conviction that one might expect from the kind of corruption alleged at Stoney. Annual budgets are often disasters: in 1997, the reserve received about $50 million in revenues (including federal funding and gas royalties) but posted a $5.6-million debt. Among other things, three Stoney chiefs received tax-free incomes and allowances totalling more than $450,000 in 1997, according to one confidential Department of Indian and Northern Affairs (DIAND) report.

Many, including Judge John Reilly, were quick to blame Chief John Snow for the reserve's continued dysfunction. First elected in 1969, Snow is only one of three chiefs, but with the exception of a four-year period between 1992 and 1996 he has been a dominant political force on the reserve for more than thirty years. "Over and over, in the conversations I have with Stoney people and non-Stoney who have worked on the reserve," wrote Reilly, "the finger is pointed at Chief John Snow."

For decades, allegations have been made about Snow's coziness with federal bureaucrats. A confidential Indian Affairs memo from 1998 reveals that "special access to senior management" had been provided to Chief John Snow on several occasions, including a private audience with DIAND's associate deputy minister. This is curious, if only for the fact that the Stoney tribe actually has three equal chiefs who lead three different band councils with a single administrative office.

"Chief Snow gives Indian Affairs a way to control the reserve," charged one community member in an interview, "and Indian Affairs gave Snow the resources to keep political control." Again, it is yet another unproved accusation against Snow—a chief who has also been credited with some important Aboriginal rights and land claim victories—but from a reserve-level perspective, it seems almost elementary: how could anyone last that long as the public figurehead of an ongoing social disaster without some outside help?

Snow himself could not be reached for comment; he rarely gives interviews. But in the wide sweep of the Stoney story, is it possible that a single person could be the author of so much misfortune? Within the context of the current reserve system— a netherworld of strange rules, bureaucratic wrangling and chronic cash shortages—political chaos seems likely, regardless who is elected chief. The same problems play out on reserves across Canada, over and over, as part of a system where account- ability is a fundamental problem. This is especially so on many reserves that have received income from natural resources such as oil and gas.

In any other sphere of public life, this inherently troublesome, legally dubious structure probably wouldn't have stretched the 125-plus years since Canada drafted its first Indian Act. But then again, Aboriginal society wasn't supposed to last this long. Nor were there supposed to be rich deposits of natural gas (and lesser quantities of oil) beneath the surface of the reserve—after treaty, valuable land was often given to whites.

"Indian Affairs have removed themselves [from Stoney], so chief and council have taken over," explains Ben Baich, a former Indian Affairs employee who worked with the Stoney and left in 1981, disillusioned with the system. "If you were chief and had four hundred people unemployed and you had a project that would employ forty—who would you hire? If you don't employ your family, you're beat."

In the confines of reserve governance and in the absence of Indian Affairs, what seems like corruption is sometimes sheer pragmatism, where natural resources like oil and gas are also tools of patronage and survival.

"The chiefs administer poverty," explains Baich. "As long as Indians are unemployed and fighting against each other, the federal government doesn't have to deal with the history and the issues."

But the government's absenteeism has come under increased scrutiny. In April 1999, Canada's auditor general criticized Indian Affairs for not being able to account for $3.6 billion in native funding. "The department is not taking adequate steps to ensure allegations of wrongdoing, including complaints and disputes related to funding arrangements, are appropriately resolved," said Auditor General Denis Desautels. Moreover, the department lacked a process to manage and respond to reserve-level concerns and allegations—some 300 allegations on 108 reserves in the previous year alone. The auditor general also raised concerns about the degree of financial risk many reserves were assuming under more extended self-government funding arrangements.

What was clear from the auditor general's report is that reserve democracy and financial management often mirror the long-standing system of Indian Affairs bureaucracy. Under the current system, thirty-year disasters like Stoney seem inevitable.

UP THE BOW RIVER VALLEY, a winter storm rolls in from the mountains. Judge John Reilly leans into the wind and works his way through the burial grounds.

He is troubled by what he sees. A number of the people buried here once stood before him in his courtroom. "For me, it was people I either knew or knew of them or knew their parents," he says. "There's not one person on this reserve that hasn't lost something."

We stand beside the final resting places of champion powwow dancers, single parents who left behind children, cousins and friends buried together.

Buffy Dawn Kaquitts: 1978–1996

Kelly Harold: 1975–1995

Patricia Bearspaw: 1972–1977

Reilly keeps walking. Two groups of people dominate this cemetery: the young and the old. It's a story that's as clear as the dates on the headstones. Elders and youth, side by side.

It was more than just a string of bad luck. Throughout the summer of 1997, newspapers kept close track of the alarming death count on the Stoney Nakoda reserve, an Aboriginal community sixty kilometres west of Calgary.

June 27: Hendrick Labelle dies in an alcohol-related accident.

July 22: Stanley Rollinmud commits suicide by walking out onto the Trans-Canada Highway.

Despite everything, Indian Affairs argued that the Stoney people required no special attention because evidence of wrongdoing hadn't surfaced. "At this stage, we see no cause or have any intention of launching an inquiry," said Indian Affairs spokesperson Jim Fleury on July 17, 1997. "We are not launching any kind of special inquiry or investigation."

A month later, then Indian Affairs minister Jane Stewart reiterated the department's position: there was no need for a public inquiry because it wasn't in the best interests of the Stoney to air their "dirty laundry." On August 7, the Stoney band council agreed to submit themselves to external financial management—known as third-party management—by the accounting firm Coopers & Lybrand, following confirmation of a $5.6-million 1996 deficit with Indian Affairs. There was still no official admission of any problems involving the reserve. A departmental communications briefing at the time argued that despite "recent deaths at Stoney, DIAND has no solid basis yet to directly connect these with unique social conditions on the reserve."

Nevertheless, young Stoney kept dying. Newspapers kept printing stories.

August 7: Carolyn Snow, niece of Chief John Snow, dies in an alcohol-related traffic accident.

August 15: Roland Ear, the driver in Snow's death, found murdered on his front lawn.

August 20: Abby Dawn Hunter killed while lying on the highway.

By August 21, the federal government relented: with the approval of Stoney council, an independent forensic audit would be conducted on the reserve in response to widespread complaints of corruption, social strife and mismanagement. Accounting firm KPMG would conduct the audit. An anonymous hotline and investigation office were set up for reserve residents: more than 343 different allegations would eventually be investigated, 43 of which were eventually turned over to the RCMP.

After decades of dysfunction, the Stoney had become an officially designated tribe-in-trouble. With its invasion of accountants, the federal government claimed that the Stoney reserve would now be squeaky clean and trouble-free. As Jane Stewart, Canada's Indian Affairs minister, reassured Alberta's worried justice minister in a December 10, 1997, letter, "Coopers and Lybrand . . . has worked with the community and the current administration to balance current year budgets and restore the fiscal health of the First Nation. Social and Education Programs are being delivered and are fully available to all community members."

It was, by all accounts, a significant moment. The federal government pledged to bring accountability and self-reliance to the Stoney reserve, in response to the scandalous summer of 1997. Matters were in good hands, everyone was told. Professional managers were going to fix things.

All of this did nothing but worry Tina Fox, a fifty-eight-year-old Stoney councillor who's been an outspoken supporter of band council reform. As the first-ever Stoney woman to be elected to tribal council, she's served six two-year terms and has seen and heard just about everything there is to know about the reserve. Surprisingly, her biggest concern wasn't Stoney Chief John Snow, whom both the media and a number of reserve residents have frequently blamed for the band's sorry state.

No, Indians don't scare her. Rather, Tina Fox fears the people who have come, once again, to solve all their problems. Bureaucrats, consultants, accountants and oil companies all have their solutions for Stoney—which seems a lot like the paternalism of the old Indian Agent system.

"Since our ancestors signed our treaties, Indian Affairs has been developing programs they think are good for us," says Fox. "But they have not been good for us—and they reject programs that we develop for ourselves.

"A lot of our money isn't taxpayers' money," she explains. "It comes from oil and gas from our reserve. But yet we still don't have control." Outsiders have a strong presence here; even the gas station and grocery store are run by non-Natives. Around us are the foothills of the Rocky Mountains, rich oil and gas territory that Stoneys once occupied as their traditional territory. Then the whites came, and Treaty 7 was signed in 1877, giving the Stoney reserve lands that were a small fraction of their original territory. The foothills were so rich in resources that even the limited reserve that was given to the Stoney yielded millions of dollars in natural gas royalties. When gas was discovered in the late 1960s, Indian Affairs auctioned off Stoney wells to the highest bidder, and large oil companies like Shell and Amoco came onto the reserve. The tribe that had been poor since treaty suddenly had huge wads of cash.

Much of that money has disappeared. And Indian Affairs helped them spend it. "With the $400 million [in tribal royalties] that we've spent over the last twenty years, we really don't have much to show for it," says Fox. "During the period when we had money, Indian Affairs did not give us any housing grants, for example. . . . We built quite a few houses out in the community with our own band funds—whereas other First Nations were getting grants."

Individual monthly payments were made to distribute the royalty money, reaching five hundred dollars a month for every man, woman and child. "We were paying our own welfare, I guess, where that money could have been saved for a future generation. It's kind of destroyed us, really."

Tina Fox lost her son to an alcohol-related accident. She's seen friends, relatives and family crippled, killed and hurt from ongoing trouble on the reserve. For years, she's kept a diary, marking the passing of every Stoney who's been killed in tragic circumstances. She remembers things that other people have forgotten. And she remembers her own residential school experience, the way she was told to reject the beliefs and stories of her elders.

Tina Fox fears Indian Affairs because it wasn't all that long ago that the department was actively trying to eliminate Aboriginal society. Until recently, Canada ran one of the world's most extensive apartheid-style systems for each and every one of its six-hundred-odd recognized First Nations; it was only during the late 1960s and early 1970s that Canada wound down its last few residential schools and annulled its official assimilation policy.

So when the government comes calling with solutions, it's not always cause for celebration. As seen at Stoney, there's plenty of bad history. Consequently, both Indian Affairs and tribal governments now find themselves wrestling with problems wrought from decades of mismanagement as well as serious, long-term strife.

This is why Tina Fox fears a department that has solemnly pledged to honour, respect and champion Aboriginal self-government—it talks the language of partnership but often demonstrates a conflict of interest in its dealings on reserves. Acting in the best interests of its Aboriginal trustees and carrying out government policy—a dual role defined by Canada's Indian Act—are bureaucratic functions at odds within the same department.

"We do have a suspicion that Indian Affairs is trying to do the best damage control they can," says Fox. "They're trying to put the lid on us here, so that our issues don't spread out to all other First Nations communities across Canada."

In other words, the Stoney reserve has become a place where even the solutions are part of the problem.

Late in 2000, I revisit Tina Fox on the reserve: she has quit band council politics and has enrolled in a university counselling program. The Stoney Nakoda nation itself is on an upswing: a number of Stoney have been promoted to key management positions, the suicide rate is down, and Judge Reilly's courtroom is hosting fewer Stoney. They are, in other words, somewhere on the road to taking care of themselves.

IN THE FUTURE, continued economic strife will mean that more and more tribes will form partnerships with private sector companies to shore up reserve economies. This is the uncertain question of self-government: if the federal government is phasing itself out and trying to limit its expenditures, how will reserves support themselves in the face of an ever-growing Aboriginal population?

"It's not that far into the future where companies will be able to deal directly with the nations without having the federal government there," says Ken Woolner, CEO and president of Calgary-based Velvet Exploration. Velvet, bought out by American major El Paso in 2001, signed an exploration deal with the Stoney for their entire reserve territory in September 1998 and considers itself a pioneer in Aboriginal-corporate partnerships. "That's an inevitable outcome of this whole process. And frankly I think it is what Indian Affairs wants as well."

Many Aboriginal leaders have decried the federal government's plans to get out of the Indian business as irresponsible and premature. Others, like Woolner, see self-government as an opportunity for partnership. It doesn't hurt that the foothills region had become one of the hottest natural gas exploration areas in Canada. According to Woolner, PetroCan announced the largest gas well in recent memory, "about fifteen miles north of our [Stoney] property. And Canadian 88 announced potentially big finds thirteen miles north and six miles north.

"Undeveloped land in this area is just going to get more and more expensive with all these discoveries. People are talking about reserves on individual wells in excess of 100-billion cubic feet of gas. There's a tremendous amount of value tied up in one of those wells. Ultimately, you have to expect that will translate into land sale prices.

"There's land directly adjacent to us that went for $430 a hectare, some for $550 a hectare. There was one three-section parcel that went for $809 a hectare. There's some pretty high prices being paid."

And what did Velvet Exploration pay the Stoney for its land? According to its own documentation, the company paid $84 a hectare, plus commitments for seismic mapping and drilling. Industry averages for the foothills region at the time of the Velvet deal were calculated at $188 a hectare. And when Velvet acquired its Samson holdings, "the land was acquired for prices ranging between one hundred dollars ($100) per hectare and one hundred sixty ($160) per hectare," says a Velvet press release, "well below industry averages."

Woolner is aware of the discrepancy and he cautions against hasty comparisons. "The thing with our permit is that you have to be careful in that we paid a land bonus as part of our business relationship—but we do other things too. We made commitments to shoot seismic and to drill wells. When companies are buying Crown land, they don't have to make any of those commitments. So when [you add] Crown land sale prices to the deal we made, you can't really compare them because ours is [a] much more extensive agreement."

Nevertheless, Velvet managed a land bonus deal that was, in some cases, almost ten times less than what was paid for adjoining, off-reserve property. "Suffice to say, we're thrilled that we got in [in] September as opposed to trying to get in later on, just because it would have made it that much more difficult," says Woolner. "Our timing was perfect."

When I wrote about the Stoney in 1999 for *Saturday Night* magazine, Velvet threatened a multi-million-dollar lawsuit.

There's nothing illegal about doing business with First Nations. History shows that it's probably better than government. And Velvet has followed through on all its contractual obligations, employing local Stoney and drilling wells as promised. It's the optics that hurt: a competitive bonus paid on Crown land would otherwise be worth celebrating, but a troubled reserve probably isn't an ideal example for what, on the surface, looks like a bargain.

BETWEEN BLACKED-OUT GOVERNMENT DOCUMENTS and private companies that threaten libel suits, there're plenty of people who'd just as well not be publicly associated with Indian trouble.

But the truth itself is fairly simple. Like many Canadian provinces, Indian reserves base most of their internal economy on exports. Once a self-sufficient nation of hunters, the Stoney people are now in the business of exporting things of value: natural resources, money for groceries, social workers and imported consultants. A significant portion of the taxpayer dollars and trust funds that have been spent on the Stoney have actually left the reserve. The 1998 KPMG audit made special note of the fact that more than half of all tribal payments went to non-Stoney individuals and suppliers. For example, in 1997 the band spent $23.8 million on payments to Stoney individuals and elected officials—including Social Services, payroll and royalty cheques—while $24 million went to off-reserve professional services, consulting fees, salaries and other services.

On this point, KPMG identified a mysterious off-reserve Company Three that received a total of $5.5 million between 1994 and 1997, disbursed via 1,448 separate cheques. It wouldn't be the first time that Aboriginal dysfunction has resulted in off-reserve profit. The horrible possibility is that the Stoney nation is, in the short term, most valuable to the white world as a disempowered "self-government" complete with constant infighting and implosions. This isn't necessarily an intentional outcome, nor is it official policy. It just happens.

Of course, money isn't everything to the Stoney. The nation has suffered from too much money, just as it suffers from too little. It's one of the many paradoxes of the reserve.

Elder J. R. Twoyoungmen is unsure about the future. "We're losing our ability to be Indians. We're caught in between—we're not good enough Indians and we're not good enough whites, either," he says. "I don't know how we can start healing ourselves. I can claim to be an Indian. I can say that. But to be thinking that way, myself, I just don't know."

Indian Affairs can't be blamed for everything. They've frequently tried to set things straight, albeit in a way that's often mystified even its own employees. "It's good that they tried to change their mandate," says elder Twoyoungmen. "We don't know—the future could have been much worse, far worse, than it is now."

WHILE SOME ENERGY-RICH RESERVES like Stoney are on the defensive, just trying to hold it together, other nations are hunting governments and companies like buffalo.

I'm sitting in a Calgary courtroom watching, with some disbelief, what is happening. No fewer than six lawyers are bickering back and forth, representing three different parties. There's oil multinational Chevron Resources, several Cree Indian bands and the federal government. And everyone is suing everyone else.

Literally, there are about five or six different lawsuits afoot, all concurrent. The oil company is suing the government. The government is suing the Indians and the corporation. And the Indians are suing the other two. It's a legal free-for-all, a nightmare of judicial procedure and accusation. People are arguing and interrupting one another. And the judge is doing his best to keep track of everything.

The provincial Court of Queen's Bench in Calgary has become the setting of a bizarre melee of lawyers, a messy collision of the kind of vested interests that now characterize Indian country. Sometime during the mid-1980s, Chevron overpaid royalties from several oil wells it operated on Cree land. The money was delivered to Indian Affairs and deposited into a trust fund for each of the four respective Indian bands. The money was spent by the bands. Chevron eventually noticed money missing from its coffers and filed for ten million dollars.

"It's the first time I've seen anything like this," says one lawyer. Despite the fact that the federal government was the primary contact—managing land leases and handling money—both Chevron and the federal government filed suit against the Indians of four reserves located near Hobbema, Alberta. "Usually companies only go after the government if there's a money problem," the lawyer said. The four Cree bands—the Samson, the Ermineskin, the Bobtail and the Louis Bull—launched counterclaims worth fifty million dollars against both Chevron and the federal government, based on their own calculations that showed outstanding royalties and faulty accounting. Thus the mess of lawyers.

Counsel for the Ermineskin nation accuses the federal government of betraying the Indian bands for siding with American-owned Chevron. "What interest is the Crown being found to protect?" asks the lawyer. "The Crown, by choice of its council, is pursuing us."

He has a point. Why is the federal government trying to collect misplaced corporate booty from Indians? You'd think that a company like Chevron—with more than $3.5 billion in Canadian assets—wouldn't need any help throwing its weight around. And isn't the federal government, bound as a trustee by the Indian Act, supposed to be acting in the best interests of Aboriginals?

There is more sniping. The government, for its part, claims that it is doing what is legally prudent: honouring the independence of the First Nations by treating them as a separate legal entity—in good times and bad. These Indian bands are the richest in Canada, notes the Crown lawyer. "The status quo gives them everything they want," he charges, "and if the Crown is in a conflict, it's because the bands tried to put them there."

The tough-love rationale impresses nobody. The company still wants its money back. And the Indians wonder why the feds are so quick to collect corporate oil money and so slow to distribute it to reserves.

Herein is the clue to understanding the next several decades of federal-Aboriginal relations. Faced with a choice between an American multinational and some uppity Indians, the government's lawyers chose the corporation. In plain terms, the federal government cannot afford to be seen plugging Aboriginal interests or setting a precedent that might bind it to future obligations. Not just because the feds have long wanted to get out of the Indian business—and $7 billion in annual Aboriginal expenditures—but because the government itself has been named defendant in $190-billion worth of First Nations lawsuits. In this melee of vested interests, it's evident that the government has the most to lose.

The largest of the four bands, the Samson Cree, is strangely subdued. With 51 percent of the Hobbema Cree population, it has the largest stake in the Chevron case. Yet the Samson keep referring to another lawsuit, something they call Victor Buffalo. Apparently, this Buffalo person is quite popular. Soon all the lawyers are talking about him.

Afterwards, nobody will comment about Victor Buffalo. A trip to the federal clerk's office reveals that the Buffalo case has been sealed to the public—a case so confidential, in fact, that no one can quite say why the court documents are closed. There's not even a statement of claim, the most basic court document. It is a lawsuit that makes the court clerk nervous.

This much is clear: Victor Buffalo is a Samson chief who, in 1989, launched a civil action for $1.3 billion in damages against the Department of Indian Affairs and Northern Development. Other details emerge, despite the high security around the case. Aboriginal leaders, lawyers, judges and bureaucrats all have their stories. Several sources disclose that although the case has been running since 1989, it only began court proceedings in April 2000. More than 150,000 pieces of evidence have been collected. And most of an office-tower floor in downtown Calgary has been reconstructed to fit a special high-tech courtroom that will accommodate this single, massive legal proceeding.

After further digging, it becomes apparent that *Buffalo* is merely the lead salvo of several potential lawsuits from Samson worth somewhere between thirty and forty billion dollars. These lawsuits extend well beyond Indian Affairs, claiming a large swath of mineral rights across central Alberta. In fact, it turns out that the Samson, the largest Cree band in Alberta, is at the forefront of a national wave of litigation and negotiation for shared control of oil and gas, timber and mining in Canada.

In addition to Cree claims for shared mineral rights in central Alberta, the Blackfoot, Peigan and Stoney of Treaty 7 have already filed suit for the mineral rights of southern Alberta— and Treaty 8 bands are positioning themselves in the north. Saskatchewan, with its strong federated tribal council, is close behind with a negotiating strategy that's saving lawsuits as a last-ditch measure.

No wonder the government hid behind Chevron. In the company of a federal security guard, I tour the empty court-room built for the Buffalo proceedings. The carpet smells new and the paint looks fresh. The judges and lawyers have large cushy seats and computer consoles built into their tables. It is a modest, one-hundred-seat theatre, designed and decorated with the same bureaucratic sensibility that governs most office build-ings. But make no mistake: it is a battle zone.

SAMSON LAWYERS WON'T RETURN my calls. The government won't release its court documents. And the Samson tribal administration won't talk to me about the Buffalo case unless their lawyers say it's okay—which obviously is not happening.

In search of answers, I manage to contact several Samson Warriors, the self-appointed official opposition of the band's tribal government. They agree to talk—but no tape recorders or cameras are allowed. The reserve is off limits because they can't be seen talking to journalists. "Too much trouble," says one.

We agree to meet at Tim Hortons in Wetaskawin, twenty minutes down the road from Hobbema.

It is lunchtime when they arrive. Six large Indians enter the doughnut shop dressed in jeans, powwow windbreakers, boots and moccasins. Several tote cellphones. Heads turn as Wetaskawin locals scope out the new arrivals; some people don't even pretend they're not staring. It's a long way from W. P. Kinsella's famous fictional Hobbema of whimsical Aboriginals and their kooky hijinks. These people mean business.

It turns out that the de facto spokesperson is actually the Warriors' only female member: Deborah Nepoose, school bus driver and grassroots activist. She explains how Indian Affairs has stepped away from the reserve, leaving the Samson to struggle with the legacy of oil money, allegations of reserve corruption and an uncertain future.

"We've been screwed by everyone: the government, Social Services, consultants—everyone who was supposed to help us," says Nepoose. "Screwed. That's the Buffalo case right there."

Between 1980 and 1989, the federal government collected more than $783 million in oil and gas royalties for the Samson Cree—almost $200,000 for every man, woman and child on the reserve—from bountiful on-reserve oil fields. Roughly half of these funds were held in trust. The rest was distributed to members and spent on various projects. Like Stoney, Canada's richest Indian nation has been blessed and cursed by its affluence:

large, modern homes dot a reserve that, until the late 1980s, was the suicide capital of North America.

To any stranger passing through Hobbema, there is little physical evidence of an ongoing social crisis. Driveways, strip malls and recreation centres gave the impression that the Samson reserve is actually a misplaced Toronto suburb. There are teepees, to be sure, but the obvious hallmarks of poverty that one associates with Indian reserves—broken-down cars, broken-down homes—are scant. A local high school provides the only clue to any trouble: "Respect Others' Property," advises its billboard. "School Under Video Surveillance."

Between 1985 and 1987, the male suicide rate was eighty-three times the national average, one of the highest rates in the world. Kids were dropping like flies in the community of six thousand, with more than three hundred suicide attempts each year. At the time, individual families were collecting roughly three thousand dollars in royalties each month and teenagers were given thirty-thousand-dollar cheques on their eighteenth birthdays. This massive influx of oil money, co-administered by Indian Affairs, came closely on the heels of residential schools. The community is still recovering—auto wrecks are common enough that the Canadian Auto Association attempted to de-insure its Hobbema drivers in 1999.

This is what angers the Warriors the most: the Samson have had more opportunity than any other First Nation in Canada, yet the windfall has meant a lost decade—ten years of drugs, alcohol, violent death and suicide. "The government knew what was happening," says Deborah Nepoose, "but they didn't care."

A 1984 study commissioned by Indian Affairs found that sudden wealth was indeed causing serious social disruption among several of Alberta's oil-producing bands. Money management and social programs were low official priorities despite the fact that these bands had never really had experience with money before. "Nobody thought about counselling when this money came in," said the report's author, Joe Dion. "I think the department was remiss and irresponsible."

The Samson Cree are now at the forefront of the next wave of Aboriginal activism mainly because few other Indian bands could afford to do so. While its oil royalties are rapidly dwindling, the nation is far from broke. The Warriors report that the band will probably spend upwards of thirty million dollars on legal fees, research and other court-related expenses over the course of a decade.

Gawkers in the Tim Hortons remain spellbound by the Warriors. There could be free Timbits and coffee being given away at the front and some of them likely wouldn't notice.

Regarding Victor Buffalo, the Warriors confirm that the Samson claim against the government is indeed huge and that the band has been amassing an army of lawyers to challenge Indian Affairs on nearly everything that's happened from the 1940s to the present.

But they're surprisingly short on details. "You probably know more about the case than we do," admits one Warrior. "Our leaders don't say anything—you have to fight for answers around here."

A YEAR LATER—JANUARY 2000—I'm lounging in the posh Calgary offices of the Samson legal team. Before me is Terry Munroe, former Indian Affairs official and long-time adviser to the Samson nation.

Munroe explains that the Buffalo case is what is known as a breach-of-trust proceeding. The Samson have claimed that the federal government drastically mismanaged Samson business interests—including the band's extensive oil and gas properties. The core of the lawsuit, then, is a simple claim for damages: the Samson charge that, between 1946 and 1989, $1.38 billion was lost due to improper negotiation, mismanagement and faulty accounting. In plain terms, the government betrayed the rights and trust of Aboriginals—as witnessed in the events of Hobbema's lost decade—and the Aboriginals have decided to fight back.

Munroe has agreed to talk because he feels the Samson have a strong case—and because details of the trial were leaked to CBC Radio a few months earlier, no small thanks to some digging around that I'd done. Regardless, I'm the first writer they've let in the door.

He's also impressed with my breeding—not my Scottish-Scandinavian genes, but my long-dead relatives: specifically, the one who authored Canada's first comprehensive Indian Act in 1876 and negotiated several prairie Indian treaties. The one who got this whole thing started.

It was in 1877 that Victor Buffalo's ancestors made treaty with my ancestor, Rt-Hon. David Laird, governor of the North-West Territories and agent of the Queen. Chief Bobtail, representing the Bear Hills Cree, today's Hobbema bands, signed his adhesion to Treaty 6 in 1877 with Laird at Blackfoot Crossing, just east of Calgary. It was a momentous event, heralded as Canada's historic accession of valuable western territory.

The treaty covered the vast expanse of what is now known as central Alberta and central Saskatchewan—some 310,000 square kilometres of Cree, Stoney and Assiniboine land. In return for agreeing to share the land—or surrender the land, depending on whose version of the treaty is being told—First Nations such as the Samson were to be put onto reserves and allowed certain rights and annual dispensations.

Sixty years after signing Treaty 6, explains Munroe, the Bear Hills Cree discovered that they were sitting on a gold mine: under their Indian reserve was one-third of a vast oil field that, at its prime, would account for 10 percent of Canada's national oil output. While officials like Laird were scoping out potential coal and gold deposits for European ownership, part of the real prize was mistakenly given away to the Aboriginals.

Yet more irony. But wait, he says, there's more. In the 1940s, the federal government unwittingly got into the oil and gas business when private oil companies applied to drill wells on Cree land. At Samson and a number of other resource-rich reserves, Indian Agents were given power to manage millions of dollars of natural resources; later, these assets were managed by a federal trust company, Indian Oil and Gas. Until the 1970s, Canada's Indian Act granted vast discretionary powers to Indian Agents in the administration of Aboriginal business interests, children, housing and land on the roughly six hundred nations across Canada.

More often than not, people who had never been near an oil well were responsible for cutting deals with large oil corporations and making sure money was accounted for. Inevitably, mistakes were made.

"They didn't have the players and didn't have the resources and basically played the tune of oil and gas companies," explains Samson lead counsel James O'Reilly. "They were an absent caretaker—it would have been a fluke if there hadn't been problems." Indian Affairs just wasn't equipped to deal with a multi-million-dollar natural resource and finance operation. Nor was Indian Affairs equipped to deal with the social trouble that came with cash windfalls.

As Indian Affairs gradually transferred a degree of self-government to reserves in the 1970s, Samson elders and councillors began asking tough questions about their assets. Few answers were forthcoming.

By 1982, Chief Victor Buffalo attempted to negotiate a return of Samson trust funds to the reserve. That failed, and in 1989 a lawsuit was filed against the government in federal court. Ever since then, the case has been locked in pretrial motions, evidence collection and other things that happen when you try to sue the government for $1.3 billion.

Money aside, it's the potential precedent of Buffalo that makes it so remarkable. After more than 150 years of assorted Indian

Act legislation, the relationship between Aboriginal people and the federal government is still alarmingly fuzzy—nobody actually knows who's responsible for what and, more important, who's ultimately responsible for the future well-being of Indian bands and reserves. Among other things, the Buffalo case will address the complicated and increasingly antagonistic relationship between government and First Nations.

Then there are the other lawsuits. The question of the Indian Act inevitably brings up the issue of Aboriginal rights—specifically, rights to natural resources that, as First Nations argue, were wrongfully taken. Although the federal government recently appraised its own risk at about $10 billion of the $190 billion claimed, many of these cases would reopen several of Canada's major Indian treaties—and likely drag provincial governments and possibly companies into the whole mess.

There is a reckoning afoot, one that involves lengthy court battles and a powerful new wave of First Nations activism. Victor Buffalo is leading the charge in an Aboriginal effort to rectify disputes that go all the way back to Confederation. From the government's perspective, it's Oka without the guns. More than money, it is a fight for self-government on Aboriginal terms: not the welfare encampments of most Indian reserves, but quasi-provincial jurisdictions with the inevitable power that comes from sharing and controlling natural resources.

Thus the national profusion of lawsuits. Many First Nations have given up on government-controlled avenues for negotiation and dispute resolution. With its high-stakes strategy, the Victor Buffalo challenge attacks the weakest point in the federal edifice—management of Indian assets—and gambles on extracting something that will make the federal cabinet sit up and take notice: money.

AS THE GOVERNMENT BACKS AWAY from Aboriginal problems and obligations, the likely outcome will be yet more confusion.

In the future, Indian bands will sue corporations in exactly the same way that companies litigate against each other: each will try to protect their own corporate interests. Already, the Stoney are suing three other major oil companies for similar damages, including Chevron. The Samson have filed their own actions against Imperial, Amoco and Chevron. This ever-growing web of civil action is partly the result of Indians' getting into the energy business.

But the real story is this: where is the government? In one courtroom the feds are pretending that Indians don't exist, then in another the feds are suing the Indians, and in yet another courtroom the feds are claiming money on behalf of First Nations. As litigant, defendant and trustee, the federal government increasingly finds itself in a conflict of interest.

In other words, a defendant that's on the hook for $200 billion in damages is also responsible for the long-term welfare of the plaintiffs. Sworn legal enemies are bound by treaty and law to find solutions to Canada's Indian Act trouble.

And while this fundamental conflict simmers, many Indian bands are falling apart. A 1998 Indian Affairs study found that, ranked as independent countries, on Canada's Indian reserves the average quality of life would fall below that of Mexico, Kazakhstan and Malaysia, based on the United Nations human development index. While Aboriginal court challenges and land claims victories have accelerated during the last decade, the social and political status of First Nations is actually slipping, relative to the rest of the population.

National policies such as Indian self-government have sometimes been unsuccessful in Canada precisely because they have been used as a tool to scale back government obligations in the name of Native rights. The Buffalo challenge goes to the heart of this problem: really, what is Canada's responsibility to Native people? It is a question that goes well beyond the management of assets and natural resources.

"Samson is a good testing ground for the whole federal challenge of the Indian Act," explains Samson counsel James O'Reilly, who engineered the historic victory of the James Bay Cree against Hydro-Québec. "Can the feds do what they want? Or do they have an obligation to provide some level of services and standards?"

What inextricably binds Canada to First Nations is a thing called fiduciary duty: the fundamental responsibilities that stem from federal-Aboriginal partnership. With the Indian Act in 1876, Indians, treatied or not, became literal wards of the Canadian state; likewise, their lands, assets and mineral rights came under the trust of the federal government. As defined by Canada's courts, the federal-Indian relationship is *sui generis:* unique, because it is a trust that exists at a deeper level than any business contract or public law, not quite like any other legal entity.

Of course, if everything had worked according to the government's original assimilation plans, there wouldn't be any more reserves, Indian bands or Indian assets to trouble the federal government. Nor would there be a growing pile of claims and lawsuits. Consequently, today's government is saddled with a complicated web of obligations and responsibilities, partly because of the Indian Act's original, all-controlling designs.

A further complicating factor is federal-provincial relations. While First Nations primarily deal with the federal government, it's the provinces that license natural resources and collect royalties. For the prairie provinces, it's been this way ever since 1930, when the Natural Resources Transfer Act gave them possession and control over the natural riches of Crown lands. (The Atlantic provinces and their offshore oil and gas deposits were not so lucky; most royalty payments ultimately go to the federal government.) Now, some Indian lawyers say that this transfer was illegal.

"If you think about the process of stripping First Nations people, the indigenous peoples, from the land, a big part of the process has been to constrain Indian peoples within the strait-jacket of wardship under control of the federal government," says Tony Hall, professor of Native studies at the University of Lethbridge. "Meanwhile, they hand off the licensing and exploitation of natural resources to a government that claims no jurisdiction, no responsibility, in Indian affairs.

"This is an issue that often doesn't get clarified, but it's really basic to how the whole process of dispossession works. The Indians are contained within the constraints of federal jurisdiction," says Hall, not mincing words. "Meanwhile, as the federal government is constraining its Indian wards within the authority of the Department of Indian Affairs and Indian reserves, the provincial governments are busy doling out licensing—essentially extending themselves into resource companies. Extending their jurisdiction through the leasing of resource companies—which, in a way, become proxies for the provincial government."

When vast sums of money and resources are at stake, conflicts of interest arise. And from the Stoney to the Samson, provincial governments eschew Indian politics because to do otherwise would open up questions about the validity of the original resource transfer and, potentially, erode ownership. "The fear of Aboriginal treaty rights essentially brings in the federal government. It not only speaks of an Indian role in the lands and resources of Canada, it potentially brings the federal government into the resource backyard, into the wealth."

WHEN DAVID LAIRD LAUNCHED the 1876 Indian Act in Parliament, he wasn't thinking about outright genocide. In fact, the politician and former journalist was thinking about responsibility. "Indians must either be treated as minors or as white men," he said. Until Aboriginal people were self-sufficient, Laird reasoned, the government had a duty to ensure their well-being and to protect their interests.

For decades immediately following, federal-Indian relations deteriorated, largely on the basis of an ever-intensifying government campaign to eliminate Aboriginal culture—a policy of "aggressive civilization" best characterized by Canada's residential school system.

In 1984, the Supreme Court took a long, hard look at the Indian Act and delivered a precedent that sent the federal government reeling. In a unanimous judgment, the Supreme Court awarded the Musqueam band of British Columbia ten million dollars for breach of fiduciary obligation. Like Quebec's deadly Oka confrontation in 1990, it all began with a golf course: the federal government, as Indian trustee, had leased Indian land to a Vancouver golf club at rates well below market value. The decision, known as *Guerin v. the Queen,* came as a shock because the government could be held to a higher standard than anyone had previously thought. The kids could sue the parents for substantial damages.

"The government realized just how vulnerable it was, how exposed it was on numerous different fronts to charges," says Rick Ponting, University of Calgary professor of sociology. "The government realized that it had to start making its way out of the Indian Affairs field. And we have various models of self-government that the federal government has negotiated in an attempt to basically offload federal government responsibilities and activities onto First Nations governments—so that the fiduciary responsibilities don't come back to haunt the federal government."

Immediately after the Musqueam decision, Indian Affairs Minister John Crosbie sent a confidential memo to Deputy Minister Bruce Rawson to inquire about the implications of the case. The internal document, entitled "Exploratory Actions Needed," outlined a number of questions that required answers "without undue delay."

"Instead of defending Indian rights or prosecuting incursions on Indian lands, the Department of Justice has often done nothing, or has actually acted against the First Nation interest," noted Crosbie in the memo. "Is the federal government violating its special obligations . . . ?"

By the government's own estimation, a challenge like Victor Buffalo appeared inevitable. "[T]he trust accounts do not have returns which an informed and prudent trustee should be able to earn," noted Crosbie, as he wondered about the likelihood of future litigation. Crosbie called for an immediate, independent assessment of Indian Affairs and its management practices.

When reports came back in 1985, the results looked somewhat grim: "The Indian Minerals West office . . . cannot effectively perform some of the most basic resource management functions."

Another 1984 Indian Affairs report advised that trouble was potentially afoot: "Potential consequences . . . are real," noted the document, "and the exposure of INAC [Indian and Northern Affairs Canada] is high."

Even if mistakes were made, chief Crown counsel Barbara Ritson makes the point that government liability is a separate issue. "We're looking at things that happened forty years ago," she says.

In other words, the legal issue isn't whether or not the government made mistakes, but against what standard should we judge the conduct of a large bureaucracy over the span of several decades? "Just because you have a fiduciary responsibility," she continues, "doesn't mean you have a duty." It might be wrong to judge the legacy of Samson oil and gas by today's sophisticated levels of financial and technical expertise.

Ritson agrees that the Samson case is important, but that O'Reilly and his team will have to produce a sizeable amount of evidence to substantiate the broad, expansive claims that have been levelled against the government. "The plaintiffs have a lot to prove," says Ritson, who has worked on the case since 1989.

Nevertheless, government ineptitude was a well-known fact among insiders at Indian Affairs. "My God, you can't imagine how the government wants to avoid this," says Robert Laboucain, now a business consultant. "They're actually going to be challenged by Indian bands. For what? Maybe one billion dollars? They've got the government by the balls and they know it."

Musqueam was the legal precedent that would eventually found the Victor Buffalo challenge. But it also helps to explain why, at the height of the Hobbema suicide crisis in 1985, the federal government chose to keep its distance from troubled Cree reserves. So badly did Indian Affairs want to remove itself from long-term obligations that even a suicide epidemic seemingly couldn't bring them to action.

A secret 1988 Indian Affairs memo outlined this policy of neglect. The top-level document spoke of "Building for the Future" and "Honouring Obligations," but "at the same time, [the government would] avoid any other commitments to expand the scope of federal financial responsibilities beyond existing arrangements."

With a violent death happening every week at Hobbema between 1985 and 1987, Robert Laboucain made public his concerns in 1986, after failing to convince his superiors to take special measures on several troubled reserves in Alberta.

"When I began to question the Department of Indian Affairs' responsibilities, I got into a number of confrontations with the senior management," he recalls. "It wasn't my place to express concern for the people that were really at the losing end of department policy."

It was a dark time for anyone at the department. But Indian Affairs seemed resolved to steer clear of the First Nations suicide mess and allegations of mismanagement and corruption.

"I'd been there for close to two years. Even the most basic human concern by the Department of Indian Affairs was totally absent," says Laboucain sadly. "It just wasn't there: the cynicism, the constant criticism, the discrimination was profound.

"And I don't see any changes in how these bureaucrats respond now than thirteen years ago. It hasn't changed at all."

I AM SITTING in an executive meeting room on the tenth floor of Edmonton's Peace Hills Trust building. Before me is Victor Buffalo, chairman of Peace Hills Trust and former chief of the Samson nation.

It is important to start at the beginning, says Buffalo.

Fine, I say. The beginning, then.

For the Samson Cree, the sense of betrayal grew shortly after Treaty 6 was signed in 1876. As a massive food shortage ravaged prairie Indians between 1878 and 1883, the federal government ran a mandatory work-for-rations program, despite an explicit Treaty 6 "famine clause" that guaranteed free supplies in the event of an emergency. As Indian commissioner, David Laird found himself presiding over a major social crisis. To many Aboriginal people, Laird is known as the guy who couldn't deliver on treaty promises, despite genuine efforts to lobby Ottawa for assistance. This made him somewhat unpopular. During the prairie famine, Laird found himself dodging bullets from an angry Cree sniper outside his Battleford headquarters. "Feed them . . . or fight them," wrote the harried governor to Ottawa.

The chiefs of the Hobbema Cree nations soon wrote their own angry appeal to Parliament, lamenting the broken spirit of the Indian treaties. "If no attention is paid to our case now we shall conclude that the treaty made with us six years ago was a meaningless matter of form and that the white man has doomed us to annihilation little by little," said Cree chiefs Samson, Bobtail and Ermineskin to John A. Macdonald in 1883. "But the motto of the Indian is, 'If we must die by violence, let us do it quickly.'"

Buffalo recounts these details matter-of-factly. After more than a decade, his case has become another part of day-to-day business, like banking or investing. While serving as chief, Buffalo launched Peace Hills Trust in attempt to ensure the long-term security of Samson assets, some $400 million, currently held by Indian Affairs. Now Canada's largest Aboriginal bank, the institution has amassed Indian-owned assets of more than $450 million.

As a young man in the 1960s, Buffalo worked at a chemical plant and then took training in oil and gas at college in Calgary. His off-reserve time in the oil patch opened his eyes to the white world of business. You have to learn how to take care of yourself.

Around us hangs a collection of modern First Nations art, something the Samson elder points out with pride. Look, he says with a wave of his hand, this is why Indians mean business—we never stopped being Aboriginal, despite everything else.

"The Indian Act never expected that Indians would have a huge amount of money," he jokes. "They didn't expect us Indians to get into business."

Victor Buffalo finds all of this quite funny. A year ago, his lawyers wouldn't return my calls. And now, as Laird's distant offspring, I've come crawling back into Samson territory to find out what kind of war plans they have in store for the Queen. Despite Buffalo's mirth—"You don't look like him," he says—I get the feeling it's payback time. Not for the last dozen years, but for the last hundred.

"I remember the elders saying that we've got to have something in place when the oil and gas is gone," says Victor Buffalo. "When we talk about self-government, we're talking about self-reliance."

The plain truth is that the Samson can't rely on the government as a partner—nor can it go back to buffalo hunting or the dwindling oil supplies beneath its reserve land. The future is closing in. "We just want to exist, not beholden," he says. "We can't hunt. We can't fish—everything is regulated. We're surrounded."

*Victor Buffalo* v. *the Queen* is the last stand in a battle to maintain the Samson Cree—to finally beat the Indian Act at its own game, assume full self-government and become economically self-supporting. But first, they have to beat the government. And after that, they will try to win shared control of off-reserve natural resources.

Like many bands across Canada, the Samson claim they never ceded mineral rights to their traditional territory in central Alberta—an area that happens to encompass some of the largest oil fields in Canada's history. Back rent is owing, they claim, on rights that were never given away.

"It's the resource wealth of Canada that made it the way it is," explains Buffalo. "Lumber, fish, oil: the resources of this country. That's what we're talking about. There's got to be an equitable distribution."

Sometime in the next decade, the Samson nation will attempt to clarify its claim to off-reserve mineral rights. These proceedings, filed separately from the Victor Buffalo lawsuit, are at least several years away from actual court time. But the total of thirty billion dollars claimed against both the federal government and the Alberta provincial government poses an interesting question: if many treaties didn't include subsurface rights, who really owns Canada's vast resource economy? And if Indians have a fair claim, how do we work out an equitable solution between business, government and First Nations?

In Alberta, Saskatchewan, Manitoba and Ontario, treaties that were assumed to be historical surrenders of the existing provincial land mass have become current again.

"It was never our intent to relinquish or extinguish our rights to the lands and resources," explains Laurence Joseph, vice-chief of the Saskatchewan Federation of Indian Nations. "That's what we're asserting today without malice: to get back our traditional territories and stewardship of the land and resources.

"Water rights and mineral rights are included in every square foot of territory that we're claiming," he says. "That's the treaty attitude. Of course the federal government likes to believe otherwise. They'd go all out to try and prove otherwise."

The 1997 Delgamuukw decision of the Supreme Court of Canada affirmed the validity of oral history in a court of law, thereby providing First Nations with a mass of new evidence and testimony. And as tribal elders move to the forefront of court challenges, it is an uncertain time for governments. The argument made by many First Nations is that the delegation of resource rights to the provinces by the federal government was done illegally, in contravention of the spirit and intent of the signed treaties.

Both levels of government could be held responsible for transferring resource rights that weren't entirely theirs. "Now, these guys are going to war," says Robert Laboucain. "They are going to war. If you can prove original Aboriginal title, then what about the retroactive payment of royalties on what has been extracted for seventy-five years? On Crown land, some companies are going to find themselves with new partners.

"The Aboriginal leadership that I've talked to have said they're not going to go after national parks, provincial parks or municipalities or private property," continues Laboucain. "They don't want that political upheaval or backlash from the Canadian public. But when it comes to Crown land, that's up for grabs."

Consequently, governments and companies have begun to take elder testimony and Aboriginal history seriously. The federal government reopened Treaty 8 in northern Alberta to address some unresolved treaty issues. Recent agreements with several bands have included resource-sharing clauses on oil and gas revenues, most notably the Vuntut Gwitchin of Yukon, who now collect 25 percent of all royalties on their traditional lands.

For its part, the Canadian Association of Petroleum Producers has been holding annual face-to-face meetings with prairie First Nations on mineral ownership. They understand the issues and look to the provincial governments—especially oil-rich Alberta—to clarify the status of resource leases that have been granted to them.

The emerging Aboriginal reality poses uncertainties for everyone—the Samson legal gambit is both risky and potentially expensive—and it will be no small accomplishment to negotiate the next several years without a war breaking out. The government tendency, so far, has been to delay and sublimate the natural resource question; it is assumed, perhaps rightly so, that votes cannot be won by cutting energy and land deals with Aboriginal peoples.

As governments dither, many Aboriginal leaders are increasingly defiant. "The treaties were signed with the understanding that we will share," says Laurence Joseph. "We will share. But we did not relinquish or extinguish our rights or ownership of these lands and resources."

This is Indian country today: armies of lawyers, high finance and elder-executives who think in Cree. "Now they forced our hand. They're going to have to contend with us," says Joseph.

VICTOR BUFFALO HAS HIS OWN MISGIVINGS about big lawsuits. They are expensive and antagonistic. And court action doesn't always solve the problem, even if you win.

"The whole thing should have been done on a negotiating basis," he says. "I didn't want to take the government to task. And I debated whether we should file claim." Canada's Indian Claims Commission, though, remains seriously backlogged, often offering reports and decisions that are ignored by federal cabinet.

"The government keeps hiding behind regulations and laws," says Buffalo almost sadly. "I didn't want this."

Already, the federal government has challenged the authority and credibility of reserve politicians. "We've got a lot of skeletons in our closet, too," says Buffalo. "And they'll come out."

To date, the federal government has made one settlement offer on the Samson case—a nine-figure sum that all four Hobbema bands promptly rejected in 1998. "I'm confident that it will be settled," says Buffalo. "It's kind of a Mexican standoff. We're willing to go all the way."

As for the bands' mineral rights claims and disputes with oil companies, time will tell. "It's hard to fight oil and gas," says Victor Buffalo. "Those companies run this country. They are powerful."

The Samson Cree have plenty of their own troubles to worry about, ones that lawsuits probably won't fix.

With intensive community work and programs, the Hobbema suicide rate dropped 74 percent by 1988. But there's the question of self-government and money. In recent years, political scandals have regularly rocked the reserve, leading to a series of inter-Samson lawsuits over election results, alleged money-for-votes schemes, as well as the misappropriation of band funds by elected officials. These, no doubt, are some of the "skeletons" that Buffalo talks about.

A year after our Wetaskawin meeting, the Warriors have reconvened at the Ponoka Tim Hortons. Ponoka locals seem equally fascinated by the Cree activists. There are roughly ten active Warriors at Samson these days—"plus backbenchers"—and they are preoccupied with trying to build Indian democracy.

The Warriors report that the tribal government situation has improved, but band elections are a complete mess. Indian Affairs, in hastily downloading self-government provisions, somehow neglected to work with Aboriginal people to leave a functioning democratic process. Consequently, Samson elections are plagued with disputes, more allegations of vote-buying and yet more lawsuits. "Indian Affairs are the ones who approved the election laws," says one Warrior, "but why did they approve them without a code of conduct or a code of ethics?"

It's a too-familiar set of themes. "They turn their cheek when there's trouble," says another. "They're trying to shy away from their fiduciary duty."

Sometimes, Indian trouble has nothing to do with First Nations or reserves; it has to do with the way Canada itself works at cross-purposes. Canada is in deep conflict with itself: while the legislative arm of government has attempted to manage damage control on First Nations issues, the executive branch—the judiciary—has been affirming indigenous rights and land title at an ever-increasing rate. This is because Canada's courts are duty-bound to protect the honour of the Crown and the integrity of Canadian law—not budgets and litigation fears. At the middle of it all are vast tracts of energy resources— hydro, oil, gas—and scores of unanswered questions about history, ownership and the obligations of government.

In the meantime, many First Nations across Canada are faced with a difficult situation: they must endeavour to improve reserve conditions with an all-powerful federal government that has demonstrated a somewhat limited interest in their long-term welfare. They must co-operate with provincial and federal governments that have also been named as defendants in major lawsuits.

In fact, it all seems like the mess of vested interests that keep eco-disasters like Lorado, the Sydney tar ponds and a growing greenhouse gas question in a state of disarray. This is one of the unique elements of Canadian life, Aboriginal or otherwise: bound by history, law and treaty, there is no alternative to the government.

# ONE LAST BOOM

# Fort McMurray

I T ' S MIDNIGHT ON THE BANK of the Athabasca River as Trish Darling manoeuvres her Haulpak through the dark moonscape of Suncor Energy Inc.'s Steepbank mine. Lit by the floodlights of her giant truck, the darkness speeds by. We pass deep craters, diesel-fired arc lights and three-storey cable-pull shovels that are eating away at the broad banks of the Athabasca River. In the truck box is a heaping four-hundred-tonne load of oil sands, a rich mixture of dirt and the molasses-like oil called bitumen that will soon become two hundred barrels of synthetic crude.

Despite the payload, we are rocking along at thirty to fifty kilometres an hour, pitching and bouncing over obstacles that would bust an axle on a car. Having tires that are almost twice my height helps, of course, as does a 2,700-horsepower diesel electric engine. "These rigs are so easy to drive," Darling says modestly, pointing to an on-board computer and a bank of automated controls. "It's just the size that's tricky—like driving an apartment."

The few normal-sized pickups that roam the mine site are duly cautious. Komatsu Haulpaks and the slightly larger Caterpillar 979s roam the pits. On at least one occasion, one of the bigger trucks mistakenly crushed a regular truck like a bug—the driver, secured high above in the cockpit, apparently didn't even notice. We hit a soft spot in the mine's loose soil and lurch sideways, and the whole truck seems afloat, rolling on a black ocean.

Darling came to Suncor seventeen years ago as a summer student from college. She was one of the first women employed in the mines, a local girl from Fort McMurray, thirty kilometres to the south, who now expertly commands some of the largest industrial hardware in the world. Darling still marvels at the sight of it all: huge trucks that roar in and out of the darkness, shovels as big as dinosaurs that can load a rig in under two minutes and the maze of ever-changing mine roads that snake up and down the valley. Three oncoming Haulpaks rumble past in high gear, fresh from delivering their cargo to mechanized hoppers that will crush the black sand and ready it for processing. The whole mine seems to shake as they pass. "It's straightforward truckin' usually," she says. "There's hard roads here—just not very smooth."

Women are often known as better drivers in the pits. "Females are tidier and keep their machines cleaner," Darling explains. "They're not trying to hot-rod." She admits that she's been driving carefully tonight so that I don't bounce off my bumper seat and bash my head on the roof of the cab. The operator booth on top of the truck is comfortable but compact. Her favourite feature, it turns out, isn't the computer display that delivers instructions and directions, nor the suspension seat that cushions the shock of the road and protects her neck from whiplash. It's the little electrical socket behind her seat that can run electronics and household appliances. Having recently returned from maternity leave, Trish Darling is still nursing her newborn son and uses the outlet to run her breast pump on coffee breaks. "It works excellent," she says. "They don't care how I spend my breaks, so I bring a little insulated bag with some bottles and sit here and fill them up with milk. That's how I've fed my baby."

Tonight, half the trucks are hauling overburden—the top layer of earth that covers the sands, anywhere from fifteen to twenty metres deep. Muskeg, soil and the gritty bitumen are shuffled around as though the mine were a giant sandbox, and drivers are constantly ferrying loads of earth to expose the oil sands as the mine expands.

Based on surface and subsurface calculations, Alberta's bitumen deposits are one of the greatest single petroleum resources in the world—some 2.5 trillion barrels of oil, 300 billion of which are recoverable—comparable to the proven crude reserves of Saudi Arabia. Over an area that stretches from Cold Lake and Lloydminster, east of Edmonton, to the upper reaches of the Athabasca River and east to the Peace River, four different deposits cover an area as large as New Brunswick. Of these, the Athabasca deposit of Fort McMurray is by far the largest: 4.3 million hectares, roughly twice the size of Lake Ontario.

Darling's load is part of what is fuelling the last and perhaps the greatest single oil boom in Canadian history. Some seventy years after the first commercial attempts to extract oil from sand, Athabasca's dark pits are the epicentre of the largest industrial expansion in living memory: more than $38 billion in new projects have been announced since 1996—a total that had risen to $51 billion by 2001. After decades of false starts, the persistent upward spiral of oil, falling production costs and tax breaks have helped to kick-start an oil sands resurgence. By 2025, the National Energy Board estimates that upwards of 70 percent of Canadian oil production will be from Alberta's bitumen deposits, much of it taken from a concentrated array of open-pit mines and underground wells that surround Fort McMurray.

Like all booms, this one will shower prosperity on many. From welders at the mines to local real estate speculators to distant shareholders in the oil companies, many are already enjoying its benefits. Since 1999, the population in the Fort McMurray region, including the construction camps, has grown from 43,000 to 51,000, and people keep coming.

But it's unclear what the boom-to-end-all-booms will mean for the ecological well-being of the area. Not only are some of the biggest strip mines in the world being carved out next to the flowing Athabasca, but air pollution is expected to rise dramatically in a place that is already a national hot spot for greenhouse gases. Combined, the two oil sands plants in production—Suncor and Syncrude—are already the fourth-largest source of carbon dioxide emissions in Canada. These emissions risk giving Canada a permanent black eye internationally for new development, in response to growing export markets, that will add additional tonnes of carbon dioxide to the atmosphere. Based on initial predictions, the carbon-intensive refining and mining process could also emit enough nitrogen and sulphur to acidify lakes and soil throughout the region. While each project is obliged to respect provincial environmental guidelines, the cumulative effects of this massive industrial mobilization threaten the ecological health of a major slice of Alberta.

Frontiers have always defined Canada, from the fur trade to hydro power, and this northern boom shows how, despite everything else, Canada is rediscovering the oil age—in the face of potentially costly consequences.

THE FLIGHT NORTH TO FORT MCMURRAY traverses the lush boreal forest of northern Alberta: below, a carpet of green and brown stretches out, spotted with small lakes and the occasional road. With few exceptions, it is a thick wilderness that does not relent until the barren tundra lands of the Northwest Territories. The muskeg looks cold and empty from above, but its murky deeps harbour an incredible biomass of plants and micro-organisms that, as ecologists have noted, rivals only the rain forest in its atmospheric curative powers.

Only at the very edge of the city does the bush suddenly transform into houses and sidewalks. With northern lights that shimmer at night and a winter sun that never wanders far from the horizon, it is closer to the Arctic than any town in Ontario—well north of the fifty-fifth parallel—but there's also a newly opened sushi bar and fourteen different shopping centres and strip malls. Out on the edge of the city, suburbs are forged out of bush and schools now stand where once only moose dared to tread. The divide between north and south in Canada—between urban dwellers huddled along the U.S. border and remote hamlets that forge a living from the hinterland—is fading.

At the oil sands, a war of attrition is being waged on the North—an army has descended and has transformed what was once unwieldy muskeg and endless forest. Fort McMurray and the nearby Aboriginal community of Fort MacKay have seen it all before. This is an area that has been trying to hit it big since the Depression: from 1930, when the International Bitumen Company shipped its first three hundred barrels south, to 1964 when the Great Canadian Oil Sands was launched on today's Suncor site, not a single commercial or experimental operation managed to deliver the promised windfall. An anticipated boom in the mid-1970s with the launch of Syncrude—the largest oil sands operation in the world—never quite materialized.

Back in the Steepbank mine control room, memories of the past booms still linger. Sitting in front of the controls while fourteen Haulpaks criss-cross paths as blips on his computer screen, dispatcher Doug Harpe recalls the ebb and flow of the city that has always been billed as the Next Big Thing. "There's been three booms," he says. "Before Great Canadian [Oilsands], there was just a dirt road through town." His dad and his uncles worked the plant for thirty years—Doug is a second-generation oil sands kid who can remember what Fort McMurray looked like before pavement.

"Then there was Syncrude—six thousand crazy construction workers running around town." He shakes his head. "Every girl in town was pregnant. Lines into all the bars, lots of crime and people living in tents." Even in the year 2000, Fort McMurray's campgrounds were once again full and, despite all the money around town, the current boom is slightly less raucous than the previous one. Residents are more settled and many people are cagier with their money. Especially developers, who haven't met the demand for housing because many are justifiably reluctant to sink money into projects based on an ever-changing set of expansion plans.

No longer are there nightly brawls in the parking lot of the Oil Sands Hotel, a legendary hot spot that still carries a reputation. The burly, beer-swilling hordes that roamed Fort McMurray during the 1970s oil sands boom have given way to a new kind of oil worker. Like Trish Darling, many have a university degree and children—and growing numbers are Aboriginal, recruited from the Cree and Chippewa communities of the region.

Around the city, help-wanted signs hang everywhere. Retail and fast-food businesses can't find employees because the cost of living is so high. People who work counter jobs are usually planning their next move; locals still talk about when the Tim Hortons drive-through window closed temporarily because of a staffing shortage. Indeed, Fort McMurray is the kind of place where someone can go from earning minimum wage to sixty thousand dollars in a single year.

This might explain why there seems to be a twenty-four-hour lineup at the Tim's drive-through window. Here, a continual orbit of trucks and minivans arrive for coffee, crullers and muffins, regardless of whether it's 9 A.M. or 1 A.M. Most of the vehicles are brand-new—top-line Chevy trucks mingle with Ford Explorers—and most seem to be arriving or returning from the mines. As dawn breaks this morning, schoolteachers rub shoulders with scruffy construction workers, and Chippewa from Fort MacKay line up behind exotic dancers from the south. A few locals tut-tut as the working girls breeze through Tim's—five phone-book pages' worth of escort services and private massage parlours have popped up around the city during the last few years. This, along with traffic jams, Toronto-priced rents and a busy casino, are the telltale signs of a boom town.

The years of boom and bust have, ironically enough, culti-
vated a more sober, work-minded populace. Despite all the
growth and upheaval, a one-year work stay often turns into a
decade. Carolyn Slade travelled from Newfoundland twenty-
one years ago during the Syncrude boom. As manager of
Suncor's Borealis Lodge, she oversees the temporary residence
for 5,000 construction workers who are currently building
Suncor's six-billion-dollar expansion. Located just down the
road from the towering construction site, the Borealis is billed
as Canada's largest hotel. But it's no place for a holiday. "The one
thing I find different than down east is that people come here to
work—they're very focused," Carolyn says as we sit in the
cavernous 2,500-seat dining room. "Nobody relaxes. You're
friends with a lot of people but it's very rare to drop by for a cup
of coffee. My dad says he can't keep up with the pace here."

Back in 1966, some two thousand men assembled on this very
site during the construction of the Great Canadian Oil Sands
(GCOS) project. In the December 10, 1964, edition of the *Fort
McMurray Oil Sands Review,* a supplement to Uranium City's
*Northland News,* writer Gareth Crandal outlined plans for "the
biggest oil boom ever . . . pitting knowledge and scientific
discovery against one of nature's most twisted secrets—the
bond which interlocks the oil with the sand." A number of key
personnel were recruited from Uranium City's failed Gunnar
mine operation for construction and field testing, just as the
home-strapped Fort McMurray barged a number of Uranium
City homes up the Athabasca during the 1980s after the closing
of the Beaverlodge mine. But in the 1960s, Fort McMurray
was the junior settlement that, according to the biweekly, was
already wrestling with a burgeoning traffic problem, as well as
an anticipated housing shortage, several years before the first
major operation even opened.

There's been a recurrent influx ever since. "Most of these
men come here because they can't find jobs where they're

located," says Carolyn, noting that an ongoing invasion of tradespeople is expected to boost the regional population by another ten thousand over the next several years. From Syncrude to Shell, all the projects feature temporary on-site accommodation to house thousands of construction workers who would otherwise be homeless.

These insta-towns on the edge of the highway compete with each other for labour; the Borealis, nicknamed "the palace," is the latest and most expensive gambit thus far. With several multi-storey wings that extend from a large dining and leisure hub at the centre, it is as though a university residence has morphed into an industrial-strength complex that serves ten thousand hot meals every day. As we stroll through the halls, the kitchen and the various common rooms, Carolyn reviews the details of her military-scale logistics planning: forty-eight cases of lunch cheese are consumed daily, along with ten thousand pastries. And for some unknown reason, a regular count reveals that three hundred steak knives go missing each week. She pauses and points at a can of evaporated milk that sits on the counter of a common-room kitchen: "This is how you know that we have lots of easterners—nobody else will touch the stuff in their coffee."

After two decades of sporadic emigration, Newfoundlanders constitute between 18 and 25 percent of Fort McMurray's population—an estimated fifteen thousand have moved here, making it Newfoundland's "third-largest city." Most have a story about a friend or a relative from down east who slept on a floor or a couch while working through fast-food shifts into a lucrative oil sands job. Out at the recently expanded Fort McMurray airport, Lori Sweeney has worked the Avis Rent A Car desk for almost a year. "I didn't like it here at first," she says. "I cried for the first day or so. But once I got a job, it was good enough. When I went back to see what I'd left, I realized that the only thing I miss is family.

"The bush and trees are pretty much the same layout—the rent is high and the groceries are cheaper," says Lori, who recently made a down payment on a double-wide mobile home. Fixing a regular address is no small achievement; a bachelor apartment that rented for $500 three years ago now runs almost $1,400 a month.

"People gather at the Newfoundlanders' Club—same as home—and you can get all the Newfie products you want here: Purity candy, salt beef, Black Horse Beer. You pay more but it's a little taste o' home."

ON A CHILLY MORNING, I drive north to the mines with Brenda Erskine, Suncor's communications manager. Leaving Fort McMurray behind, we speed along a newly opened four-lane highway that snakes along the Athabasca River valley. Every day, up to 240 buses ferry workers out to the Syncrude and Suncor oil sands sites, which lie just across the road from each other. Until recently, the twice-daily rush hour would clog up and stop traffic on the highway, just like Toronto's notorious expressways.

Already, there's talk of a new six-lane highway, tacit recognition of what is probably Canada's most northerly case of chronic gridlock. When conventional oil supplies start to decline around 2007, says the National Energy Board, oil sands production, already supplying 50 percent of the nation's oil, will be roaring. Canadian subsidiaries of the anglo-Dutch company Shell, and of U.S. corporations Mobil and Koch Industries, have all announced new projects. "Better make that an eight-lane highway," jokes Erskine, as we pass another convoy of trucks.

We crest a hill at Poplar Creek to the sight of a huge pink and brown cloud hovering over the highway, an air mass so thick that it throws a shadow on the road and blots out the other side of the creek valley. Plunging into it, we follow the road down along the bottom of the valley and up the other side. The cloud is flat-topped, and its low altitude signifies a cold-weather inversion, common to these parts. But the pink-brown cloud is not smog. The pollution is of mysterious origin—there are no forest fires at this time of year, and the local lumber operation doesn't appear to be burning anything.

Erskine drives along in embarrassed silence. She has just finished briefing me on Suncor's environmental gains, which, for an oil company, are considerable. Back in 1996, it installed a state-of-the-art sulphur scrubber system that removes 95 percent of the sulphur dioxide—a noxious gas that contributes to acid rain—from its electricity and steam-generation plant. It was a major pioneering investment for the region.

As the Suncor plant comes into view at the bottom of the river valley—a city of pipes, tanks and towers that throws steam and smoke more than a hundred metres into the air—it's pretty obvious that the smog came from down the valley. Several kilometres away, Syncrude's giant stacks belch out the same pinkish brown muck that we drove through earlier.

"They've had a tough year," says Erskine cautiously, reluctant to comment on her competitor's operations. "They're not running at efficiency," meaning that technical troubles have wreaked havoc with the plant's coking and processing systems.

The previous fall, an explosion inside a Syncrude fractionator tower, which separates hydrocarbon vapours, crippled operations. This, in turn, has made production more expensive, the bane of oil sands operations. At the end of 2000, one of Syncrude's investors said the production problems had caused a temporary jump in operating costs from $12.64 a barrel to about $17. Still, that's a far cry from the 1980s, when it cost $26 to produce a barrel. (By contrast, at press time, the world price for different grades of crude ranged from $24 to $28 a barrel.)

Only later do I discover that in the month of July 2000 alone, Syncrude exceeded provincial air quality limits of sour gas no fewer than twenty-four times, including peak levels in excess of 80 parts per billion (ppb)—eight times the guideline—as well as several smaller sour gas incidences measured at the station closest to Suncor. Within two more months, another twenty-three sour gas incidents were measured in the area, including a 99-ppb peak next to Syncrude.

With human risk currently confined to the thousands of employees and contractors who live and work on site, the pattern of recurrent emissions spikes has not slowed the pace of development. In 1998, Syncrude—a ten-company consortium that includes the Alberta Energy Company as well as Canadian subsidiaries of the Exxon and Chevron corporations—announced a six-billion-dollar plan to double its annual output to 155 million barrels by 2007. Already the world's largest oil sands operation, Syncrude has an environmental Web site that reassures readers that "in 20 years of operation, it has never had a fine, sentence or control order imposed on it for non-compliance."

As we roll into the Suncor complex, our truck is dwarfed by the massive scale of the oil sands plant: in between pipelines and power lines that weave across the ten-kilometre site, there are a power plant, extraction plants, coking towers, fractionating towers, storage tanks, a laboratory and nearby tailings ponds. Between the construction site and the mine expansion across the river, seventy-four different cranes tower overhead and huge silver coking drums point skyward like rockets, ready to be lifted into position by a small army of workers. It all resembles an earthbound space station—or a science experiment that's run amok. There are even street signs within this city of steel: Bitumen Heights, Tar Island Avenue, Diesel Alley and Refinery Row.

It's hard to ignore the giant flares that burn off sulphur-laden gases and a plethora of other hydrocarbon waste. Before the addition of sulphur scrubbers, studies conducted between 1976 and 1985 showed that a number of sensitive lichens, considered a bellwether for air quality, had disappeared within five kilometres of the Suncor plant.

Despite all the expensive hardware of today's operations, squeezing oil from sand still requires all manner of extreme heat, hot water and pulverizing force to produce marketable crude for the south. When earth is dumped into a hopper at the edge of the mine, two sets of five-metre-long rotating teeth grind it into a paste, rejecting boulders and sending it down a water-fed pipeline to the main plant. There, the raw bitumen slurry is fed into a series of huge rotating drums. It is as though one has entered a dark, sulphuric laundromat. Every grain of sand is covered in a thin layer of oil; as the drums infuse the sand with steam and hot water, the oil begins to separate. It's a process that was invented by Dr. Karl Clark in 1923 and is still widely used. Even Suncor's $2.8-billion expansion plans call for more of these steel drums.

For a period during the 1950s, though, nuclear weapons were given serious consideration as an extraction process. "One imaginative tar sands enthusiast dreamed up the idea in 1957 (while gazing at a flaming sunset in the oil fields of Saudi Arabia) of using the power of an underground nuclear blast to get the bitumen flowing," Larry Pratt recounts in his 1976 book, *The Tar Sands: Syncrude and the Politics of Oil*. "For a time the idea was touted by Richfield Oil Company, one of the principals in the Syncrude project, but the scheme ran afoul of Canada's disarmament image about 1960."

Churned bitumen froth from Clark's tumblers is pumped into a series of separator cells. These are steel cones that stand twenty-four metres tall and allow sand, clay and water to sink to the bottom: at the top is a four-metre head of pure, unrefined bitumen that's skimmed off like cream. Roughly 6,500 tonnes of oil sand moves through these cells every hour in a building that tops fifty degrees Celsius in the summertime. Afterwards, a maze of high-pressure filters and centripetal spinners infuses the separated bitumen with naphtha—carrying a smell that would offend the dead—and the clay-hydrocarbon-sand waste water mixture is piped off to five large tailings ponds at the edge of the site.

In the upgrading process, the whole operation begins to resemble a conventional oil refinery, where complex hydrocarbon molecules are cracked by heat and separated within a series of tall fractionating towers. Different kinds of molecules for gasoline, kerosene and naphtha are captured as they float up through the towers—heated at 675 degrees Celsius—and are then diverted into separate holding tanks.

"Everything is used—even the waste gases off the fractionator," explains Lorne Bernardo, as he mixes a shipment of crude for pipeline delivery to Edmonton where it will be refined further and pipelined off to customers in Canada and the United States. During the local refining process, sulphur is often added, along with hydrogen: extra hydrogen molecules create synthetic crude, and the extra sulphur, if the customers order it, adds energy. Although some sour gas gets recycled back into the plant and some is flared outside, adding sulphur to gasoline is, Bernardo explains, necessary to accommodate the network of old refineries that import the oil sands crude for processing.

Oddly, some of the crude will return to Fort McMurray. There's no local refinery that can produce automotive-grade gasoline, so gas retailers must import from the south. Consequently, those who live next to the world's largest hydrocarbon resource usually pay more for gas than Calgary or Edmonton.

ON PAPER, THE OIL SANDS look like one of the best things that has ever happened to Canada: fossil fuels are a necessary part of our economy, good or bad, so we might as well produce them here at home. Athabasca Oil Sands Developers (AOSD), the regional planning group, estimates the oil sands are responsible for the creation of 44,000 new jobs across Canada—and a total of $216 million in public revenues stemming from the first $33 billion to be spent.

And despite the massive scale of development, the impression is that nothing has been left to chance. "Oil sands developers are among Canada's largest investors in new environmental technologies," reports the AOSD in its landmark June 2000 study, *Progress in Canada's Oil Sands*. "Their environmental performance is competitive among the world's oil producers.

"In the past 5 years, oil sands developers have invested 30 cents of every dollar on technologies that enhance environmental performance," AOSD continues. "And $CO_2$ emissions per barrel of oil produced will be reduced 45 per cent from 1990 levels."

But the truth is that in the face of an industrial expansion that has few rivals anywhere on earth, there's nothing that can stop a steady increase in greenhouse gases. The region's various projects are expected to collectively produce three million barrels a day by 2015. And by the same year, the National Energy Board estimates that total greenhouse gas emissions from oil sands synthetic crude and bitumen will be forty-nine megatonnes—more than double the output of 2000.

Under the terms of the international climate-change agreement first negotiated in Kyoto, Japan, Canada agreed to reduce its greenhouse gas emissions to 6 percent below 1990 levels by

2010. Oil sands developments, however, are taking us in the opposite direction; current projections show that Canada will miss its goal by between 140 and 185 megatonnes. As much as a quarter of the overshoot will comprise emissions from oil sands projects.

Yet it would be hard to describe the two resident companies as reckless; they have expanded as markets and investors dictated, under the rules and guidelines set out by provincial and federal regulators. Indeed, of all the energy corporations operating in Canada, Suncor is often considered the most environmentally friendly. In anticipation of Canada's international commitment to reduce the industrial emissions that are accelerating global warming, Suncor has invested in wind-power projects, rain-forest cultivation and biomass generation. The amount of sulphur it emits per barrel produced has declined considerably—some 75 percent since 1990—thanks to expensive stack scrubbers. Suncor is also reducing its carbon dioxide emissions, from 1.045 tonnes per unit of production in 1990 to half that by 2005.

Despite these efforts, all other emissions continue to climb in sync with Suncor's burgeoning industrial expansion. The operations are getting cleaner, relatively speaking, but they are expanding, so the volume of pollution is increasing. Daily emissions of nitrogen oxides increased by 54 percent between 1994 and 1998. And Suncor's growth is driving its greenhouse gas emissions through the roof: from 4.9 megatonnes of carbon dioxide in 1990 to nearly 10 megatonnes by 2002. Nearby at Syncrude, with almost double the capacity, emissions are already close to the 8-megatonne mark.

But unlike some oil corporations that indiscriminately drill wells and disappear, fixed-site operations like Suncor don't have escape plans. This, says Vice-president Kevin Nabholtz, is why both Suncor and Syncrude can be trusted to maintain healthy standards: most of their executives and workers live here permanently. "I know most of the senior executives here," he says. "They're all people with kids and family—and they don't want health impacts."

Both companies hope to reduce their rate of carbon dioxide output and collect enough carbon offsets, such as renewable energy investments, to soften the bottom line. Suncor sports a new cogeneration power plant that burns natural gas to simultaneously generate electricity and steam, achieving an energy efficiency of approximately 85 percent, compared with conventional utility plants, which sometimes extract only 30 percent of their fuel's true energy value. Syncrude has had a cogeneration plant for years.

Reducing consumption is one part of the climate change imperative; energy savings is the other. Still, vast profits have been made from decades of wasteful energy consumption. Oil sands, of course, inject new life into the energy status quo: Canada can now burn gasoline for the next one hundred years. In 2010, for every day's supply of oil sands crude that is consumed by cars, trains and planes across North America, an estimated total of 1.5 billion kilos of carbon dioxide—1.5 megatonnes—will have been released from strip mine to tailpipe. As with other fossil fuels, the majority of emissions from a hydrocarbon molecule come from combustion, not production or refining.

UP AT THE SYNCRUDE SITE, an enormous network of open-pit mines, tailings ponds and extraction plants edges towards the Aboriginal community of Fort MacKay, now less than twenty kilometres away. Ron Pauls, a Syncrude environmental scientist, stands next to a paddock of wood bison that inhabit the region's largest land-reclamation project. The 270-head buffalo ranch was set up in 1993 as a co-operative project between Syncrude and Fort MacKay. Sometime in the future, says Pauls, the people of Fort MacKay will run the 330-hectare bison farm themselves.

Land reclamation has become a big issue, says Pauls, precisely because of the enormous expansion that's been launched—and because so much of the existing strip mine remains to be reclaimed. "Just from the sheer land space disturbance, it's huge—three hundred square kilometres alone," he says of Syncrude's expansion. "That's the big issue: what's the landscape going to look like once the mine site is reclaimed?"

Syncrude's old mine is a five-by-seven-kilometre crater in the earth—nearby tailings ponds that settle out waste water, hydrocarbon and sand cover some twenty-five square kilometres. "Reclamation thirty years ago was football fields of grass." Pauls looks out over the rolling hills and low bush of the new land. "The science of it stalled before mining—so they're now learning about refugia, smaller plots of land, terraforming. Muskeg, for example, contains all sorts of seeds and spores needed for reclamation, so you don't garbage it any more." It's not boreal forest, he admits—muskeg, marsh and fens can't yet be reproduced—but it does offer an opportunity for wood bison to thrive. (Ironically, climate change is slowly pushing grassland terrain north into the boreal forest—so the synthetic grasslands of Fort McMurray are ahead of their time.)

"The other issue is emissions," Pauls says, acknowledging Syncrude's recent troubles. "When you get flammable liquids under great pressure, accidents do happen. But I'm always amazed that somebody always knows what's coming from those pipes."

Indeed, the region boasts one of the world's most extensive live-monitoring systems for airborne pollution: the Wood Buffalo Environmental Association, run by companies and community members. Essentially, Syncrude and Suncor have paid millions so that within hours of an emissions spike, everyone on the planet can read about it via the Internet, although only one fine has ever been levied—against Suncor in 1982.

Pauls points to a recent two-million-dollar Alberta Health study that found Fort McMurray's air quality and the health of its residents comparable to those of other like-sized cities. Essentially, he says, locals have more to worry about from forest fires and smoking. Readings from live monitors near Fort McMurray are manageable, despite periodic jumps.

In fact, the oil sands seem to be largely self-regulating. Although the official regulator, the Alberta Energy and Utilities Board (EUB), examines each individual project (with the input of Alberta Environment), it has yet to delay or stop any projects on environmental grounds.

Locally, there is a complex and sometimes antagonistic set of relations between stakeholders: First Nations, community members, governments and companies are collectively charged with managing the fate of the region. Personal fortunes, jobs and environmental health are all on the line. Pauls chairs the air quality committee of the Cumulative Effects Management Association, the regional task force that's grappling with all the region's environmental and social concerns. It is a mind-boggling responsibility; some seventy-three different issues have been identified, from acid emissions to ecosystem sustainability, heavy metals and air contamination. Like Pauls, most participants are knowledgeable, but they already have full-time jobs. So things are a little behind schedule.

"There is the possibility that projections of cumulative effects will arrive after the projects have begun," Pauls admits. "The EUB says that things might have to change later on."

IN MAY 2001, ALBERTA ENVIRONMENT Minister Lorne Taylor paid his first visit to the oil sands. He wasn't there to run tests or scold polluters; he was there because he wanted to speed up Alberta's regulatory approval process for large industrial projects. Along with a rush demand for new power plants, many of the $51 billion in proposed oil sands projects hadn't yet been approved. Alberta wanted to shorten the waiting time by kicking its bureaucracy into high gear. "A shortened time line does not mean less rigorous," he assured the local daily, *Fort McMurray Today*. "We'll become more rigorous as we go forward in the years to come." Taylor promised an extra $3 million to make sure that enough consultants could be hired to expedite the official evaluation process.

Some five hundred kilometres to the south, at Alberta's Pembina Institute—an independent energy watchdog and think-tank based in Drayton Valley—Tom Marr-Laing worries about Fort McMurray, the city in which he spent his high school years. Unlike Taylor, Marr-Laing worries about the true cost of moving too quickly to cash in on American and Canadian energy demand.

"You can't reasonably decide to go ahead on projects when we don't know the effects," he says, explaining that the "guided development" philosophy of oil sands regulation leaves too many unanswered questions. In addition to the climate concerns—which are considerable—Marr-Laing estimates that the cumulative-effects evaluation is about three to five years behind schedule.

"A year ago, the estimated daily output was 1.6 million barrels a day by 2010," he says. "Now they are saying it is going to be 3 million, which will exceed Alberta's acidification limits." Marr-Laing is referring to a potential regional acid-rain problem from over-deposition of sulpher and nitrogen oxides that could stretch from Fort McMurray, across the Saskatchewan border and north to Fort Chipewyan, on Lake Athabasca. Based on initial projections, the most affected region would be the immediate 1.1-million-hectare area surrounding Fort MacKay and Fort McMurray.

It's difficult to estimate the potential damage, because some parts of the boreal forest are more sensitive than others. "It's a real patchwork of different ecological systems, very different from other parts of the country," says Marr-Laing, recalling his youth spent tromping around the bush. "You walk fifteen feet, and you're in a different wetland—and all respond differently to acidification."

Moreover, some of the largest new projects are underground extraction wells, known as in situ projects, which are less intrusive than open-pit mines but haven't been fully evaluated for their effects on the boreal forest, underground-water quality and airborne emissions. Nevertheless, this is the way of the future, since most oil sands reserves lie well beyond the reach of shovels and trucks. A single project—Suncor's Firebag in situ—will cover a staggering 839 square kilometres.

Efforts to manage growth on the fly don't seem to worry Bob Scotten, executive director of the Wood Buffalo Environmental Association. Scotten says that, according to readings from live monitors near Fort McMurray, development is manageable, despite periodic spikes. "When you're investing billions and if you don't have a sustainable environmental policy, you're not going to last here," he says. And for the future? Newcomers will have to learn how to co-operate with regional and local authorities to ensure public health and environmental responsibility.

The teamwork ethos in Fort McMurray is impressive—the ups and downs of the oil sands have knit people together in a unique way. But really, some of the world's largest corporations have converged in a process where nobody can accurately predict outcomes. Isn't that cause for concern? "Right now, I don't think we have an understanding of how it all might come together," admits Bob Scotten.

Bob stresses that accurate and timely information is vital. This doesn't change the fact that, when queried about local environmentalists, he immediately lists a number of company scientists and consultants. I rephrase my question: there's no lack of friendly experts here, Bob, but I'm looking for someone who doesn't have a vested interest in non-stop expansion. He offers up the name of the Wood Buffalo Environmental Association's sole community representative from Fort McMurray, Anne Dort-Mclean.

Anne is the president of the Fort McMurray Environmental Association (FMEA), a lonely posting in a resource-driven boom town. When I visit her at her day job as manager of the local

Boys and Girls Club, Anne questions the 2000 Alberta Health report and its rosy picture of Fort McMurray's air quality. "I think their process was a little flawed, the methodology wasn't explained." With all of Fort McMurray's new residents, a significant portion of the sample more accurately reflected the health situation of other communities: the persistent turnover in Fort McMurray's population makes it difficult to accurately appraise cumulative health effects. Anne recalls community members who suffered severe asthma—including former FMEA members who left Fort McMurray precisely because of health concerns. There's no epidemic per se, but it might not be long, she says, before Fort McMurray develops a big-city air-quality problem.

And despite all the studies and committees, it has become more difficult to question development. "For a while it was okay to be an environmentalist—it was never popular—but lately it's become a dirty word," says Anne. "You want to stop programs, stop jobs, people say—but of course it's not about that.

"Because it's a one-industry town, there's an unhealthy paranoia to say anything bad—say if you've got a brother at a camp. Employees are reluctant."

As kids pour in downstairs for after-school activities, Anne wonders if the whole environmental evaluation process isn't already a foregone conclusion. "Even with good intentions, I don't know if they can do anything before the damage is done."

BERTHA GANTER IS A FORT MACKAY Chippewa who grew up on traplines that are now being eroded by a growing web of access roads and construction traffic. As environmental representative for Fort MacKay's Indian Resource Council, she negotiates environmental and socio-economic agreements with nearby companies in an effort to moderate the impact of development.

"It's scary. At MacKay, we're uncertain about what the future holds," she says. "The community is situated on lands that aren't claim-settled. And when you look ten to fifteen years down the road, maybe sooner, this place is not going to be healthy to live in."

We're sitting in Smitty's restaurant in downtown Fort MacKay—all around us are local families and business meetings. Everyone seems alive and flush with the fruits of the boom. There is a sense of optimism here that Bertha and others from Fort MacKay—and even downriver in Fort Chipewyan—don't necessarily share. "I know there is great concern among the elders: they blame industry for their illnesses, but there's no way to actually prove it," she says. "They keep saying they never had these kinds of illnesses before industry came—thirty, thirty-five years ago. There was no asthma before.

"I never had asthma. My kids never had asthma—I raised them on a farm near Edmonton. But my two oldest grandchildren in Fort MacKay have asthma and skin problems. So I question what might be doing that."

Up until the 1960s, the people of Fort MacKay lived off the land. But they quit fishing the Athabasca River forever in the early 1970s after the federal government put out an advisory about high mercury concentrations that had likely leached from pulp mills and, some argue, nearby tailings ponds. They were advised to eat only one meal of fish every week. "So when the elders heard that they just said—forget that, don't eat anything, because if it's bad once a week, then it's no good at all.

"Years ago, before industry, we used to camp all along the river: the men would hunt—moose, rabbits, whatever—and the women would pick berries. We'd be there all summer—like summer holidays. With the fishing being lost, there's nobody camping on the river any more."

In addition to the loss of the river and the disappearance of moose, more subtle changes are happening. Elders notice that the plants are drying up, says Bertha. In the winter, they see black soot on the snow, so they don't use snow for water in the traplines; they carry it in with them. "Whenever we go out to the trapline, I bring water. I wouldn't drink the water here, even in the small creeks."

Alberta's boreal forest face is part of an industrial transformation that people at Fort MacKay have been witnessing for thirty years. The area has been carved up by forestry, access roads and drill sites, and the influx of oil sands extraction is yet another strain on Canada's largest ecosystem, a network of 100,000 species whose carbon-scrubbing biomass is 50-percent water. In Alberta's boreal, for example, only 9 percent remains wild. In Manitoba and Quebec, hydro dams have flooded or damaged one-fifth of the boreal swath that stretches from Labrador to Yukon, an affected area the size of Lake Ontario that includes no small amount of traditional First Nations territory.

The sense of loss is pervasive. "Trapping doesn't make sense as a business any more," says Bertha. "But those traplines are where we teach our kids all the traditional things."

Every year Bertha takes MacKay's elders on tours of the plants to inspect what's happening and see what's growing. "Last year we took them to Suncor's Steepbank mine—and where you see that bridge that was Tar Sands Hill: the best blueberry patch in the whole region. It was just blue—cranberries, raspberries. And when we took elders across there, a couple of them cried. Their blueberry patch was gone forever. It's hard on them."

"We were planning to take them to Albian Sands [a new project site] just recently cleared. It was a beautiful spot, but nothing left. So I've been putting off taking them. But they should see it. When I first went out there after the clearing, it really bothered me: about fifty to seventy-five square kilometres emptied flat.

"It's history lost, it's culture lost—values are changing with industrialization: fewer family get-togethers, everybody working to keep up with the pace. I mean, the speed of development up here is just unreal."

Despite everything, some Fort MacKay elders advise companies on reclamation: they choose plants that were native prior to strip mining and give grudging approval to projects that slice up traditional traplines. They've been accused of compromise, but they're achieving results. Unlike Hobbema's legal war of attrition, the strategy of co-operation and company partnership has meant that local employment is high, thanks to community projects signed into company agreements and ongoing corporate efforts to hire Aboriginal workers. Educating companies about the land has also meant that Aboriginal peoples have been able to see more integrity in reclamation efforts: knowledge from elders is increasingly being incorporated into terraforming. Just a few months ago, says Bertha, some elders happened upon a patch of wild strawberries on reclaimed land.

She's not sure what's next. "It seems like at every meeting I'm going to, I'm pushing more to slow things down—but we don't even have time to catch up from one project to the next."

The truth is that the First Nations and Métis of the region, barring any major legal battles, have little choice but to go along with the long-term development plans set by government and industry. "When the government approves a project, they usually say 'we see minimal environmental effects due to this project' and they shouldn't say that," she says. "Just tell it as it is.

"They are going to go beyond the threshold here if they don't say 'No' to a project soon. But money talks."

ON THE VERY DAY THAT Alberta's environment minister announced plans to streamline regulatory measures, Syncrude CEO Eric Newell was travelling to Washington to sell the resources of northern Alberta. He said he was "surprised" at how high the level of interest in the oil sands industry was. It was also the day that George W. Bush launched his U.S. power plan, a manifesto of continental energy expansion. Speaking with senior energy policy advisers in the U.S. capital, Newell said it had been twenty years since he'd last seen so much interest in trans-border power. "People were just absolutely fascinated." Most of the $51 billion in projects announced are owned or proposed by American companies or American subsidiaries already. But more capital is required "to develop these high-cost resources that wouldn't otherwise get developed."

A month later, in June 2001, Newell arrived in Ottawa to meet with Liberal cabinet ministers. Concerns had been raised by the David Suzuki Foundation and several other public advocacy groups about the vast oil sands expansion and the diminishing possibility that Canada, under such an industrial regime, could decrease its output of greenhouse gas emissions. If northern Alberta carries the fossil load for the production of three million barrels daily—the majority for export—Canada will have a serious handicap in meeting its international emissions obligations. And any company that profits from growing emissions while Canada spends billions to reduce greenhouse gases will effectively enjoy a new kind of subsidy: a carbon dispensation possibly worth millions or billions of dollars. It's "an outrageous contradiction between Canada's commitment to reduce greenhouse gases and its desire to meet massive US demand for more energy," says a 2001 Suzuki Foundation report on the oil sands.

Liberal ministers were much more sanguine, said Newell to *The Globe and Mail*. Based on his reception in Ottawa, the industry would expect no trouble from the federal government. In meetings, even Environment Minister David Anderson reportedly supported the argument that Canada's climate change strategy should focus mainly on the consumption of energy while producers proceed as usual. In other words, unmitigated oil sands expansion would be accommodated within Canada's official climate strategy. "We certainly view climate change as a potential issue for us," said Newell. "We have to make sure that anything we do under the Kyoto protocol does not penalize our industry or impair our competitiveness."

Europeans floated down the Athabasca in the 1700s and noticed black tar seeping from the riverbanks, and the early accounts of Canada's oil sands have proven prophetic. "Where now the almost unbroken wilderness holds sway," wrote one unnamed explorer, "industrial plants may arise and tall stacks may dominate the landscape."

The largest single Canadian petroleum resource is actually a continental property, a fact that seems to have tremendous impact on government policy. Early on, Canada intended to claim the sands exclusively. The Athabasca and Mackenzie valleys to the north are "the most extensive petroleum fields in America, if not the world," reported one cabinet member to the Canadian Parliament in 1888. "The uses of petroleum and consequently the demand for it by all nations are increasing at such a rapid ratio that it is probable this great petroleum field will assume an enormous value in the near future." Canada's newly confederated government recognized the mineral riches of the region and made special arrangements to sign treaties with local Indians before their land became too valuable. ("They will be more easily dealt with now than they would be when their country is over-run with prospectors and valuable mines discovered," noted one 1897 internal report.)

The modern age of the oil sands began with the arrival of American capital. In 1954, the Sun Oil Company of Philadelphia, bought its first oil sands leases on the banks of the Athabasca. By 1967, Alberta Premier Ernest Manning and J. Howard Pew, chairman of American Sun Oil, launched "the world's first oil mine" on the site of today's Suncor plant. In front of a crowd of five hundred, Pew lived up to his reputation as a champion of industry and enemy of godless Communism. "No nation can long be secure in this atomic age unless it be amply supplied with petroleum," he said. "If the North American continent is to produce oil to meet its requirements in the years ahead, oil from the Athabasca area must necessarily play an important role." Pew sank $240 million into the Great Canadian Oil Sands in 1963 because he believed the investment would reduce U.S. dependence on foreign oil.

The resource transfer from Aboriginal to private, mostly American, companies took all of sixty-six years to happen, beginning with an intensified continental energy market in the 1950s—and a province keen to unload mineral leases. "By the early 1960s most of the prime acreage in the tar sands was under the control of the major oil companies," recounts Larry Pratt in his 1976 book, *The Tar Sands*. To this day, only a few major players in the oil sands are Canadian: independents like PanCanadian and the Alberta Energy Company, quasi-national Petro-Canada, as well as Suncor, with 50-percent Canadian shares, represent domestic producers.

On the eve of what some have described as the world's first great energy crunch—the final run of affordable fossil fuels—Canada has limited control over its largest petroleum resources. Under the North American Free Trade Agreement (NAFTA), exports and domestic supply are linked—meaning that unless Canada is willing to risk a trade war, exports can't be cut back in an effort to avoid crushing domestic prices. Back in 1989 when Brian Mulroney signed NAFTA, "few Canadians cared about losing energy sovereignty," wrote *The Globe and Mail*'s Eric Reguly as crude prices neared a ten-year high in October 2000. "Because (a) Canada was apparently blessed with an endless supply of oil and natural gas, and (b) the tradeoff was guaranteed access to the world's biggest energy market.

"To the Americans, Canada would become a welcome rival to OPEC," he noted. "Eleven years later, you've got to wonder whether Canada's free-trade negotiators had a clue what they signed." It turns out that free trade isn't free anymore: Canada, under existing trade agreements, can never curtail its exports without a radical reduction in domestic consumption.

As J. Howard Pew foretold on the banks of the Athabasca, Canada is the custodian of an important continental resource, one that is just now being called to market. Today, an integrated continental network of pipelines means that Fort McMurray crude can flow directly to Houston, New Orleans or Montreal, depending on the customer.

"It is a hemispheric issue and it needs to be elevated to the presidential," said president-elect George W. Bush of the growing energy trade. Canadian officials seemed to concur. "We are in a very advantageous position being in North America, being a good friend and ally," said Natural Resources Minister Ralph Goodale after a high-level meeting with the U.S. Secretary of Energy in March 2001. "The potential here is to do billions of dollars in new business. The investment, the jobs and growth that comes from that advantage are terrific from a Canadian point of view."

GIVEN THE STRICT TERMS OF TRADE that govern Canada's largest petroleum resource, it would be patently unrealistic to invoke nationalist policies of the past—such as the controversial National Energy Policy of the 1970s that rigidly imposed separate foreign and domestic energy pricing. Yet it would be prudent to reconsider the generous tax breaks, royalty holidays and potential greenhouse gas subsidies enjoyed by some of the world's largest companies as they ready Canadian energy for export. Do companies really need extra incentives to develop non-renewable sources?

For much of the 1990s, as Alberta reduced conventional oil and gas royalty rates, federal tax subsidies continued to pour forth, even though they served no urgent purpose but to ensure that Canadians paid for their gas twice: once as taxpayers, and again as consumers. In 1995, for example, Ottawa handed out $336.6 million to the oil industry in the form of direct grants and equity, $259.3 million in the form of various support programs and $362 million in tax breaks—more than $1 billion in total. Based on industry estimates, provincial oil sands royalties collected between 1996 and 2025 will account for only 9 percent of all government revenue collected, all federal and provincial taxes included. Under special credits given to mining operations, noted the federal Commission of the Environment, oil sands tax concessions could be as much as $40 million per billion spent.

If government wanted to create jobs, there's certainly cheaper—and more sustainable—means: as one 1995 study reported, only five to nine jobs are created for every million dollars spent on heavy energy such as oil sands (imported machines, high energy costs). The same capital invested in wind technology would create ten jobs, and labour-intensive residential energy retrofits (to improve home efficiency) would produce roughly twenty jobs with the same cash.

The final cost borne by taxpayers is the potential expense of enforced greenhouse limits, as per the 2001 international treaty on climate change. Even though the world will be trying to deter countries from accumulating carbon dioxide in the future, industry estimates show a strong trend towards a continental carbon imbalance, with Canada saddled with production (but not consumption) emissions created from exported oil. Of the 17.6-megatonne increase of carbon dioxide between 1991 and 1999 from the oil sands, for example, only 21 percent came from increases in Canadian demand or production increases to replace conventional crude supplies, notes a June 2000 report from the industry group Athabasca Oil Sands Developers. The rest, some 13.8 megatonnes, was created from crude export to the United States, "replacing declining U.S. conventional oil." Someone will likely pay for the extra carbon created by oil exports—and there's a good chance that taxpayers will shoulder at least part of the expense.

And in an age where successful climate savings are often achieved through energy efficiency, the power-intensive mining and extraction process seems like energy upgrading as much as oil production: oil sands production requires more than double the energy needed to produce and refine conventional gasoline. Although the process has become much more efficient since the 1970s, one could still power 2.23 million Canadian homes for a year (with an electric furnace) with the amount of energy the oil sands consumed in 1995 to produce 121 million barrels of synthetic crude—of which roughly half was exported to American customers.

Considering that the oil sands "industry" during the 1990s was essentially two companies, it is an enormous scale of consumption. Power is actually produced on site in the oil sands—all fossil: gas turbines and coal—and companies like Syncrude and Suncor have been racking up healthy profits selling electricity into the volatile Alberta grid. By 2000, the impressive fleet of the world's largest trucks—each consuming upwards of forty hectolitres of diesel during an eight-hour summertime shift— and the thundering factories that separate oil from sand were already sucking up more power than food, beverage, plastics, textiles and clothing industries combined.

The oil sands have been billed as Canada's energy insurance plan, but it's a slight one. In the short term, a steady supply of synthetic crude will ensure that Canada's economy doesn't immediately suffer as world supplies dwindle. But from gasoline to natural gas, Canadians already pay as much as everyone else on the continent (pre-tax) for their own resources—gathered, processed and sold largely by foreign corporations. Aside from royalties and an influx of investment capital, the national benefit of the oil sands—or Arctic gas or Sable Island gas, for that matter—is somewhat limited. It is the vast supply of the resource, not its Canadian origins, that will temporarily offset rising energy costs. Over the long term, the main beneficiaries of the continental fossil fuel market will likely be the companies themselves. And we'll still be stuck with the job of converting to renewables.

AT THE BOOMTOWN CASINO in downtown Fort McMurray, slot players emerge from the early evening darkness and station themselves in front of their favourite machines. By 10 P.M., there will be lineups at the machines and card tables. The rush often runs in sync with a shuttle bus that travels back and forth between the casino and the construction camps. "When they come here, they come hard," says one security guard, dressed in a suit. "These guys come off the job flush, no family here and long hours—so they rip loose." It's not uncommon for some to unload several hundred dollars in a few minutes. In a glass room off to one side, an ongoing high-roller game picks up a few more players.

By contrast, there's a national gambit afoot in the oil sands like nothing we've ever seen. With mega-infusions of capital and a city bursting at its seams, this is what an oil rush looks like in the twenty-first century: global companies that can marshal an army of workers and equipment, and governments that are surprisingly generous with public money and regulatory approvals.

The truth is that Canada needs the oil sands over the short term because our economy just isn't ready for the future; unlike many European nations that have invested in alternatives such as wind power and comprehensive public transportation, Canada remains heavily dependent on petroleum to fuel its economy.

Nevertheless, we continue to spend billions to sustain an energy system that, by many accounts, will not last beyond the end of this century.

Difficult questions lie ahead. As expansion roars across the oil sands, who will cover the true cost of carbon dioxide emissions that currently contribute to Canada's failure to meet international climate obligations? Companies like Suncor have already made initial steps towards covering their own offsets and investing in renewable energy, but it's hard not to wonder if Canada's fossil fuel industries won't turn out to be the Sydney tar ponds of the new millennium: an expensive environmental legacy whose liability is ultimately borne by government and taxpayers.

Indeed, at the other end of the city, in the old suburb of Waterways, lies a remnant of the uranium boom—an old radioactive waste site enclosed only by a chain-link fence and a few anonymous signs that warn people to leave the area. On the edge of the Athabasca River is an old loading dock where uranium—and, earlier, radium—were unloaded from barges travelling down from Great Bear Lake and Uranium City. Radioactive ore fell off the barges and rail cars and onto the riverside property, still owned by Canadian National. The waste wasn't discovered until 1992, roughly sixty years later.

The signs at Waterways mention nothing about radioactivity. "WARNING," they say. "Contaminated Land—Do Not Stay in This Area. For information, call collect: 613-998-9442."

This city rides a boom that been foretold ever since explorer Peter Pond mapped the area in 1778. One gets the feeling that stakes are high. Back at the casino, after-work gamblers occupy the floor; they're an orderly bunch who impassively empty barrels of loonies into video slots, pausing only to purchase drinks or snacks from a roving cart. Like most casinos, winners are showered with riches, free drinks and access to a private lounge with a big-screen TV. Losers, as always, remain anonymous.

# CLOSING KEMANO

## British Columbia

M ID-MORNING IN THE DEPTHS of a hydro power plant, Marlene Nielsen recalls how her daughter tried to save the B.C. company town of Kemano. After nearly a half century of maintaining the massive hydro turbines buried inside the base of Mount DuBose, Kemano was suddenly slated for closure. A company-wide effort to cut costs resulted in an announcement in 1999 that Kemano—a remote town of 220, some six hundred kilometres north of Vancouver—would be closed forever in July 2000. But for 80 families, it was still home. Nielsen's youngest daughter, aged eleven, offered to help pay the difference if it would keep her town alive.

"She was willing to donate her piggy bank—$3.47," says Nielsen, an engineering clerk. "She wrote a letter to the company president and said, Hey, if it's a matter of money, we'll vote on it and we'll pay more."

We are four hundred metres inside Mount DuBose, next to a man-made underground waterfall that plunges from a tunnel near the top of the mountain and spins eight turbines with a force of nearly 760,000 kilopascals (110,000 pounds per square inch). The water follows a vertical drop that's sixteen times the height of Niagara Falls. The hum of the hydro plant—five hundred tonnes of moving parts—sends a dull rumble through Nielsen's underground office.

Like many townsfolk, she's sad to leave her home of fourteen years. "This is a nice place, a safe place," she says. "You know, the real world is scary if you're a single mom; out there it's scary and here it's like milk."

Accessible only by water or air, Kemano was a classic company town, existing for the express purpose of churning out vast quantities of electricity for Alcan Aluminum Limited's Kitimat smelter—the largest in North America—about eighty kilometres southeast of Kitimat. At peak capacity, some 840 megawatts of electricity is carried out of the mountain and over alpine passes to Kitimat. Excess capacity, usually 170 megawatts, is sold to a local pulp mill and BC Hydro, Kemano's connection to an electrical grid stretching from Prince Rupert to Los Angeles.

Ever since 1957, a small isolated version of the Canadian Dream had prospered in Kemano—the kind of place where people didn't bother to lock their doors, bowling and golf were major pastimes, and where residents enjoyed the stable income of old-fashioned jobs. With a small shopping mall, a rod and gun club, a Brownie troop, an elementary school and a curling rink, Alcan once boasted that Kemano was "a combination of wilderness lifestyle with 20th century conveniences close at hand."

Some British Columbians will remember Kemano for the $1.3-billion hydro expansion that Alcan unsuccessfully championed during the 1980s and early 1990s. Others might even recall the heady days of Kemano's original construction, back when the hydro plant made international headlines as a shining example of Canada's bright industrial future. The subterranean powerhouse, the lightning electrical current that flowed over mountain passes and the gleaming aluminum, a wonder metal that rolled from the molten pits of Alcan's Kitimat Works—all of this represented the promise and ingenuity of the twentieth century. It was everything that the architects of Confederation could have wanted, the pinnacle of Canada's postwar dreams: wilderness conquered by contentment and cheap, invisible power.

Power was the ideology of modern Canada—of luxury, progress, knowledge and health—that transformed a semi-frozen nation of people who, quite literally, lived in the dark. It was a test of our ability to control and improve upon natural environments, to extract prosperity from the landscape. But at some point, the founding vision gave way to something else: a highly centralized, corporate-dominated system based largely on waste production and environmentally unfriendly technologies. We no longer fully control this machine.

There have been inevitable questions: What have we lost in the wake of material gain? What is the real cost of progress?

As we sort through Canada, the energy nation, it's important to remember why we bothered to erect power plants, transmission grids and pipelines in the first place. Kemano's tidy neighbourhoods, steady jobs and community values provide some clues. There was a dream here, of a sort, something that flickered throughout the town's final days.

KEMANO'S ENDURING LEGACY has been to survive as a slice of small-town normalcy in the middle of nowhere. "The only thing you have to worry about out here is a bear," says Nielsen. "There are no bad people—every child has fifty moms and dads, aunts and uncles. And many people came here because of that."

In many ways, it seems like a town frozen in time, circa 1960: strong community bonds, a low crime rate and excellent schooling have inspired many past Kemanoites to stay until retirement. Which is why the closure announcement on April 29, 1999, was so painful. Many, like Neilsen's young daughter, have never lived anywhere else.

"Man, it hit the community hard," Nielsen says. "That afternoon was very dark: they closed the school, the powerhouse— basically, the whole town closed for the afternoon. It was an open-door policy: people wandered in and out of each other's homes asking, 'What happened?'"

Nielsen's office, deep within the labyrinth of chambers, corridors and machine rooms inside the mountain, has no windows.

"We asked for a skylight once," she jokes. But it's no cave. Amid standard office trappings, you can see signs of settlement and change—crayon drawings and goodbye cards mix with cardboard file boxes and a paper shredder. This is how Kemanoites have lived for more than forty-five years: they make themselves at home, despite everything else.

It's hard to imagine that this quiet community was once the centre of world attention. Back in the 1950s, aluminum was considered a miracle metal—and a commodity central to national security. On the eve of the Korean War, government and industry anticipated a surge in demand for aluminum, and the Kemano project was fast-tracked. By the time Kemano's first turbines were installed in 1954, the Nechako watershed was already flooded.

Alcan has prospered ever since—and its B.C. operations at Kitimat have enjoyed some of the cheapest power in North America. But Kemano's 840 megawatts haven't come without controversy. Diverting up to 70 percent of the Nechako's flow through the Kemano powerhouse has caused salmon stocks to suffer significant losses. In 1999, almost fifty years after the Kenney Dam went up on the Nechako, the Outdoor Recreation Council of British Columbia listed the Nechako as the province's eighth-most-endangered river: only three million sockeye, a fraction of pre-1951 stocks, have returned to the watershed in peak years. (The International Pacific Salmon Commission estimates that with improved water flow, the Nechako system could produce up to thirty million sockeye and become the largest salmon-producing tributary of the Fraser River.)

It is June 2000, one month before the last boat leaves Kemano. Like most non-union staff, Nielsen is losing her job—and all are losing their homes and a beloved community. Some say they will even miss the company that pulled the plug.

While Kemano's adults try to grapple with the final days of their small-town paradise, kids continue to offer loonies and quarters to stave off closure. "To this day, some of the younger ones want to give their allowance to help keep the town," says school principal Ken Allison. "The kids just don't understand the fiscal issue. [Former Alcan president] Mr. Jacques Bougie could never explain the economic rationale. It was a luxury to keep this community open, but that's a hard sell to everyone—especially the kids."

MOST PEOPLE ARRIVE IN KEMANO by boat. The two-and-a-half-hour boat trip from Kitimat to Kemano aboard the MV *Wachwas* is a rite of passage for most residents. The thirty-seven-metre cutter, a former Arctic exploration ship, can ferry sixty people and enough cargo to keep Kemano well stocked with groceries. It glides along the Gardner Canal, a fjord accented by waterfalls, mountain goats, hot springs and clear-cuts, slicing deep into the Coast Mountains. It is an ancient route taken by the Haisla people to oolichan fishing camps at Kemano and the Kitlope watershed.

"Last week we had a killer-whale pod swim alongside us," says Captain Ralph Kerman, who has served on the ship since 1992. Up in the wheelhouse, Ralph and engineer Gifford Grey admit they will miss the twice-weekly trip to Kitimat—"the big city," jokes Ralph—almost as much as they will miss Kemano. The boat is the community's lifeline and all good things—groceries, mail, supplies and trips to the outside world—come from its passage. "Let's just say that people notice if the boat is a few minutes late," says Ralph. "We're pretty popular around here."

Gifford has been rooting around in the guts of the ship. A mechanic's cap is perched on his head as he sets down a huge wrench. "Diesel is aromatherapy," he says. "There's nothing better than an engine room going full bore."

Grey recalls welding on the original Kemano turbines in 1955, back when he was a junior tradesman in Vancouver.

"Kemano was the big news back then," he says. "The eighth wonder of the world, people said."

The project actually encompassed several separate feats of engineering: the Kenney Dam, which plugged the Nechako River and created 910 square kilometres of inland reservoir; a 16-kilometre-long concrete tunnel through Mount DuBose, which carries water over an 800-metre plunge to Kemano's sea-level powerhouse; the 213-metre-long underground power-generation chamber, designed to shelter Kemano's turbines from nuclear attack; and a high-voltage transmission line strung across 82 kilometres of Coast Mountain wilderness to Alcan's smelter at Kitimat.

It was "the most expensive project ever attempted by private industry," heralded *National Geographic* in a 1956 feature. "[Canadians] had dammed a river, run it backwards through a mountain, dropped it down a man-made waterfall 16 times higher than Niagara, and then released it into the Pacific." It was a construction job worth five billion in today's dollars.

It doesn't bother Ralph and Gifford that the announcement of the town's closing barely garnered headlines. The outside world is still distant—and the news of the closure has only brought a more relaxed atmosphere to an already laid-back community. For example, Ralph hasn't worn his captain's uniform in months; like the rest of Kemano, he's winding things down. "I kind of lost interest when they said they'd close the town," he says. "This year, nobody is looking after their yards or gardens: people aren't even cutting their lawns, which was never really heard of before. Alcan actually cuts my front yard because they can't stand looking at it any more."

The boat passes Cornwall Point and heads down a fjord towards Kemano. Two hours later, a small harbour comes into view and we pass a natural earthen jetty that still serves as a Kemano-Haisla fishing camp and traditional cemetery. The MV *Wachwas* pulls up alongside a dock and a small crowd of residents picks up supplies and family members from the boat. The arrival feels routine, but it isn't—only eleven round trips until the final departure on July 28. Oh yes, says Captain Ralph, the boat is for sale, too—only $680,000 (U.S.).

These days, it is the departures that matter most: several families have already left and most will leave within the next few weeks. We've arrived on the last-ever day of school, an event that launches an intensive month-long period of moving trucks, suitcases and final goodbyes. In Kemano, summer holidays are the beginning of the end.

LIZ HARDY, A FORMER KEMANOITE who was brought in by Alcan to manage the closure, is waiting for us at the dock. As we drive the sixteen-kilometre road into town, she explains the emotional roller coaster that's gripped Kemano ever since the 1999 announcement. "It was almost as though there had been a death in the family," she says. "We had to go through the grieving process: the anger, the denial and the gradual realization that this thing has happened."

The end of school today marks a new phase. "I think we went through the resignation process about two months ago and now it's actually happening," Liz says. "We are moving their friends and neighbours out. So this is perhaps the hardest part."

Some things continue as normal. We pass a few trucks on their way back to the dock—two black bears have been spotted nearby and, as always, Kemanoites flock to view local wildlife. But it's not just for love of nature; the bears are often tipsy from nibbling on overripe mountain ash berries and they stumble around, drunk, offering hijinks that you won't find on the Discovery Channel.

"We've had two grizzlies 'at it' just down the road," Liz says of a pair of mating bears. "Everybody and his dog were out there taking pictures. Someone even took three rolls; the developers in Kitimat must be wondering what's happening here in Kemano. You go down to the dock and a couple of otters are doing the same thing."

Liz Hardy grew up in England in the 1950s hearing and reading about the wonders of Kemano. Her father was a forty-year Alcan employee. "It was one of the reasons I came to Canada," she says. We drive by a deserted campsite from the failed Kemano Completion Project, a $1.3-billion hydro expansion that would have drained much of the remaining Nechako watershed—the river system that feeds the huge reservoir on the other side of Mount DuBose—and jeopardized a significant portion of the Fraser salmon run. In 1995, the project was halted after $535 million was spent in construction. It left a tangled web of political interests and bruised community relationships. Liz helped close that operation too—sent one thousand workers packing.

"Ten years ago I stood on the helipad after having sold everything to come here," she recalls. "My whole life was two Eddie Bauer bags and a box—so I know what it's like to have it dragged from underneath you."

Of all the jobs here, hers is perhaps the most solitary. "The first few months were really tough," she says. "I had to realize the anger directed at me wasn't personal."

We pass by the bowling alley and curling arena as we approach the townsite. "One of the things that has impressed me is the professionalism of some of these people," she says. "We've tried to keep the community as whole as possible until the end. Many people, although they've been in pain, have kept their enthusiasm up. They said they wanted to make this The Best Year Ever—that's been the slogan."

Indeed, the dizzying array of Kemano clubs and activities has continued almost right to the end. Tonight, for example, the pottery club will convene in the recreation centre. The Kemano tae kwon do club/dojo will award new belts tomorrow. And there's an after-school golf lesson today, even though there's no more school. Events are advertised on the Kemano TV channel, a scrolling local weather and news broadcast. Few details escape its grasp: Reporter And Photographer Set To Visit Kemano, says one headline.

When the company announced Kemano's demise in 1999, many thought they'd been betrayed: angry words were exchanged, some abandoned the community early to protest the closure. Others, such as the Kemano Brownie troop, were more pragmatic: they would carry on, soldiering away at games and crafts until it was time to get on the boat to Kitimat. A lone posting on their Web site reads:

> We are the Kemano Brownies/Sparks. We have 2 Brownies & 5 Sparks in our group. We love to do crafts. Our town will not be a town in September 2000.
>
> The company running the town is closing it. Therefore this will be the final year for the Kemano Brownies/Sparks. We will make it the best year ever.

THE TOWN SUDDENLY APPEARS before us, an orderly, wayward suburb transplanted from another era. Neat, two-storey houses line the streets—some eighty residences—and several minivans and camper trailers are parked out front. Off in the distance are the school and the recreation centre. And behind that sits Mount DuBose and the subterranean powerhouse.

The setting is spectacular: black granite mountains spring up on both sides of Mount DuBose, rivalling the alpine scenes of Jasper and Banff. Waterfalls shower down from small glaciers and empty into the Kemano River, where hawks and deer gather.

A few young children ride their bikes in the middle of the street, weaving left and right as they chase each other, oblivious to traffic. Liz points towards the school. "Every time my spirits got down, I'd go there," she says. "Right from the beginning, it was clear that the school was the heart of the community." We arrive at the school and it appears deserted: summer holidays have already begun and the school's thirty-three kids, between grades one and eight, have scattered throughout town. Inside, Kemano's teachers are packing up boxes and sorting through files.

"We had a little ceremony today," says principal Ken, touring us through classrooms, a computer lab and a library. "At the end of the day, each kid stuck a pin in our map, so everybody knows where they are going." Some are moving to nearby Kitimat, while others are travelling as far as Ontario and Quebec.

Having rehearsed for this moment all year, today's ending seemed almost normal. And not everyone is sad about leaving— especially a few of the teenagers in grades seven and eight. "The more senior students are ready to roll," Ken says. "We can't provide the opportunity for socializing that teens need."

"Without TV, we'd be dead," confirms Richard Mitchinson, fourteen. He's hungry for the outside world. "I can name every-one in my school—even the young ones. You just know it.

"It's tougher on the younger kids," he says. "But I don't think I'll miss it much—you can do almost anything out there."

His younger sister, Alexandra, is almost in tears about leaving. "I just don't want to go anywhere else," she says. Alexandra and her friends, Madeline and Anne-Marie Jones, painted a giant sign on the road in front of her house today: a large heart that said inside "WE LOVE KEMANO" and, next to it, a larger painted circle, as wide as the road, that proclaimed, "Heck No We Won't Go."

For the past year, Kemano's kids have been putting up signs all around town, part of a school project to help them celebrate their community and prepare for the end. Many feel they are losing the comfort of a large family. "In here, because they all know each other so well, it's like brother and sister—so they have brother-sister-type relationships," explains principal Ken. "It's pretty love-hate sometimes, but they're all really great kids."

It is a cozy town, for better or worse. "You go off to the top of a mountain and someone else is walking on the other mountain, and you know who it is," says teacher Chris Kalnay, a ten-year resident. He's closing up his classroom, packing up papers and organizing desks.

He admits that there are few secrets in Kemano—and it's not always pretty. "Everybody knows everybody," he explains, "but everybody doesn't necessarily like everyone else."

It's true: in less than a day, and through no real effort, I've managed to accumulate a fair pile of gossip. Who went to local wife-swapping parties in the 1970s, for example, and which of these swingers might still live in Kemano.

Madeline and Anne-Marie, age thirteen, don't mind Kemano's fishbowl at all. The closeness of the town gave them a kind of freedom that few children enjoy. "School is boring sometimes," says Madeline. "But you can stay out as long as you like—unless there's a bear."

Kemano's kids have grown up trading e-mail messages on the Microsoft Network—"all the girls are into it," says Richard—while living in the kind of old-fashioned community that's almost disappeared from the rest of Canada.

Even adults have fun. "I'm the curling club champion two years running and I've never curled before," says ship hand Raymond Stohl, a former fishing captain who moved from Prince Rupert two years ago. "It's small enough that it doesn't matter how bad you are, you're going to win something. And they've got so many draws and prizes that everybody wins something all the time. It's just a neat place to live."

"The neighbourhood I grew up in [in] Orillia was a lot like this," recalls teacher Debbie Allison, who is married to principal Ken. "You climbed apple trees, ran barefoot and rode bikes.

"And most of the people from the outside will tell you that's what is missing from their lives."

THERE'S CAUSE FOR CELEBRATION at the pub night, a twice-weekly gathering of Kemanoites at the volunteer-run bar in the recreation centre. The town's newest newlyweds are toasting their third month of marriage. "I never believed in love at first sight, but it was pretty much right away," says Tammy Boomars, an Alberta girl who met her husband-to-be, Kemano tradesman Shaun Boomars, on a holiday in the Dominican Republic. It was February 1999. "We got home and talked on the phone—1,700 minutes in two weeks."

By August, they were engaged and Tammy had moved to Kemano. They returned from a Mexico wedding ceremony last April to find that the town had organized a wedding reception—one that included a few surprises. "We didn't realize until halfway through the first dance that they'd brought over our whole family," says the bride. "My parents drove nineteen hours to get here. It was Kemano's longest secret."

Inside the bar—which doubles as a bingo parlour and community hall—there's still a sense of disappointment. "I came out just in time for the announcement," Tammy says. "You're starting a life together and you have bean counters up there that have no idea of what's going on."

Kevin Mitchinson, a control-room operator who's been in Kemano since 1990, says he decided to leave Alcan altogether, even though as a union employee he was guaranteed a job in Kitimat. "I understand why they want to change the way they do business," he says. "But what helped me decide not to remain with the company was their treatment of people here—I can't work for a company or a manager that I can't trust."

"It's not so much that they're shutting the place down," explains one powerhouse worker. "It's the way they're going about doing it."

Some Kemanoites report that several laid-off employees have still not received settlements (these would come through at the last minute), and remaining community members complain that they were ambushed with the closure, despite previous assurances that Kemano was a sound, profitable operation. Those who were terminated didn't find out until several months after the announcement.

"They don't know me without my number," says control-room operator Blair Maguire, "75888—might as well tattoo it on my forehead."

The company just doesn't need Kemano's 220 people any more. After technological upgrades, a rotating camp of twenty-five people will operate the power plant. That's all that will remain: a field crew, three holes of golf and an empty recreation centre. Most homes will be burned to the ground over the next two years as part of a drill for B.C. firefighters—a detail that many parents haven't yet told their kids.

But on a deeper level, everyone involved in the project—workers and management—still seems shocked at how quickly things can change. For decades, Alcan was landlord, mayor, security guard, hospital and grocery store. Along with cheap rent—$175 a month—Kemanoites enjoyed top-notch facilities and the chance to put money in the bank. But it was never their town. "It's like Big Brother," says a senior staffer at the bar, who wished to remain anonymous. "You give up a certain amount of control over your life here, so it's so much more personal—it's like being thrown out by your parents." It's little comfort that Jacques Bougie's total compensation in 2000 was $23.9 million, not quite double the annual cost of running Kemano.

By January 2001, after Kemano's townsite was partly razed, occupied by only a skeleton crew, Bougie shocked the business world by abruptly resigning as Alcan's president and chief executive. His only explanation was that he wanted to spend more time with his family.

FOR SOME, KEMANO WAS TROUBLE from the beginning. The Cheslatta Carrier Nation, whose traditional territory spans the Nechako region, hardly saw the flood coming: some communities had less than two weeks' notice in the late 1950s to clear out of their homes and move to higher ground. With the decline of traditional hunting and fishing, the Cheslatta witnessed the erosion and submersion of traditional burial grounds. As the Nechako reservoir rose, high water and flooding unearthed the remains of Cheslatta ancestors, sometimes leaving washed-out graves and coffins floating on the water.

Following a 1950 provincial agreement with Alcan, the Department of Indian Affairs brokered the transfer of lands to Alcan and administered the forced migration of families, scattering the band across a 240-kilometre span. It was only in 1990 that overwhelming evidence emerged that the federal government had forged signatures on Cheslatta surrender documents, resulting in an out-of-court settlement in 1993 for almost seven million dollars.

"I am acutely aware of the perceived injustices and deep emotional scars left in the community from the original Kemano project," said John Watson, a former Indian Affairs official, to British Columbia's Utility Commission in 1993. "I think they are something that none of us, as Canadians, can be proud of."

The Haisla of Kitimat fared better after the arrival of Alcan, but their traditional territory—which includes Kemano and the town of Kitimat—are currently under treaty claim. Tom Robinson, hereditary chief of the Kitimat Haisla, remembers the days before whites lived in the region. "We were dormouse poor," he recalls. "Nobody cared if we existed—not even Indian Affairs.

"Alcan was a godsend, compared to fifty years ago: people got jobs, health services became available—it used to take seventeen hours to get to a hospital."

More than eighty years of unsettled treaty issues have left Robinson cynical about the future. "You people are outright greedy: if you could take it all back and imagine how little it would have cost for them to settle it in the 1920s." It's a simple issue, he says, an arrangement that has benefited both company and government. "If they were honest, they would have settled it."

A GLOBAL SPATE OF DOWNSIZING and restructuring in the aluminum industry is behind Kemano's demise. Just after the April 1999 closure announcement, Alcan unveiled plans to amalgamate with two other global companies and become the world's largest supplier of aluminum. The merger was later narrowed to Alcan and Algroup of Switzerland, which will form a conglomerate worth $12.4 billion (U.S.). Fluctuating global aluminum markets and the financial pressures of the multi-billion-dollar merger sent shock waves all the way to Kemano. Alcan says that it must save $50 million annually to stay competitive. And although cheap electricity—a primary cost in aluminum smelting—has made Alcan a world leader, Kemano's closing puts Alcan's shareholders $13 million closer to that goal, explains Doug Groves, a senior manager from Kitimat. He was also brought in to facilitate what he admits has been a difficult and sometimes confusing process.

"Yes, it is hard, but I'm doing it to look after the people here in the way I think they deserve," he says. "I also know that from a management perspective, this is the right decision for the company to make. It's become very costly to run the community. We've kept an appliance repairman on site for years because there's more than one hundred stoves and one hundred fridges—and a plumber, schoolteachers, a security force and a registered nurse, pharmacy and clinic."

At one time, the biggest challenges in Kemano were dealing with pesky bears and the occasional troubled worker. Groves, whose first job was at Kemano, recalls one employee from the 1960s who tried to smuggle a whole Caterpillar tractor by mail, piece by piece. "He mailed just about every single part to an associate in Kitimat. And they didn't catch him until he tried to mail the blade—that was his undoing."

As someone who got his start in Kemano, he hates to say it but technology has made his town obsolete. "When this place was built, it was very experimental," says Groves. "No one had ever harnessed a 2,600-foot waterfall before—every day we produce the same power that Vancouver consumes and we can now control most of it from Kitimat."

Both he and Liz Hardy, Alcan's two front-line managers for the shutdown, are themselves losing their jobs at the end of it all, through retirement. But after thirty-two years of working for Alcan, Hardy isn't ready for early retirement.

"My dad had forty years with Alcan and I was hoping that I'd make forty as well," she says. "It's been a great company. But there are things you'd like to do differently—or things out of one's control. By and large, we've done a lot of things right here and a lot of things wrong."

She has organized job fairs, moving vans and counselling for Kemano's displaced families, while she's had little idea what her own future will be. "The irony has been trying to communicate to people that it's not scary—and actually being scared witless myself."

THE FEAR OF THE UNKNOWN—the modern working world of sporadic unemployment, short-term contracts and nomadic career paths—hangs over Kemano like a cloud. Every year, more company towns in Canada disappear. It's a fact of Canadian life: resource and industry towns live and die on financial decisions and market fluctuations that are globally influenced more and more. While BC Hydro juggles power contracts in California, producers like Cominco (and, reportedly, Alcan) are cutting back production to sell power to the United States. Employees sit idle because it's sometimes more profitable for a few managers to feed power into the 150,000-megawatt electricity grid that now runs to northern Mexico. It used to be that a town was as good as its factory—but in the calculus of an accelerated world marketplace, it's impossible to assume anything.

Back at the pub, teacher and volunteer bartender Robert Cheater is getting ready to close up shop. It's midnight, and most people have left for home. He sits to talk. He's weary from being sleepless; it's less than a month until he moves out, and he hasn't found a job yet. With a newborn daughter, the town's latest addition, Cheater has four kids and a wife to support.

Tonight, he's not so sure that he made the right decision to come to Kemano. "When I took the job, I had lots of questions about the future of the town," he says. "I had a good situation in my previous teaching job." Cheater had been given a five- to seven-year commitment—he was even being groomed to become principal of the Kemano school. He gave up seniority and the security of a public school job to come work for Alcan. And, as he closes the pub, he says that it's all just a little too much sometimes.

"Even though I love it here in Kemano, in a way I regret coming here," he says. "Maybe that's just the way I'm feeling right now. Some nights I'll wake up thinking about the whole situation: where are we going to? Will we be able to survive?"

It's time to start stacking chairs. "You think that as long as you're together, everything is going to be fine," he says. "But the world does still revolve around having employment and making money—you've got to be able to support your family."

ON THE SLOPE ABOVE THE TOWN, perched on top of the single-run ski hill, is the Kemano Star, a thirty-year-old beacon made of light bulbs and wood that never goes out. "People put it up there, so that no matter how bad the weather got, they could always see a star," says Don Carlyle, Kemano manager.

It's another clue as to why so many people, past and present, have formed a close, personal bond with this hydro-power plant: Kemano's electricity carried this town for forty-five-odd years, ultimately providing for almost everything here, sprung from healthy Alcan revenues. The humming generators inside the mountain offered something uniquely symbiotic: people tended the power plant and the plant, in turn, took care of them.

But by December 2000, water levels in the Nechako reservoir had reached record lows, leaving Alcan—and its newly auto-mated hydro station—with a power shortage. Moreover, Alcan would default on its contract for thirty million dollars in annual electricity sales to BC Hydro, which in turn needed the extra power for its peak domestic demand—and to sell, at considerable profit, to California. With Canada's only southbound transmission line west of Saskatchewan, BC Hydro needed Kemano's surplus power.

The water shortage came as some surprise, because Alcan's original Kemano expansion project called for a near doubling of hydro capacity, based on the sheer size of the Nechako water mass. But even now, what once seemed like an endless resource has literally shrunk in size, following erratic precipitation trends that have been linked to long-term climatic shifts.

Following Kemano's mixed fortunes, BC Hydro itself appears to be getting out of the megaproject business. Where earlier Socred governments built huge dams like the W.A.C. Bennett and the Mica, today's BC Hydro puts its efforts into managing and trading electricity. Installations like Kemano will probably never be undertaken again, purely on the economic reality of megaproject funding. This, perhaps, is an ancillary benefit of deregulation and high public debt: governments are now much less inclined to throw public money at large power projects such as hydro and nukes. (The one clear exception is Quebec, whose power keepers seemingly never quit dreaming of large concrete cathedrals.)

Some have identified the massive offshore oil and gas deposits in the open water west of Kemano at the Queen Charlotte Islands as British Columbia's next energy source. Worth an estimated three billion dollars each year in production revenue, British Columbia's subsea collection of oil, natural gas and frozen gas (hydrates) is a fossil resource that could supply forty years of fuel. Even with a drilling moratorium on the Charlottes, ten billion barrels of oil and 1.3 trillion cubic metres of gas may not be resources that will be embargoed forever.

With megaprojects on the wane, the national dearth of alternatives could push Canada's energy status quo back towards fossil fuels. As of 2001, all of Canada's emissions reduction programs remain voluntary. There are no special tax incentives for renewable power to compete with the millions spent on fossil capital credits. And an inconsistent regulatory and environmental framework tolerates a broad range of unrestricted emissions and exposures, from greenhouse gases to coal-fired mercury to low-level radioactive waste. Even basic provisions currently enjoyed by many American states—like low-sulphur gasoline, local wind-power programs, incentives for hybrid cars—are still years away in most parts of Canada.

The past is full of futuristic visions, rapid expansion and discovery—the industrial dream of abundant energy and progress. The present is the nadir of institutionalized power—large energy utilities, large corporations, megaprojects—reflecting the industrial scale, corporatization and complexity of Canadian life. The future is, by contrast, much more diffuse, a potential unravelling of the past; from climate change to rising gas prices, the nature and shape of power will inevitably change.

The only guarantee is that things won't fix themselves. That's perhaps the nostalgia of Kemano, that people run the energy system and not the other way around. This was a place where people were, until recently, still a central part of the power process. Human scale is the lost treasure of Kemano: pedestrian-friendly streets, green spaces, community events, locally produced power, and quality education and recreation. With Kemano's renewable hardware hidden under a mountain, the town was most prominent, conveying a balance missing from places such as Lorado, the oil sands and most parts of urban Canada.

And like the former Kemanoites, we can't rely solely on megaprojects and bulk power—the inevitable climate and energy crunch means that we are being forced to assume responsibility. For better or worse, we are being kicked out of our own comfy powerhouse into an unfamiliar world.

EARLY MORNING ON KEMANO'S DOCK: locals gather for another departure of the MV *Wachwas*. Robert Cheater drops off his wife and kids for a trip to Kitimat—doctor's appointments, errands—and it all seems like a dress rehearsal for the inevitable. Several families boarding the boat today are never coming back.

"It's the beginning of the end," says Diane Hoyles, Kemano's registered nurse. She will send off the last boat on July 29 and decommission the clinic herself in the deserted town before being airlifted by helicopter. She stands on the dock and waves to the people on the boat. "It's a community where it's one minute you're happy and one minute you're sad," she says.

Molly Baruta is leaving Kemano today, along with her husband, Evan, and their two young boys. They've been preparing for months, but this morning's departure for Kitimat is like nothing they've ever done before. "It's been hard," says Molly. "It's sort of unreal until you have to get on the boat."

The Barutas could have left Kemano months ago. But they chose to stay. Molly points to the crowd on the dock—tears well up. "We wanted to be here because they were the only ones who understood," she says.

It's time to go. Deckhands throw off the ropes and the ship slowly drifts towards the channel.

Robert waves at his wife and children, who disappear into the distance. He's thankful that Kemano didn't close sooner. "A lot of people said that they wished Alcan had wrapped things up quickly," he says. "But by my way of seeing, I'm glad we had time to enjoy things and say goodbye."

# SELECTED BIBLIOGRAPHY

**INTRODUCTION: Ellesmere Island**

Agnew, Thomas, et al. "Record Reduction in Western Arctic Sea-Ice Cover in 1998: Characteristics and Relationships to Atmospheric Circulation." Environment Canada, Apr. 1999.

Etkin, David. *Climate Change and Extreme Events: Canada*. Toronto: Environment Canada, 1999.

International Panel on Climate Change, Working Group II. *Technical Summary, Climate Change 2001: Impacts, Adaptation and Vulnerability*. Geneva, Feb. 2001.

National Energy Board, *Canadian Energy—Supply and Demand to 2025*. Calgary, 1999.


**OFFSHORE: The North Atlantic**

Kenchington, Trevor J. *A Review of the Marine Environmental Effects of the Sable Offshore Energy Project*. Musquodoboit Harbour, Nova Scotia: Gadus Associates, Mar. 1997.

Milligan, T.G., et al. *Fate and Effects of Offshore Hydrocarbon Drilling Waste*. Halifax: Department of Fisheries and Oceans Canada, 1996.

Porter, Ian. "Offshore High: Sable Natural Gas Project Puts Nova Scotia on the Global Energy Map almost Overnight after Years of Waiting." *Oilweek,* 1 June 1998.

United States Energy Information Administration. *Canada Energy Overview*. Feb. 2001.


**NEW STORMS: Sable Island**

Drinkwater, K.F. *The Effects of the NAO on the Continental Shelves off Eastern Canada and Their Impacts on Fish Stocks*. Dartmouth: Bedford Institute of Oceanography, 2000.

Environment Canada. "Sable Island Ground-Level Ozone Statistics: 1992–1997." Personal correspondence, 2001.

Environment Canada. *Towards a Conservation Strategy for Sable Island*. Canadian Wildlife Service, Atlantic Region, Mar. 1998.

Hurrell, James W. "The North Atlantic Oscillation." National Center for Atmospheric Research, presented at National Academy of Sciences, 12th Annual Symposium, Oct. 2000.

Hurrell, James W., and Robert R. Dickson. "Climate Variability over the North Atlantic." *Ecological Effects of Climate Variations in the North Atlantic.* N.C. Stenseth, G. Ottersen, J.W. Hurrell, and A. Belgrano, eds. New York: Oxford University Press, 2001.

International Panel on Climate Change, Working Group II. *Summary for Policymakers, Climate Change 2001: Impacts, Adaptation and Vulnerability.* Geneva, Feb. 2001.

Kerr, Richard A. "Climate: A New Driver for the Atlantic's Moods and Europe's Weather?" *Science Magazine,* 7 Feb. 1997.

Lucas, Zoe. "Vegetation & Terrain Management on Sable Island." Nova Scotia Department of Natural Resources, 1998.

Marshall, John, and Yochanan Kushnir. "Atlantic Climate Variability: A White Paper." Massachusetts Institute of Technology, Apr. 1997.

Nova Scotia Department of Education. "Sable Island Shipwreck Map." <http://collections.ic.gc.ca/sableisland>

Nova Scotia Offshore Petroleum Board. "Scotian Shelf Exploration Licences Map." <http://agcwww.bio.ns.ca>

United Nations Environment Programme. "Impact of Climate Change to Cost the World $US 300 Billion a Year." 3 Feb. 2001.

Various authors. "Chapman Conference on the North Atlantic Oscillation, Abstracts and Proceedings." American Geophysical Union, 2000.

## UP FROM THE UNDERGROUND: Cape Breton

Barlow, Maude, and Elizabeth May, *Frederick Street: Life and Death on Canada's Love Canal.* Toronto: HarperCollins, 2000.

Cameron, Silver Donald. "Last Call for Cape Breton Coal." *Canadian Geographic* Nov.–Dec. 1999.

Engler, Robert. *Brotherhood of Oil.* Chicago: University of Chicago Press, 1977.

Johnson, David. "Industrial Policy and the New Economy." Louisberg Heritage Society, 1995.

Jones, David C. *Feasting on Misfortune.* Edmonton: University of Alberta Press, 1998.

Macgillivray, Don. *Mining Photographs and Other Pictures, Glace Bay 1948–1968.* NSCAD Press, 1983.

Maritime Fishermen's Union. "Fishermen say NO to Oil/Gas Exploration on Cape Breton's Coastline." Press release, 7 Sept. 2000.

Natural Resources Canada. "Backgrounder: History of the Cape Breton Development Corporation," 2001.

Nova Scotia Power Inc., Voluntary Challenge and Registry, Action Plan Update 2000.

Nova Scotia Standing Committee on Economic Development. Transcript, Halifax, 11 May, 1999.

Royal Commission on Canada's Economic Prospects. *The Nova Scotia Coal Industry.* Ottawa, 1956.

## THE ARCTIC VORTEX: Iqaluit, Resolute, Eureka

Agnew, Thomas, et al. "Record Reduction in Western Arctic Sea-Ice Cover in 1998: Characteristics and Relationships to Atmospheric Circulation." Environment Canada, Apr. 1999.

Arms, Myron. *Riddle of the Ice: A Scientific Adventure into the Arctic.* New York: Anchor Books, 1998.

Broecker, W.S. "What if the Conveyor Were to Shut Down? Reflections on a Possible Outcome of the Great Global Experiment." Lamont-Doherty Earth Observatory, Columbia University, 1999.

Chan, Hing Man. "Mercury in the Traditional Diet of Indigenous Peoples in Canada." Centre for Indigenous Peoples' Nutrition and Environment, McGill University, 2000.

Delworth, Thomas L., and Keith W. Dixon. "Implications of the Recent Trend in the Arctic/North Atlantic Oscillation for the North Atlantic Thermohaline Circulation." GFDL/NOAA, Princeton University, May 2000.

Deser, Clara, and Marika Holland. "Decadal Variations in Labrador Sea Ice Cover and North Atlantic Sea Surface Temperatures." National Center for Atmospheric Research, Boulder, Colorado, 2001.

Environment Canada. "Arctic Ozone," June 2000.

———. *Canada Country Study: The Arctic Region,* Nov. 1997.

———. "Eureka Weather Normals: 1961–1990."

———. "High Arctic Weather Stations—50 Years of Operation," 2000.

———. "Resolute Climate Normals: 1961–1990."

———. "State of the Canadian Cryosphere," 2001.

Fast, Helen, and Fikret Berkes. "Climate Change, Northern Subsistence and Land Based Economies." Environment Canada, Oct. 1998.

Hansen, J., et al. "Forcings and Chaos in Interannual to Decadal Climate Change." *Journal of Geophysical Research* 102, 1977.

International Panel on Climate Change, Working Group II. *Technical Summary, Climate Change 2001: Impacts, Adaptation and Vulnerability.* Geneva, Feb. 2001.

Jones, Helen. "Open-Ocean Deep Convection: A Field Guide." Massachusetts Institute of Technology. <http://puddle.mit.edu/~helen/oodc.html>

Pollard, Wayne, and Trevor Bell. "Massive Ice Formation in the Eureka Sound Lowlands." Seventh International Permafrost Conference, 2000.

Rothrock, D.A., et al. "Thinning of the Arctic Sea-Ice Cover." *Geophysical Research Letters,* 1 Dec. 1999.

Shindell, D.T., et al. "Northern Hemisphere Winter Climate Response to Greenhouse Gas, Ozone, Solar and Volcanic Forcing." *Atmospheres,* Aug. 2000.

Shindell, D.T. "Climate and Ozone Response to Increased Stratospheric Water Vapor." *Geophysical Research Letters* 28, 2001.

Thorpe, Natasha, and Sandra Eyegetok and Lena Kamoayok. "Tuktu and Nogak Project." 10th Arctic Ungulate Conference. Iqaluktuutiaq, Nunavut, 28 Sept. 1999.

Vevatne, Jonas. *Canada on the Brink: From Frontrunner to Laggard?* Olmos Cicerone, June 2000.


## AFTER THE ICE STORM: Quebec

Canadian Energy Efficiency Alliance, *2nd Annual Report Card on Government Activities*. Ottawa, 2000.

Coalition of Citizens of Val Saint-François. Press release, 14 Jan. 2000.

Desbarats, Peter. *René: A Canadian in Search of a Country*. Toronto: McClelland & Stewart, 1976.

Hornung, Robert. *Provincial Government Performance on Climate Change: 2000*. Ottawa: Pembina Institute, 2000.

Hydro-Québec Inc. Annual Report 2000.

———. *The LOOP*, Feb. 2000.

Intergovernmental Panel on Climate Change, Working Group II. "Summary for Policymakers, Climate Change 2001: Impacts, Adaptation and Vulnerability." Geneva, 2001.

Lapointe, Paul-André, in *States, Firms and Raw Materials: The World Economy and Ecology of Aluminum*. Bradford Barham, ed. Wisconsin: University of Wisconsin Press, 1994.

Mallett, Nathan, and Roger Burford. "Ice Storm Mayhem." *Electrical Business*, Mar. 1998.

McCully, Patrick. *Silenced Rivers: The Ecology and Politics of Large Dams*. New Jersey: Zed Books, 1996.

Patterson, J., et al. "Battlelines." *Alternatives Journal*, summer 1999.

Patterson, W. "Full Circle." *Cogeneration and On-Site Power Production*, Jan.–Feb. 2000.

Patterson, W. "Transforming Electricity." Royal Institute of International Affairs/Earthscan, 1999.

Raphals, Philip. "Power from the People." Helios Center for Sustainable Energy Strategies, 22 May 2000.

Sixth Report to Parliament under the Energy Efficiency Act: 1998–1999, June 2000.

Young, Robert H. "Statement Representing the Vermont Joint Owners." Press release, 21 Aug. 1999.


## THE WINDMILL AND THE REACTOR: Toronto

Adams, Tom, and Michael Hilson. "Ontario Hydro Bound for Bankruptcy—Again." *National Post,* 17 Nov. 2000.

Anderson, Michael. "Arduous TREC." *Alternatives Journal*, spring 2000.

Atomic Energy Control Board. Staff response to Dr. David Hoel (BMD 00-08.9A).

Auditor General of Canada. "Canadian Nuclear Safety Commission: Power Reactor Regulation." Office of the Auditor General, 2000.

Babin, Ronald. *The Nuclear Power Game*. Montreal: Black Rose Books, 1985.

Bramley, Matthew. *Greenhouse Gas Emissions from Industrial Companies in Canada: 1998*. Ottawa: Pembina Institute, Oct. 2000.

Caton, Lisa. *Energy Co-operatives: Opportunities for Co-op Development in Ontario's Energy Sector*. Toronto: Canadian Co-operative Association, June 1996.

Caton, Robert, et al. *Clearing the Air: A Preliminary Analysis of Air Quality Co-Benefits from Reduced Greenhouse Gas Emissions in Canada*. Vancouver: David Suzuki Foundation, Mar. 2000.

Commissioner of the Environment and Sustainable Development. *Government Support for Energy Investments*. Ottawa: Office of the Auditor General, 2000.

————. "Smog: Our Health at Risk." Ottawa: Office of the Auditor General of Canada, May 2000.

Dillon Consulting Limited. "Wind Turbine Evironmental Assessment, Screening Document: TREC and Toronto Hydro," April 2000.

Ginsburg, Jessica, et al. "A Solar Strategy for Toronto Hydro," Dec. 1999.

Healthy City Office. "SMOG: Make It or Break It." City of Toronto, April 1988.

Hoel, Dr. David. "Affidavit," 9 Dec. 1999.

Hornung, Robert, and Matthew Bramley. "Five Years of Failure." Drayton Valley: Pembina Institute, Mar. 2000.

McClearn, Matthew. "The Competition." *Canadian Business*, 5 Mar. 2001.

National Energy Board. *Canadian Energy—Supply and Demand to 2025*. Calgary, 1999.

Nuclear Awareness Project. Press release, 17 Aug. 1997.

Ontario Clean Air Alliance. *Countdown Coal: How Ontario Can Improve Air Quality by Phasing out Coal-Fired Electricity Generation*. Toronto, Oct. 2000.

————. "Nanticoke: Ontario's Number-One Polluter." Toronto, Oct. 2000.

Ontario Medical Association. "The Illness Costs of Air Pollution in Ontario." 27 June 2000.

Ontario Ministry of Energy, Science and Technology. *Direction for Change: Charting a Course for Competitive Electricity and Jobs in Ontario*, November 1997.

Ontario Power Generation Inc. "Pollution Release Report." Pollution Watch Scorecard, 2001.

————. *Annual Report*, 1999.

————. *Progress Report*, 2000.

————. "Pickering Nuclear Unit Leak Stopped—Unit Remains Shut Down." Press release, 24 Aug. 1999.

Pembina Institute. "Taking Stock 1998: North American Pollutant Releases and Transfers, Analysis and Highlights." Drayton Valley, July 2001.

Roberts, Wayne, and Susan Brandum. *Get a Life!: How to Make a Good Buck, Dance around the Dinosaurs and Save the World While You're at It*. Toronto: Get a Life Publishing House, 1995.

Rubin, Norman. "Why Pickering-A Should Not Be Restarted Without Approval by an Independent Panel Review." Energy Probe's comments to the Canadian Nuclear Safety Commission on the Pickering-A return to service, 14 Dec. 2000.

Sierra Club of Canada, Toronto Environmental Alliance. *Green Report Card on Electricity Restructuring in Ontario.* Toronto, 2000.

Torrie, Ralph. *Power Shift: Cool Solutions to Global Warming.* Vancouver: David Suzuki Foundation, April 2000.


## TWILIGHT ON FISION AVENUE: Uranium City

Auditor General of Canada. *Atomic Energy Control Board: Canada's Nuclear Regulator.* Ottawa: Office of the Auditor General, 1994.

———. *Atomic Energy Control Board: Canada's Nuclear Regulator.* Ottawa: Office of the Auditor General, 1994.

———. *Federal Radioactive Waste Management.* Ottawa: Office of the Auditor General, 1995.

Beak Consultants Ltd. "An Assessment of the Radiological Impact of Uranium Mining in Northern Saskatchewan." Environment Canada and Atomic Energy Control Board, June 1986.

———. "Assessment of Lorado," 1989.

Canada Mortgage and Housing Corporation and Health Canada. *The Canadian Guideline for Radon in Homes,* 1997.

Canadian Environmental Assessment Agency. *Report of the Joint Federal-Provincial Panel on Uranium Mining Developments in Northern Saskatchewan,* Nov. 1997.

Chambers, Douglas B., et al. "Long Term Population Dose Due to Radon from Uranium Mill Tailings." The Uranium Institute, Twenty-Third Annual Symposium, Sept. 1998.

Cohen, Mark Francis. "Nuking the Atmosphere." *Mother Jones online,* 23 May 2001.

Environment Canada. "Abandoned Gunnar Uranium Tailings." Briefing, undated.

———. "Abandoned Lorado Uranium Tailings (Nero Lake)." Briefing, undated.

———. "Vegetation (Trees, Shrubs and Lichen)." Briefing, undated.

Environment Canada–Health Canada. *Priority Substances List, Assessment Report: Releases of Radionuclides from Nuclear Facilities (Impact on Non-Human Biota),* July 2000.

Environment Protection Agency (U.S.). *Biological Effects of Ionizing Radiation (BEIR) VI Report: The Health Effects of Exposure to Indoor Radon: Public Summary,* 1998.

Goldstick, Miles. *Wollaston: People Resisting Genocide.* Montreal: Black Rose Books, 1987.

Gray, Earle. *The Great Uranium Cartel.* Toronto: McClelland & Stewart, 1982.

Health Canada. *Uranium in Drinking Water.* Public Comment Document, Jan. 1999.

Kaihla, Paula. "Nuclear Confusion." *Canadian Business,* 12 Nov. 1999.

Makhijani, Arjun, Howard Hu, and Katherine Yih, eds. *Nuclear Wastelands: A Global Guide to Nuclear Weapons Production and Its Health and Environmental Effects.* A special commission of International Physicians for the Prevention of Nuclear War and the Institute for Energy and Environmental Research. Cambridge: MIT Press, 1995.

Natural Resources Canada. "Detailed Findings: Contaminated Sites." Audit 2001.

Vance, Robert. *Canadian Minerals Yearbook 1998: Uranium*. Natural Resources Canada, 1998.

Various documents. *Historical Review of the Beaverlodge Mining Area of Northern Saskatchewan*. Province of Saskatchewan.

## THE OIL PATCH WAR: Alberta

Alberta Energy and Utilities Board. *Regulatory Highlights: 1999*, 2000.

Alberta Energy Company Limited. "Industrial Terrorism: 'A Creeping Sickness That Must Be Eradicated.'" Press release, 14 Sept. 1998.

Commissioner of the Environment and Sustainable Development, *Government Support for Energy Investments*. Ottawa: Office of the Auditor General, 2000.

Finch, David, et al. *The Great Oil Age: The Petroleum Industry in Canada*. Calgary: Detselig Enterprises, 1993.

Intergovernmental Panel on Climate Change, Working Group II. *Technical Summary, Climate Change 2001: Impacts, Adaptation and Vulnerability*. Geneva, Feb. 2001.

Jaremko, Gordon. "Stevie Wonder: Alberta Energy Ministry Swings to Virtuoso of Limited Government." *Oilweek*, May 1997.

Marr-Laing, Thomas, and Chris Severson-Baker. *Beyond Eco-Terrorism: The Deeper Issues Affecting Alberta's Oil Patch*. Drayton Valley: Pembina Institute, Feb. 1999.

Nikiforuk, Andrew. "Big Oil, Meet Big Trouble." *Canadian Business*, 29 May 2000.

————. "Pure Profit." *Canadian Business*, 3 Apr. 2000.

*R v. Ludwig*, court documents, 2000.

Royal Canadian Mounted Police. Various documents, 1997–2000.

## ANOTHER NATION: Stoney Nakoda, Samson Cree

Chalmers, John West. *Laird of the West*. Calgary: Detselig Enterprises, 1981.

Department of Indian and Northern Affairs. Various documents, 1982–1997.

KPMG. Audit of Stoney Nakoda, 1997.

Treaty 7 Elders and Tribal Council. *The True Spirit and Original Intent of Treaty 7*. Montreal, Kingston: McGill-Queen's University Press, 1996.

*Victor Buffalo v. the Queen*, court documents, 2000.

York, Geoffrey. *The Dispossessed: Life and Death in Native Canada*. Toronto: Vintage, 1990.

## ONE LAST BOOM: Fort McMurray

Canadian Industrial Energy End-Use Data and Analysis Centre. *A Review of Energy Consumption in Canadian Oil Refineries and Upgraders*. Burnaby: School of Resource and Environmental Management, Simon Fraser University, 2001.

Foley, Dermot. *Fuelling the Climate Crisis: The Continental Energy Plan*. Vancouver: David Suzuki Foundation, 2001.

Marr-Laing, Tom, and Gail MacCrimmon. *Patchwork Policy, Fragmented Forests: In-Situ Oil Sands, Industrial Development and the Ecological Integrity of Alberta's Boreal Forest*. Drayton Valley: Pembina Institute, May 2000.

McCrank, Neil, chairman, Alberta Energy and Utilities Board. "Regulatory Issues Associated with Oil Sands Development." Presented to the Canadian Heavy Oil Association, June 2000.

National Energy Board, *Canada's Oil Sands: A Supply and Market Outlook to 2015*. Calgary, Oct. 2000.

Nikiforuk, Andrew. "Alberta's New Oil Boom." *Canadian Business*, Aug. 1997.

Pembina Institute. "Environmental Watchdog Calls for Strong Federal Role in Oilsands Developments." Press release, 11 Dec. 1998.

Pratt, Lawrence. *The Tar Sands: Syncrude and the Politics of Oil*. Edmonton: Hurtig Publishers, 1976.

Suncor Inc. Environment reports, 2000.

Syncrude Canada Ltd. *Innovation in Energy: 1998– 2008 Reduction*, 2001.

## CLOSING KEMANO: British Columbia

Alcan Aluminum Limited. *Alcan in BC*, 1999.

Christensen, Bev. *Too Good to Be True: Alcan's Kemano Completion Project*. Vancouver: Talonbooks, 1995.

Hume, Mark. *The Run of the River*. Vancouver: New Star Books, 1992.

# INDEX